UNDERSTANDING PEDAGOGY AND ITS
IMPACT ON LEARNING

Understanding Pedagogy and its Impact on Learning

edited by

Peter Mortimore

P·C·P
Paul Chapman
Publishing Ltd

Selection and editorial material © Copyright 1999 Peter Mortimore
Chapter 1 © Copyright 1999 Chris Watkins and Peter Mortimore
Chapter 2 © Copyright 1999 Iram Siraj-Blatchford
Chapter 3 © Copyright 1999 Caroline Gipps and Barbara MacGilchrist
Chapter 4 © Copyright 1999 Susan Hallam and Judith Ireson
Chapter 5 © Copyright 1999 Michael Young and Norman Lucas
Chapter 6 © Copyright 1999 Jenny Corbett and Brahm Norwich
Chapter 7 © Copyright 1999 Ronald Barnett and Susan Hallam
Chapter 8 © Copyright 1999 Toni Griffiths and David Guile
Chapter 9 © Copyright 1999 Ann Hodgson and Maria Kambouri
Chapter 10 © Copyright 1999 Richard Noss and Norbert Pachler
Chapter 11 © Copyright 1999 Judith Ireson, Peter Mortimore and Susan Hallam
First published 1999

Paul Chapman Publishing Ltd
A SAGE Publications Company
6 Bonhill Street
London EC2A 4PU

SAGE Publications Inc
2455 Teller Road
Thousand Oaks, California 91320

SAGE Publications India Pvt Ltd
32, M-Block Market
Greater Kailash - 1
New Delhi 110 048

British Library Cataloguing in Publication data

A catalogue record for this book is available from the British Library

ISBN 1 85396 452 2
ISBN 1 85396 453 0 (pbk)

Library of Congress catalog card number available

Typeset by Anneset, Weston-super-mare, Somerset
Printed and bound in Great Britain by Athenaeum Press, Gateshead

CONTENTS

Acknowledgements

I wish to record my thanks to the authors – all busy with teaching duties, research commitments and administrative tasks – for the positive way in which they approached the challenge of drafting and revising these eleven chapters. I also wish to thank Jo Mortimore for help with the final manuscript. Finally I wish to pay tribute to Ranjna Patel for her patience in managing the many texts and disks involved in this project.

Preface

This book has grown out of a series of discussions with colleagues at the Institute of Education. On numerous occasions over the last few years we have bemoaned the lack of a collection of writing about pedagogy. This most important of topics – affecting the way hundreds of thousands of learners of different ages and stages are taught – has been neglected. Instead of systematic collections of evidence, teachers have had to rely on ideological positions, folk wisdom and the mantras of enthusiasts for particular approaches. At the beginning of 1998 we felt the time had come to stop bemoaning this lack and do something about it. Accordingly we decided to create a book. I am grateful to the commissioning editor of Sage Publications who shared this view and has made the idea into reality.

The purpose of our collection of eleven chapters is to encourage debate about pedagogy in England today. We are contributing our initial work but are well aware that much more needs to be said and done. We are academics – although we all have professional backgrounds as teachers – and part of our job is to think about educational issues and how they might be resolved. We are very conscious that the debate about pedagogy must involve two other groups: practising teachers and policy makers. It must involve teachers because they are involved with pedagogy every working day of their lives. Teachers have a great deal of knowledge about pedagogy and have often learned the hard way what does and does not work. Policy makers representing, as they do, the wider society of parents, employers and citizens must also participate in this debate. We believe such participation is essential even though we deplore the idea that pedagogy should ever be prescribed by policy makers and fear the negative impact of 'top down diktats'.

Our book consists of an introductory chapter in which we explore the context of pedagogy and recount some of the shifts in thinking that have occurred over recent years. We also point up the differences in approach between academics, practitioners and policy makers. This introduction is followed by a series of chapters in which we trawl the published literature for evidence about the impact of pedagogy on the development of differently aged learners and those learning in different contexts. We depart from this age/context classification in order to include two further chapters: one focusing on learners with special educational needs; and another which addresses some of the issues of pedagogy arising from the use of information and communications technology (ICT). In the last chapter, we endeavour to address the big picture. What do we know about the impact of particular pedagogies and, as importantly, what do we still not know? Given the structure of the book, we also ask whether there are important differences between the pedagogy used for learners of different ages and stages. Finally, we use the information from the separate chapters to ask whether there are any lessons for the future. Our focus is mainly on England and, although many of the papers we cite are from North America or mainland Europe, we are conscious of this limitation. Some of the issues to which we draw attention are common to all systems but others are culture specific.

As with all edited collections, we authors share a sense of frustration. Having completed our chapters we feel we are at the beginning rather than the end of our work. Nevertheless, despite such limitations we offer the book as a contribution to an important debate. We look forward to discussing our ideas with practitioners and policy makers and taking forward into the new century such collective thinking on pedagogy.

Peter Mortimore
Institute of Education
University of London

Notes on Contributors

Professor Ronald Barnett is Dean of Professional Development and Professor of Higher Education at the Institute of Education. He worked in higher education for twenty years, as a researcher and an academic administrator before joining the Institute. He is the author of many books on higher education including two prize winning volumes *The Idea of Higher Education* and *The Limits of Competence*, both published by Open University Press.

Dr Jenny Corbett is Senior Lecturer in Special and Inclusive Education at the Institute of Education. She worked in secondary schools and in special education before moving into further and higher education. Her major research interests are in language and power discourses relating to special needs and inclusive policy and practices within the post-school sector. Current research projects involve an analysis of the ideological history of inclusive education and an investigation into vocational training for young people with learning disabilities in France and Cyprus. Her most recent book *Special Educational Needs in the Twentieth Century* is published by Cassell.

Professor Caroline Gipps was Dean of Research at the Institute of Education until 1998. She trained as a psychologist and worked as a primary school teacher before going into research. For over twenty-five years she has carried out research on issues around assessment and testing and the links among assessment, teaching and learning. She is currently Deputy Vice-Chancellor at Kingston University.

Toni Griffiths is Director of Education and Professional Development at University College London. She was previously Dean for New Initiatives at the Institute of Education, University of London, and Senior Research Fellow at the University of Warwick. She has been involved in European research and development projects in the field of work-based learning, particularly work experience, for the past ten years.

David Guile is a Research Officer in the Post 16 Centre of the Institute of Education. He is co-chair of the New Learning for New Work Consortium.

He has been a deputy head of an inner London comprehensive school and a consultant for London East Training and Enterprise Council, and undertook an industrial secondment with British Telecom. His research interests are Work-based learning, Education-business partnerships and ICT. His latest monograph *Information and Communication Technology and Education* is published by the Institute of Education.

Dr Susan Hallam is Senior Lecturer in the Psychology of Education and Assistant to the Dean of Professional Development at the Institute of Education. She has been involved in educational work for almost thirty years and has experience as a teacher and LEA co-ordinator in addition to lecturing and researching in higher education. Her research has been concerned with learning and teaching in a range of educational environments, truancy and exclusion from school and the effects of listening to background music on behaviour, a reflection of her background in music.

Dr Ann Hodgson has worked as a teacher, lecturer, editor, civil servant and LEA advisor. She now works as a lecturer in adult and lifelong education at the Institute of Education and writes on education policy issues such as reform of the 14–19 curriculum, widening participation in learning, organising and funding adult and lifelong learning and value-added approaches to achievement.

Dr Judy Ireson is Senior Lecturer in Psychology of Education at the Institute of Education. She has many years' experience of teaching and research in psychology and education, in this country and overseas. Her main area of expertise is in psychological and educational aspects of learning, with research interests in the relations between educational contexts, teaching and learning; individual tutoring and the teaching of reading. She is currently undertaking research on the impact of ability grouping in schools.

Dr Maria Kambouri is a lecturer in Research Methods in Psychology and Education. Prior to joining the Institute, she worked in educational establishments in Greece, Belgium and the USA as tutor, consultant, researcher and student. Her main research interests are adult learning and the use of ICT and other media in learning and teaching. She has directed several research projects for the Basic Skills Agency on adult literacy and numeracy issues.

Norman Lucas is a lecturer in Post 16 Education at the Institute of Education. He was an elected member of the Inner London Education Authority and a former Further Education lecturer. His research and publications include initial teacher education and professional development, issues of professionalism, Further Education funding and management.

Dr Barbara MacGilchrist is Dean of Initial Teacher Education at the Institute of Education. She has worked in the education field for over thirty years and was a teacher, headteacher and LEA Chief Inspector before joining the Institute as Head of In-Service Education. Her major research interest is school effectiveness and improvement. Her latest book *The Intelligent School* is published by Paul Chapman.

Professor Peter Mortimore is the Director of the Institute of Education. He has worked in the education field for over thirty years and has been a teacher, local authority officer and school inspector as well as a university teacher and researcher. He is an expert in school effectiveness and improvement. His latest book *The Road to Improvement* is published by Swets and Zeitlinger.

Professor Brahm Norwich is Professor of Special Needs Education at the Institute of Education. He has worked as a teacher and educational psychologist. His interests are in the education of children and young people with disabilities and difficulties in learning, support systems in schools, motivational and emotional aspects of teaching and learning and the theoretical and practical contributions of psychology to education.

Professor Richard Noss is Professor of Mathematics Education at the Institute of Education. He was a mathematics teacher for nearly ten years, before turning to research in mathematics education in the early 1980s. He is an expert on the educational potential of digital technologies and has authored and edited several books. Most recently he is the co-author of *Windows on Mathematical Meanings: Learning Cultures and Computers*, published by Kluwer.

Dr Norbert Pachler is Lecturer in Languages in Education at the Institute of Education with responsibility for the Secondary PGCE in Modern Foreign Languages and the MA in Modern Languages in Education. Prior to moving into higher education he worked for the inspectorate and advisory service of a London local education authority on curriculum development and in-service training and taught in secondary and further education.

Dr Iram Siraj-Blatchford is Senior Lecturer in Early Childhood Education within the Child Development and Learning Group at the Institute of Education. She has been a teacher in primary and nursery classes and an advisory teacher. She has lectured and published widely on ECE. She is editor of the *International Journal for Early Years Education* and co-director of the major longitudinal study Effective Provision of Pre-school Education (EPPE) Project funded until 2003 by the DfEE.

Chris Watkins is Head of the Assessment, Guidance and Effective Learning Group at the Institute of Education. He has been a mathematics teacher in a large secondary school, a teacher in charge of a unit for pupils whose effect on school was disruptive, and a trained school counsellor. Current work in the field of pedagogy includes effective learning in classrooms, mentoring, tutoring and school behaviour.

Professor Michael Young is Head of the Post 16 Education Centre at the Institute of Education. Before joining the Institute as Lecturer in Sociology of Education, he taught science in London secondary schools. His recent research has concentrated on the post compulsory curriculum and in particular on different national strategies for overcoming the academic/vocational divide. His latest book *The Curriculum of the Future* was published in 1998 by Falmer Press.

Pedagogy: What Do We Know?

Chris Watkins and Peter Mortimore

The aim of this chapter is to highlight a number of issues in the use of the term pedagogy and to outline some of the ways in which the word is used. We will discuss the research literature on pedagogy and suggest there is a trend amongst writers towards an increased recognition of the complexity of pedagogical activity. We also detect an increasing awareness of the need to take into account the context in which pedagogy occurs. We will compare the views of some of these academic writers with those of practitioners and, finally, consider public and policy-makers' apparent views about pedagogy. In writing this book we are conscious that a large number of issues will be raised and only a few resolved. We hope, however, that we will contribute to an important debate about different approaches to teaching and, ultimately, to ways of improving learning for learners of all ages.

PEDAGOGY: A CONTESTED TERM

The term pedagogy is seldom used in English writing about education. Where writers have used the term, they have often been criticized for using an ill-defined and poorly developed idea. We do not recognize this criticism as fair. Rather, we recognize that, as with other complex ideas, pedagogy will be difficult to define – even in the formal literature on the subject. The boundaries of the concept may seem unclear, but the ways in which different writers have drawn them may itself be instructive.

'Pedagogy', derived from French and Latin adaptations of the Greek [παισ, παιδ (boy) + αγωγοσ (leader)], literally means a man having oversight of a child, or an attendant leading a boy to school. This meaning is now obsolete. Moreover, the gendering, appropriate in ancient Greece – where the formal education of girls was unusual – is inappropriate for modern times. The limitations of the literal meaning of the term have encouraged leading contemporary writers to invent broader terms, such as 'andragogy', for education (Knowles, 1980).

Modern day usage of the term 'pedagogy' is more common in European countries, in particular, in French, German and Russian-speaking academic communities, than in English-speaking ones. In continental

pedagogical institutes are to be found alongside, and within, university departments. Academic awards in pedagogy are also common. A scan of *Zeitschrift fur Padagogik*, a European journal seemingly addressing this area of work, shows, however, that few articles actually do focus on what to many British readers would be central: classroom teaching. The boundaries of pedagogy in mainland Europe, it appears, are defined very broadly. As one Swedish academic notes: 'Pedagogy as a discipline extends to the consideration of the development of health and bodily fitness, social and moral welfare, ethics and aesthetics, as well as to the institutional forms that serve to facilitate society's and the individual's pedagogic aims' (Marton and Booth, 1997, p. 178). Even in France, a country which has taught pedagogy since 1883, the director of its *Institut National de Recherche Pédagogique* has described how the term is subject to changing connotations and pressures (Best, 1988).

In the context of these cultural differences, there have been accusations of 'neglect of pedagogical studies in England' (Simon, 1994, p. 147). Simon locates the reason for this neglect in the outlook of the dominant public schools and their traditional concern with character formation rather than with intellectual development. A more parsimonious explanation may be that the term has not found a stable working use amongst British educators.

Brief definitions of pedagogy are offered from time to time. A common example is 'the science of teaching'. However, the brevity of this phrase may create its own difficulty, since such a definition depends on the reader's assumptions about 'science' and their conceptions of 'teaching'. In this chapter, we wish to avoid an overly positivist view of science based, as it would be, on an experimental methodology, the formulation of 'laws' and a technical approach which portrays itself as independent of the prevailing social order.[1]

We are anxious not to exclude other forms of understanding simply because of the definition we adopt, for example, inadvertently excluding the arts because we refer directly to the sciences. In order to overcome this problem, we will adopt an inclusive approach more like that which characterized the first appearance of the term 'pedagogics' in 1864: 'the science, art or principles of pedagogy' (*Oxford Shorter English Dictionary*, 1993). We also wish to draw attention to an alternative way of thinking about pedagogy which is neither science nor art: this is seeing pedagogy as a craft, an approach suggested by writers who recognize uncertainty and the limits of predictability (McDonald, 1992; Marland, 1993).

In a similar way we do not wish to define the term pedagogy in a way which stresses only the teacher's role and activity – this would be better described under the more limited term of didactics. We believe that it is help-

---

[1] We welcome, however, views of science embodying uncertainty, relativity, complexity and chaos and recognizing the role of creativity and social construction in knowledge-creation (Fleck, 1935; Latour and Woolgar, 1986).

ful to our discussion to focus our attention on teaching but we also need to take the learner into account. Thus the basic premise from which we wish to begin our definition of pedagogy is: 'any conscious activity by one person designed to enhance learning in another'.

RESEARCH LITERATURE ON PEDAGOGY

Conceptions of pedagogy have become more complex over time. By this we mean that our growing knowledge has simultaneously become both more differentiated and more integrated. In other words, we believe that we now know more of the different elements which are needed to compose an adequate model, and can also integrate them into the whole by describing the relations between them.

We suggest four main phases, although it would be misleading to suggest that these phases represent a smooth progression towards greater understanding.

The literature to which we will refer has been generated by academics, working mainly in universities, and is available through our access to formal knowledge codified in libraries and world-wide databases. We recognize that this is not the common knowledge base of an everyday classroom practitioner nor of an educational policy-maker. We consider that teachers and policy-makers are likely to view pedagogy in different ways. We will discuss such differences in perspective in later sections of this chapter.

Phase 1: A focus on different types of teachers

Early studies of teaching adopted a focus on the teacher's 'style'. A common way to do so was to construct what are sometimes termed 'polarized typifications' of teachers. Such typifications have often reflected key concerns of their time. During the inter-war and post-war years, for example, concerns about 'authoritarianism' and 'democracy' were reflected in studies of group leadership style. A much-quoted study characterized approaches as being either 'authoritarian' or 'democratic', although the investigator added a third style, 'laissez-faire' (Lewin et al., 1939). Other studies divided teachers according to whether they were 'integrative' or 'dominative' (Anderson and Brewer, 1946). This conceptualization of pedagogy was simple in its attribution of impact to a teacher's personal style.

Such a polarized categorization, perhaps, reveals that the underlying purpose of these exercises was to identify 'good' and 'bad' approaches. Interestingly, such studies have rarely been accompanied by advice about how any 'bad' pedagogue might be made 'good'! Perhaps the sole focus on the teacher helps to elicit derogatory connotations such as those of 'pedantry, dogmatism and severity' which attach to the noun 'pedagogue' (Oxford Shorter English Dictionary, 1993). Polarized conceptions of teachers continued into some studies carried out in the 1960s and 1970s. Bennett, for example, having argued strongly against 'ill-defined dichotomies' (Bennett and Jordan, 1975) later collapsed twelve separate clusters into one 'informal-formal' dimension (Bennett, 1976).

The move away from attempts to categorize significant features of pedagogy by polarized and over-simplistic descriptions of teachers' approaches coincided with the advent of studies which, with the development of mainframe computers, were able to analyse large data-sets. One such study applied multiple psychometric measures to a sample of over 6,000 teachers (Ryans, 1968). The study found a significant correlation between teachers receiving a uniformly high assessment of their classroom behaviour and the frequency of their involvement in avocational (non-work) activities (p. 393). Such findings illustrate both the potential and the limitations of correlational analysis. They also demonstrate the limitations of a too-personal focus on the teacher.

Later it became clear that prevalent modes of pedagogy depended on much more than the style of the teacher. Contrary to the received wisdom that classrooms had become 'progressive' and 'child-centred', surveys were revealing that 'traditional' practice remained the dominant form of teaching in primary schools in the United Kingdom (Barker Lunn, 1984; Galton, 1987). Similar evidence was presented in the USA (Cuban, 1984), together with an analysis that such constancy of approach could be identified over a number of decades and, perhaps, reflected some basic features of the classroom situation. A productive focus on pedagogy, therefore, should incorporate an additional recognition that teachers are influenced by their context.

Phase 2: A focus on the contexts of teaching

Research studies which adopted a detailed focus on life in the classroom established a more sophisticated approach to understanding the complex interactions of pupils and teachers. Smith and Geoffrey's (1968) research, for example, described the detail of life in urban classrooms. Kounin's work, which also highlighted the complexities of classroom life, has remained influential for twenty years (Kounin, 1977).

Doyle provides an overview of studies which have focused on classroom contexts:

> Classrooms are crowded and busy places in which groups of students who vary in interests and abilities must be organized and directed. Moreover these groups assemble regularly for long periods of time to accomplish a wide variety of tasks. Many events occur simultaneously, teachers must react often and immediately to circumstances, and the course of events is frequently unpredictable. Teaching in such settings requires a highly developed ability to manage events.
>
> (Doyle, 1990, p. 350)

This phase of research added the managerial and organizational aspect of teachers' classroom work to the view of pedagogy (Arends, 1994). It highlighted how teachers orchestrate a complex situation, oversee numerous events and manage multiple activities. This broader view of pedagogy enables the classroom to be viewed as an 'activity system', which teachers need to establish and manage. Different profiles of classroom activities can be seen, and may relate to what had previously been called different 'teaching methods' (for which a convincing categorization has yet to be created). Classroom activities are constructed from the key elements (shown in Figure 1.1). The most important element in determining the coherence of an activity is its goals: successful managers of activities communicate a clear programme of action for participants (Doyle, 1984).

Brophy, an experienced analyst of teachers and teaching, has suggested that the knowledge base of how teachers plan and manage multiple learning tasks and complex activities is still under construction (Brophy, 1992). It appears, from many accounts, that when experienced teachers plan their work they focus on the activity and the content rather than using a rational and linear model of beginning with *goals*, moving through *planned actions* towards anticipated *outcomes*. In the complexity of a live classroom, the direction can be more one of *actions* leading directly to *outcomes* before the *goals* have been considered. In this way the goals become symbols of, and justifications for, what has already been achieved.

Teachers display significant differences in how they cope with this complex environment. They differ in their responses to the simultaneous events, with their multi-faceted nature, and the need for immediate action. Experienced teachers monitor and interpret such events and demands in greater detail – and with more insight and understanding – than do their less experienced colleagues: they respond effortlessly and fluidly (Sabers *et al.*,

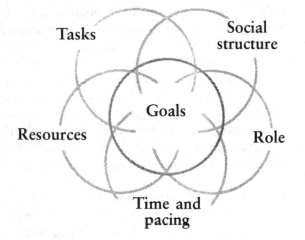

Fig. 1.1 Elements in teaching activities

1991). Experienced teachers' understanding of classroom processes is more connected and complex. For example, they do not separate issues of classroom management from pedagogy in the way that beginner teachers do (Copeland et al., 1994). Teachers who actively accept the complexity of the classroom orchestrate events in their classes more successfully than those who do not (Doyle, 1977). All teachers, however, need to be able to handle uncertainty in the classroom setting (Floden and Buchmann, 1993).

Recognition of the influence of the classroom context has enhanced our understanding of classroom change. Although classrooms are very dynamic, they can also be very resistant to change. Simple interventions, such as adding a specific teacher skill or changing the content of the curriculum, often show little lasting impact. It even remains an open question whether major interventions, such as the introduction of new technology, will significantly change classroom practice (Cuban, 1993).

We have also come to understand two additional ways in which context has influence. First, research into school differences and the analysis of how school learning differs from learning in other contexts (Resnick, 1987) have led to a recognition that the school context can influence pedagogy (Talbert et al., 1993). We now understand more about how, for example, the secondary school setting – with its age-graded, subject-centred, self-contained classrooms – has a powerful and seemingly enduring effect on the nature of its pedagogy. The generation of different metaphors of schooling; as 'gardens in which children grow'; 'factories in which children are made' and 'hospitals in which children are cured of their ignorance' illustrates the different conceptions of schooling and hence the different contexts for learning that can be created.

Second, recognition that the content of what is taught influences *how* it is taught has led to a greater focus on teachers' knowledge of subject-matter. Since, however, the subject-matter of schools will change in various ways, such knowledge must be dynamic and context-dependent rather than static. According to Carlsen (1991), teachers hold multiple representations of subject concepts and, in their teaching, select those based on their understanding of the context of instruction and their prior knowledge of what is likely to be effective for particular learners. So researchers into pedagogy not only endeavour to investigate how teachers organize subject-matter in their own minds, but are also interested in the teachers' ability to understand and apply the subject-matter in different ways, according to the context of their classes, the sequence of lessons, and their knowledge of the learning groups and individuals.

This phase of research, despite the influence of the most recent studies, is still focused on a limited view of pedagogy and on only one of its forms: instruction. The learner and the process of learning remain relatively unexamined.

Phase 3: A focus on teaching and learning

Recent developments in our understanding of cognition and meta-cognition have influenced the conceptualization of pedagogy. In part, this reflects our increased awareness of the need to think of learners as active constructors of meaning. Bruner (1996) has identified dominant models of learners which have held sway in our times, and has spelled out the implications of each model for pedagogy. He puts forward two models which reflect recent research into cognition:

1. Seeing children as thinkers, constructing a model of the world to help them construe their own experience. The model considers what children think and how they arrive at what they believe. Pedagogy is to help the child understand better, more powerfully: this is fostered through discussion and collaboration, the process of sharing knowledge in an unthreatening community. Truths are the product of evidence, argument and construction rather than of authority.

2. Seeing children as knowledgeable, testing whether hypotheses stand up in the face of evidence, interpretation and existing knowledge. Teaching helps children grasp the distinction between personal knowledge, on the one side, and 'objective' knowledge (what is taken to be known within the culture) on the other. 'This perspective holds that there is something special about "talking" to authors, now dead but alive in their ancient texts – so long as the objective of the encounter is not worship but discourse and "going meta" on thoughts about the past.' (Bruner, 1996, p. 62).

The implications for pedagogy of these two models are that they shift the focus from simply trying to transmit information to a group of individual learners to the process of building a community of learners engaged in the generation and evaluation of knowledge and in which the teacher makes explicit her knowledge at the same time as promoting access to other sources.

The first model noted above, which identifies children as thinkers, focuses on sharing knowledge within the discourse of a particular community. It links us to another understanding in cognition, that *what* is learned relates strongly to the situation in which it is learned. 'Situations might be said to co-produce knowledge through activity' (Brown *et al.*, 1989, p. 32). This view has led to an approach – sometimes called 'cognitive apprenticeship' – which makes deliberate use of the social context in which knowledge can become an authentic tool. It sees learning as being embedded in the activity of particular environments. This argument challenges the idea that abstract or procedural knowledge can be taught for later application in another situation. Indeed Cox (1997) argues that unless learners are building up their understanding of situations – through understanding the variations between them – knowledge learned in one context is unlikely to pass to any other.

Other studies have demonstrated that effective learners may be proactive in their metacognitions – their thinking about their thinking – and their own process of learning. These effective learners may have a more fluent understanding of their own learning than others and may possess the ability to 'talk themselves through' difficulties which arise.

Knowledge about the promotion of such effective learning has been described in relation to four themes: active learning, collaborative learning, learner responsibility, and meta-learning or learning about learning (Watkins *et al.*, 1996). Not all of this is new; the first three of these themes were well represented in a fifty year old publication (Miel and Wiles, 1949). However the fourth theme adds a potentially transforming element to the conceptualization of pedagogy. The intention would be to eliminate the likelihood of hearing from a student 'It's not that I haven't learned much, it's just that I don't really understand what I'm doing' (Rudduck *et al.*, 1995). An explicit pedagogical focus on the learning process advances the learner's conceptions of learning, improves what they learn and increases the likelihood that they will see themselves as active agents in learning, as findings have demonstrated from pre-school onwards (Pramling, 1990).

Phase 4: Current views of pedagogy

At this point in the development of the research literature on pedagogy, a suitably complex model is in sight. On the one hand it offers an increasingly integrated conceptualization which specifies relations between its elements: the teacher, the classroom or other context, content, the view of learning and learning about learning. Such a model draws attention to the creation of learning communities in which knowledge is actively co-constructed, and in which the focus of learning is sometimes learning itself. This model of pedagogy would also be increasingly differentiated by details of context, content, age and stage of learner, purposes, and so on.

Such a model does not offer simple prescriptions for action but it does provide guidelines for desired outcomes. Rather than suggest a simple linear causal chain, which is unlikely to explain the links between teaching and learning, it recognizes that influences are often partial and can be reciprocal. Different versions of pedagogy may be best understood as different clusters of relations between the elements of the model.

Given that such a model reflects mainly the views of researchers and academics, it is now important to ask how other people's knowledge of pedagogy compares with this picture. In what ways might the perspective of teachers be similar to, and different from, this model and how might this be explained?

PRACTITIONERS' VIEWS OF PEDAGOGY

What is the view of the teacher – the everyday pedagogue? McNamara (1991) calls this view 'vernacular pedagogy'. It would be reasonable to expect to find some differences from and some similarities to the formal models that we have discussed, since researchers and teachers – although seeing pedagogy from different standpoints – are both influenced by the same public modes of thinking about teaching and learning.

Teachers sometimes talk about 'teacher styles' in much the same way as researchers did. In their everyday work, many teachers perceive their style as very personal. Without an agreed framework in which teaching can be discussed, teachers may simply describe their approach in terms of a contrast with the style which they attribute to others. So the simplified bi-polar concepts such as formal-informal are likely to be found in their conversations. Jackson (1977) has described this as teachers 'thinking in twos', and has suggested that the phenomenon reflects teachers' response to the complex but fragmented context in which they work. (This certainly seems a valid observation of occasions when a school staff discusses ideas for change when the speed of creating coalitions for and against a proposal can be breathtaking.)

When asked about the qualities of a good teacher, teachers have used up to thirty important and distinct categories. However, the relative frequencies in their choice is illuminating: beginner teachers' views seem to reflect 'unrealistic optimism' (Weinstein, 1989), with high priority given to the teacher-pupil relationship and to pupil self-esteem, in contrast to the views of experienced teachers which are more likely to emphasize organization and creativity rather than personal qualities such as patience or effort. Here the experienced teacher's perspective resonates with the trend noted in our earlier discussion of the research literature – bringing the classroom context and its demands into the picture.

Johnston (1990) found that when he interviewed teachers about their work, his respondents cited the following elements: grouping of pupils; physical and social climate; learning centres and activities; classroom management; pupil evaluation; teacher morale; pupil achievement; instructional practices; teacher planning; and the teacher/student relationship. This list conveys well teachers' awareness of the multidimensional nature of classroom life.

Concern about time is a dominant theme in teachers' talk about management of the classroom, even for those teaching pre-school and primary classes. The amount and pace of lesson content is the most pervasive time-related issue. Here, again, the influence of the context can be seen. A common response by teachers is to orchestrate a situation in which teacher-led activities play the dominant role and student-centred activities the minor role (Langer and Applebee, 1988). Concern about time translates to a concern about 'covering the curriculum', in which teachers focus on their own teaching activity rather than on the learning activity of their students.

Teachers' conceptions of teaching have more recently been elicited. Samuelowicz and Bain (1992) have located these conceptions on an ordered continuum:

1. Imparting information
2. Transmitting knowledge

3. Facilitating understanding
4. Changing students' conceptions
5. Supporting student learning.

These conceptions represent different profiles on five dimensions: the learning outcome, the view of knowledge, the role of students' knowledge, the degree of reciprocation, and the control of content. There is a similar continuum to be found in a study of teachers' views of science learning (Roth, 1987). Here, approaches to pedagogy were grouped within three categories of teachers: fact acquisition teachers; content understanding teachers; and conceptual development teachers.

Teachers' conceptions of teaching are an important focus. There is some evidence that they relate significantly to the teaching strategies which a teacher operates in the classroom (Trigwell and Prosser, 1996). This relation should not be taken for granted, however, since there are many occasions when human rhetoric does not match human action in a particular context.

Experienced teachers view their educational purpose as increasing the quality of students' thinking, engaging them in the processes of learning, and improving their disposition towards learning (Copeland et al., 1994). Schools which focus predominantly on learning are more successful (Rosenholtz, 1991). Indeed, this is one of the lessons from the set of case studies undertaken by the National Commission on Education (NCE, 1996) as well as from the literature on school effectiveness and school improvement (Mortimore, 1998).

The central question in understanding vernacular views of pedagogy might be: 'How do teachers' views of learning relate to their views of teaching?'

In seeking to answer such a question, we cannot take for granted what is meant by 'learning'; a variety of views exists. Two decades of studies have consistently identified five broad categories of what people generally assume 'learning' to mean (Säljö, 1979; Marton et al., 1993):

A. Getting more knowledge
B. Memorizing and reproducing
C. Acquiring and applying procedures
D. Making sense or meaning
E. Personal change.

Before tracing the use of these categories further, we need to recognize that such everyday conceptions are open to critical analysis in the light of what is known in the formal literature about learning. For example, a distinction between knowledge and meaning may be illusory. The learning of 'simple factual knowledge' requires learners actively to construct meaning, even when those around them may view such meanings as perfectly obvious. Similarly in areas which, for the great majority, are unproblematic (such as learning to read), children who experience difficulty illustrate that learning may re-quire significant personal change in their view of themselves and their relations with parents, siblings or peers. Aspects of self, social relations and purpose all influence the learning in hand, and may need to be given attention for the best results.

If the distinctions between these five different views of learning do not stand up to critical scrutiny, it would be inappropriate to adopt the idea that they indicate distinct learning goals which each match distinct pedagogies. The common idea that we can teach facts first by one method (usually 'telling') and then promote understanding by another method has been challenged. Facts cannot exist without understanding so any pedagogy based on the principle that it is helpful to 'learn the basics first' may be wrong. It may be better to regard the conceptions of learning which are first in the list as more incomplete, and the latter as more complete. This way of conceptualizing can be paralleled by also identifying more incomplete or more complete approaches to pedagogy. Incomplete methods of teaching may sometimes achieve the lower order goals, but they do so on the assumption that the higher order processes of making meaning and handling personal change are irrelevant. This is an unsafe assumption on many occasions and can disadvantage particular groups of learners. It is only a safe assumption when the higher order processes have already been established with learners.

So what of the relations between teachers' conceptions of teaching and their conceptions of learning? Trigwell and Prosser (1996) offer two interesting findings. First, those teachers who saw a strong connection between pedagogy and learning were those who viewed teaching as mainly transmitting the syllabus and learning as accumulating knowledge in order to satisfy external demands. The adoption of simple conceptions allowed a high degree of agreement. However, in another sense, the connection is weak since teachers with these views had distinct difficulty in focusing on learning. Second, those teachers with more sophisticated conceptions saw teaching and learning as different but inextricably linked processes. Although such teachers held more sophisticated conceptions of learning, they sometimes adopted lower level approaches to teaching – whereas the teachers with simpler conceptions of learning rarely adopted higher level approaches.

Both these findings can be interpreted as teachers' simplifying the relationship between pedagogy and learning. In the first case, many teachers adopt lower-order views of teaching in response to, for example, examination pressures and organizational constraints. They simplify the goals in order to cope with the demands. In the second case, teachers simplify practice in order to cope with the complexity of the classroom. Teachers are aware of this tendency to simplification for, although some describe their ideal as using pupil-centred methods, they cite the everyday constraints of the classroom as being the reasons for their actual choice of methods (Chandra, 1987). Sometimes teachers will offer the rationale that students prefer directive teaching although there is little or no direct evidence of such a preference (Larsson, 1983). Pupils may indeed have their own strategies for simplifying classroom demands and, especially, may work to reduce any ambiguity in tasks in which they will be assessed (Doyle, 1983). Recent research, however, suggests that pupils' general preferences are for active and collaborative work which, although it is less frequently used in classrooms, is seen as more likely to lead to learning (Hughes, 1997).

So, at the end of this section, we have identified some possible tensions between the formal and the vernacular views of pedagogy. While the trend amongst writers has been moving towards a model which supports the active construction of meaning and endeavours to help learners learn about learning, we have also seen that teachers may adopt a simplified model of practice in the face of contextual constraints.

DIFFERENT VIEWS, DIFFERENT COMPLEXITY

Roland Barth (1997) has suggested that the researcher's knowledge base is perhaps a mile wide and an inch deep in contrast to that of the classroom practitioner's which is an inch wide and a mile deep. This comment helps identify a key difference between an academic considering pedagogy and a practitioner doing likewise. The former strives to gain a multi-contextual view so as to construct an overall model. In contrast, the practitioner is concerned with the particular features of his or her context and in its daily rhythms. The cross-situation complexity which the researcher aims to create in explanatory models is of a different nature to the within-situation complexity which the practitioner creates. The implications for action may also differ in important ways with the researcher seeking a long-term indirect impact, while the practitioner is faced with the need for short-term immediate action. These points may be illustrated diagrammatically in Figure 1.2.

Thus the relationship between these two parties is not a direct exchange of similar forms of knowledge about pedagogy. When engaged in work together they are not trading in exactly the same currency: research and practice simply do not stand on the same logical footing. Researchers try to use theories to generate insight into problems, not as solution banks. They offer frameworks and models to the practitioner in the hope of helping them – in the light of the broader picture they can provide – to frame a problem, review their current practice and challenge themselves to extend their repertoire.

Practitioners will always have a role to play in the selection and translation

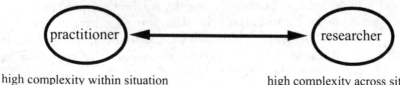

high complexity within situation
short-term immediate action

high complexity across situations
long-term indirect action

Fig. 1.2 Practitioner and researcher knowledge

of frameworks and models to specific contexts. They need to challenge researchers on the validity of their models. Seen in this light the relationship between researchers and practitioners should be productive and able to move beyond some of the archetypal misunderstandings, such as teachers criticizing academics for not being 'practical' (or its inverse 'teaching me to suck eggs') and academics becoming disappointed that their proposals were either rejected or varied beyond their recognition.

In our experience, teachers welcome collaboration with people who will work as hard to understand classroom events as the teachers do to conduct them. This demands recognition that teachers possess important expertise and that professional learning is an adaptive process. This process is long-term and is critically influenced by contextual factors in the school and local area. At its best, professional development helps teachers to understand their school and to contribute to school-based improvement efforts. In such undertakings the researcher can help the professional to enhance their own knowledge-generation capacities. This style of relationship has sometimes been characterized as one of 'critical friend' though this term is not always clearly understood: some seem only to read the word 'critical' while others seem only to comprehend the word 'friend'.

Having compared the formal and the vernacular views of pedagogy and discussed the criteria for profitable exchange, we turn to recognize other players in the story.

POLICY AND PEDAGOGY

Recent decades have seen politicians and policy-makers develop an increased interest in the details of pedagogy. This trend began some thirty years ago with the publication of the Plowden Report (Central Advisory Council, 1967), nowadays regarded as the report which gave birth to the traditional-progressive distinction in policy and public debate. However, current perceptions that a romantic view of social relations in small groups informed the recommendations is not accurate. Rather, the Report's suggested increase in group work was actually a measure designed to help teachers trying to reach all their children:

> Sharing out the teacher's time is a major problem. Only seven or eight minutes a day would be available for each child if all teaching were individual. Teachers therefore have to economise by teaching together a small group of children at the same stage (paras. 754–5)

A polarized view of teaching styles can still be detected in policy debates and media reports but a 1986 House of Commons Select Committee noted:

> we hope the simple argument between styles, whether formal or informal, individual or class teaching, child-centred or subject-centred, can be left behind: none is sufficient by itself.
>
> (House of Commons Science and Arts Committee, 1986, p. 115)

Since 1986, the attitudes of politicians have changed. Using the rhetoric of 'secret gardens' and the call for increased financial accountability in public services, governments have promoted new forms of monitoring and control. In the context of reducing levels of trust in Britain (Inglehart, 1990, pp. 35 and 438), an additional fear has been added to the occupational hazards of teaching – the fear of public censure and shame. So although as recently as 1991 a Secretary of State could state that 'questions about how to teach are not for government to determine' (Clarke, 1991) the State's influence on classroom practice has been pursued through a variety of routes. Without direct legislation, impact on pedagogy has come though government agencies, their formal inspection frameworks and models of teacher competence. These have been supported by less formal modes of opinion-forming through direct and indirectly attributable media coverage.

Recent policy-makers have focused on actions which, they claim, achieve results. Policy-makers thus need to simplify pedagogy if they are to take such a role. In so doing they appear to have reverted to a nineteenth-century model which centred on the 'object lesson' – a set piece deemed to have universal application. This stance has created an interesting set of relations between teachers, academics and policy-makers themselves (see Figure 1.3).

The dynamics in this triangle are sometimes characterized by critical friendship, with acceptance of different perspectives, open communication and equal respect. On other occasions, practitioners feel treated as functionaries and the stance of policy-makers towards teachers is one of a 'hostile witness'. At the same time, researchers have been accused of acting like 'collusive lovers' towards the teaching force.

Ministers have only engaged in proffering pedagogical advice in recent times but local advisers, trainers and writers have done so for many years. Their roles and careers elicit and encourage such behaviour. However, the

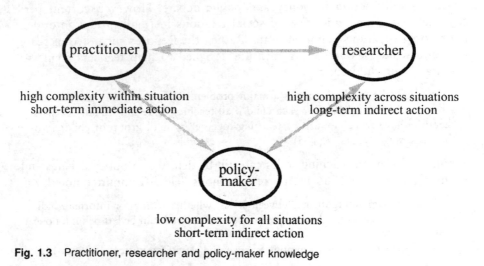

Fig. 1.3 Practitioner, researcher and policy-maker knowledge

impact of simple advice for all situations is often short-lived since it encounters powerful features of the school and classroom system:

– prescriptions which are significantly less complex than the prevailing practice have decreasing effects, since they do not embed into the continuing practice of the context;
– prescriptions are always modified and interpreted to fit the local conditions and culture, thus maintaining local effects. For example when we asked twenty science teachers to exchange their 'Schemes of Work' their major realization was that they were not all teaching the same National Curriculum;
– prescriptions often neglect teachers' roles as professionals able to select and adapt methods according to their reading of the needs: instead they cast teachers in the role of functionaries, with consequent damage to professional morale;
– the imposition of prescriptions on human systems has some predictably negative effects: causing teachers to become more prescriptive or controlling and this can lead to increasing inequalities in the system's performance;
– prescriptions do not carry a message of, or invitation to, continued learning in the future.

Since prescriptions are a simplification, it is no surprise that they generally embody a partial, mechanical, view of learning. They risk the adoption of a particular view, a 'folk pedagogy', which Bruner (1996) identifies as probably the most common practice today. This is the view that children learn only from didactic exposure. It incorporates the belief that pupils should be presented with facts, principles and rules of action. These are to be learned, remembered and then applied. Pupils are assumed not to 'know' about the topic; knowing can be conveyed by telling; and the learner's mind is passive.

Its principal appeal is that it purports to offer a clear specification of just what it is that is to be learned and, equally questionable, that it suggests standards for assessing its achievement. More than any other folk theory it has spawned objective testing in its myriad guises. (Bruner, 1996, p. 55)

It remains to be seen what long-term effects such a pedagogical approach will have.

CONCLUDING COMMENTS

In this opening chapter, we have discussed some of the general issues which influence our current conceptions of pedagogy. We have noted how pedagogy has been understood at different periods of history in increasingly complex ways. We have recognized that 'expert' teachers display great complexity in their handling of classroom processes, although we have also drawn attention to the tendency to simplify approaches to teaching in response to the constraints and demands of the situation.

We hope that readers will be interested to follow these and other issues through the chapters of this volume, and that the importance of complexity and context will be kept in mind. We believe that they are necessary antidotes to over-simple orthodoxies.

Life continues to change at an increasingly fast pace. The global knowledge base is growing exponentially and the social fabric of our societies is being altered by the massive expansion of communications. Pedagogy must change to keep up with these developments. It must seek to engage those who would otherwise be excluded. It must also support all learners to generate knowledge and to learn what to do when faced with uncertainty.

The nature of work is also changing. There are now fewer of the manual and unskilled jobs which had previously been taken by many males. Individuals in employment need to possess the skills to work well with others and to go on learning, as well as having high levels of literacy and numeracy. An increasing proportion of employees will need to be skilled in the use of information technology. Since multi-national companies can easily locate in areas where skilled work forces are available more cheaply, part of the response in this post-industrial era is to move from high-volume to high-value production, and to develop the requisite skills. Educators, just as they had to respond to the demands of industrial revolution, are now being required to respond to all the implications of modern life. Their learning curve is increasingly *steep* – social, technological, economic, environmental and political changes are all underway (Watkins, 1997).

Arguments are frequently made that if educational standards in a country are perceived to be low, industries may move elsewhere thus causing a detrimental effect on the country's economy. In the richer nations there is currently much political pressure on educational systems to 'raise academic standards'. If maintaining employment requires high educational standards, then governments will try to ensure that those standards are attained and subsequently maintained. International league tables of educational performance make it relatively easy for crude comparisons to be made – especially by those unaware of their methodological difficulties (Bracey, 1998).

In the landscape of future learning, we believe that formal organizations for learning – such as schools – will increasingly be seen as but one element. Such bodies may be called on to justify their special position, which may be an advance on them being treated as scapegoat or saviour in turns. This greater expectation may be met if the major contribution of schools is to enhancing quality and not just quantity. In such a fast-moving scenario, schools and colleges need to help citizens learn about their learning in all contexts of their lives so as to enhance a state of self-efficacy.

For this to happen, schools and colleges have to function more like learning organizations than like learning factories. Information and communications technology will need to play its part in accessing information, promoting dialogue and creating new communities for co-constructing knowledge. Teachers will be expected to possess a full repertoire of pedagogic options in order to create high-achieving environments for the maximum number of diverse learners. Only in such a fashion will our definition of pedagogy – 'any conscious activity by one person designed to enhance learning in another' – remain suitably vibrant and become suitably distributed for a post-industrial context.

The following chapters will explore, at a more detailed level, a number of issues to do with the pedagogy currently employed in different phases of education. Our focus on pedagogy in different educational settings – what it has been, is and might be – is surely long overdue.

REFERENCES

Anderson, H.H. and Brewer, J.E. (1946) *Studies of Teachers' Classroom Personalities. – 2: Effects of Teachers' Dominative and Integrative Contacts on Children's Classroom Behavior*, Stanford CA: Stanford University Press.

Arends, R.I. (1994) *Learning to Teach*, New York: McGraw-Hill.

Barker Lunn, J. (1984), Junior school teachers: their methods and practices, *Educational Research*, 26(3): 178–188.

Barth, R. (1997) Presentation at launch of the London Leadership Centre, Institute of Education, 30 January 1997.

Bennett, N. (1976) *Teaching Styles and Pupil Progress*, London: Open Books.

Bennett, N. and Jordan, J. (1975) A typology of teaching styles in primary schools, *British Journal of Educational Psychology*, 45: 20–28.

Best, F. (1988) The metamorphoses of the term 'pedagogy', *Prospects*, XVIII(2): 157–166.

Bracey, G.W. (1996) TIMSS: The Message and the Myths, *Principal*, 77(3): 18–22.

Brophy, J. (ed.) (1992) *Advances in Research on Teaching – Vol. 3: Planning and Managing Learning Tasks and Activities*, London: JAI Press.

Brown, J., Collins. A. and Duguid, P. (1989) Situated cognition and the culture of learning, *Educational Researcher*, 18(1): 32–42.

Bruner, J.S. (1996) Folk pedagogy, in *The Culture of Education*, Cambridge MA: Harvard University Press.

Carlsen, W.S. (1991) Subject-matter knowledge and science teaching: a pragmatic perspective in Brophy, J. (ed.) *Advances in Research on Teaching – Vol. 2: Teachers' Knowledge of Subject Matter as it Relates to Their Teaching Practice*, London: JAI Press.

Central Advisory Council (The Plowden Report) (1967) *Children and their Primary Schools*, London: HMSO

Chandra, P. (1987) How do teachers view their teaching and use of teaching resources?, *British Journal of Educational Technology*, 18(2): 102–11.

Clarke, K. (1991) *Letter to schools regarding the enquiry on primary teaching*, London: DFE.

Copeland, W.D., Birmingham, C., Demeulle, L., Demidiocaston, M. and Natal, D. (1994) Making meaning in classrooms: an investigation of cognitive processes in aspiring teachers, experienced teachers, and their peers, *American Educational Research Journal*, 31(1): 166–196.

Cox, B.D. (1997) The rediscovery of the active learner in adaptive contexts: a developmental-historical analysis of transfer of training, *Educational Psychologist*, 32(1): 41–55.

Cuban, L. (1984) *How Teachers Taught – Constancy and Change in American*

Classrooms, 1890–1980, New York: Longman.

Cuban, L. (1993) Computers meet classroom – classroom wins, *Teachers College Record*, 95(2): 185–210.

Doyle, W. (1977) Learning the classroom environment: an ecological analysis, *Journal of Teacher Education*, 28(6): 51–55.

Doyle, W. (1983) Academic work, *Review of Educational Research*, 53(2): 159–199.

Doyle, W. (1984) How order is achieved in classrooms: an interim report, *Journal of Curriculum Studies*, 16(3): 259–77.

Doyle, W. (1990) Classroom knowledge as a foundation for teaching, *Teachers College Record*, 91(3): 347–60.

Fleck, L. (1935) *The Social Construction of Scientific Thought*, Chicago: University of Chicago Press.

Floden, R. and Buchmann, M. (1993) Between routines and anarchy – preparing teachers for uncertainty, *Oxford Review of Education*, 19(3): 373–382.

Galton, M. (1987) Change and continuity in the primary-school – the research evidence, *Oxford Review of Education*, 13(1): 81–93.

House of Commons Science and Arts Committee (1986) *Achievement in Primary Schools*, London: HMSO.

Hughes, M. (1997) *Lessons are For Learning*, Stafford: Network Educational Press.

Inglehart, R. (1990) *Culture Shift in Advanced Industrial Society*, Princeton NJ: Princeton University Press.

Jackson, P.W. (1977) The way teachers think, in Glidewell, J. (ed.), *The Social Context of Learning and Development*, New York: Gardner Press.

Johnston, J.M. (1990) *What Are Teachers' Perceptions of Teaching in Different Classroom Contexts?*, paper given to Annual Meeting of the American Educational Research Association: Boston MA.

Knowles, M.S. (1980) *The Modern Practice of Adult Education: From Pedagogy to Andragogy*, Wilton CN: Association Press.

Kounin, J.S. (1977) *Discipline and Group Management in Classrooms*, Huntington NY: Krieger.

Langer, J.A. and Applebee, A.N. (1988) *Speaking of Knowing: Conceptions of Learning in Academic Subjects. Academic Learning in High School Subjects*, Washington DC: Office of Educational Research and Improvement.

Larsson, S. (1983) Paradoxes in teaching, *Instructional Science*, 12(4): 355–365.

Latour, B. and Woolgar, S. (1986) *Laboratory Life: The Social Construction of Scientific Facts*, Princeton NJ: Princeton University Press.

Lewin, K., Lippitt, R. and White, R. (1939) Patterns of aggressive behavior in experimentally created social climates, *Journal of Social Psychology*, 10: 271–299.

Marland, M. (1993) *The Craft of the Classroom*, Oxford, Heinemann Educational.

Marton, F. and Booth, S. (1997) *Learning and Awareness*, Mahwah NJ: Lawrence Erlbaum.

Marton, F., Dall'Alba, G. and Beaty, E. (1993) Conceptions of learning, *International Journal of Educational Research*, 19(3): 277–300.

McDonald, J.P. (1992) *Teaching: making sense of an uncertain craft*, New York: Teachers College Press.

McNamara, D. (1991) Vernacular pedagogy, *British Journal of Educational Studies*, 39(3): 297–310.

Miel, A. and Wiles, K. (1949) *Toward Better Teaching*, Washington DC: Association for Supervision and Curriculum Development of the National Education

Association.

Mortimore, P. (1998) *The Road to Improvement: Reflections on School Effectiveness*, Lisse: Swets & Zeitlinger.

National Commission on Education (1996) *Success Against the Odds: Effective Schools in Disadvantaged Areas*, London: Routledge.

Oxford Shorter English Dictionary (1993) Oxford: Clarendon Press.

Pramling, I. (1990) *Learning to Learn: A Study of Swedish Preschool Children*, New York: Springer-Verlag.

Resnick, L.B. (1987) Learning in school and out, *Educational Researcher*, 16(9): 13–40.

Rosenholtz, S.J. (1991) *Teachers' Workplace: The Social Organization of Schools*, New York: Teachers College Press.

Roth, K. (1987) *Helping science teachers change: the critical role of teachers' knowledge about science and science learning*, paper given to Annual meeting of AERA, Washington DC.

Rudduck, J., Harris, S. and Wallace, G. (1995) 'It's not that I haven't learnt much. It's just that I don't understand what I'm doing': metacognition and secondary-school students, *Research Papers in Education*, 10(2): 253–271.

Ryans, D.G. (1968) *Characteristics of Teachers: Their Description, Comparison and Approval; A Research Study*, Washington DC: American Council on Education.

Sabers, D.S., Cushing, K.S. and Berliner, D. (1991) Differences among teachers in a task characterised by simultaneity, multidimensionality and immediacy, *American Educational Research Journal*, 28(1): 63–88.

Säljö, R. (1979) *Learning in the Learner's Perspective I – Some Common Sense Perceptions*, University of Göteborg.

Samuelowicz, K. and Bain, J.D. (1992) Conceptions of teaching held by academic teachers, *Higher Education*, 24(1): 93–111.

Simon, B. (1994) 'Some problems of pedagogy revisited' in, *The State and Educational Change: Essays in the History of Education and Pedagogy*, London: Lawrence & Wishart.

Smith, L. and Geoffrey, W. (1968) *The Complexities of the Urban Classroom*, New York: Holt Rinehart & Winston.

Talbert, J.E., McLaughlin, M.W. and Rowan, B. (1993) Understanding context effects on secondary school teaching, *Teachers College Record*, 95(1): 45–68.

Trigwell, K. and Prosser, M. (1996) Changing approaches to teaching: a relational perspective, *Studies in Higher Education*, 21(3): 275–84.

Watkins, C. (1997) *Schools of the Future and How to Get There From Here*, presentation at Hampstead School Conference, September.

Watkins, C., Carnell, E., Lodge, C. and Whalley, C. (1996) *Effective Learning*, London: Institute of Education School Improvement Network (Research Matters series) (download free from http://www.ioe.ac.uk/iseic/research.pdf)

Weinstein, C.S. (1989) Teacher education students' preconceptions of teaching, *Journal of Teacher Education*, 40(2): 53–60.

2

Early Childhood Pedagogy: Practice, Principles and Research

Iram Siraj-Blatchford

This chapter seeks to identify the pedagogical principles and practices which are most frequently adopted and considered most relevant in early childhood education. The second half of the chapter addresses the most commonly promoted alternative early childhood programmes (UK and other countries) and their pedagogical implications; the opportunities and limitations they afford; and the ongoing challenges they pose for research. Early childhood education (ECE) in the UK generally refers to children from birth to eight. In this chapter pre-school education denotes under-fives care and education settings (under-six in the case of most other countries), including reception classes in U.K. primary schools.

In Chapter 1, Mortimore and Watkins refer to the way in which different models of learning have led to the generation of different metaphors of schooling; as 'gardens in which children grow'; 'factories in which children are made' and 'hospitals in which children are cured of their ignorance'(p. 6). Such metaphors have been as pertinent in early childhood as in mainstream schooling although they have more often been expressed in terms of the more limited binary opposition of 'education' and 'care' approaches to provision. As we shall see, this controversy has run parallel, and is in many ways resonant with, the debate over the relative merits of 'child centred/progressive' and 'traditional' methods of teaching in primary schools.

To be an effective pedagogue means to be skilled in the selection of appropriate teaching techniques in order to facilitate learning, and in schools it is generally recognized that a range of 'techniques' are required for the effective transmission of different forms of knowledge. In the pre-school context, however, this simply cannot be taken for granted. In childcare institutions modelled on the 'kindergarten' ('children's garden') model, the idea of 'transmission' is seen to have little relevance. The most extreme and romantic childcare perspectives that have been adopted in some care-orientated settings have therefore offered only a minimal role for pedagogy. In some pre-school settings 'education' itself has come to be considered didactic and inappropriate for young children, as Chazan *et al.* (1987, p. 11) have put it:

> The adverse reaction displayed by some teachers of young children to structured programmes . . . stems, probably, from their dislike of direct teacher instruction.

This development has been encouraged by the unfortunate historical division in state funded pre-school provision between the social services 'care' sector and the education sector. The independent and voluntary sectors have also historically been divided between the 'care' orientated playgroup sector and the less numerous but more education (or even prep-school) orientated private nurseries. At their best, the exclusively childcare orientated settings have provided rich environments where children are allowed to play and to develop at their own pace, as closely to their natural instincts as safety will allow. The adult's role has been limited to caring for the child and protecting them from injury. As we shall see, while this has often been justified in terms of respecting the child's 'right to play' or their 'right to childhood', various forms of 'free' and 'free-flow' play can also be encouraged in settings where adults take on a much more structured educational role.

For the time being it is enough to note that it is not uncommon to find that early childhood educators recoil at the thought of pedagogy as 'teaching'. Most would be satisfied that there is a consensus around an individualized play-based curriculum and that adults should be non-directive and only 'facilitate' learning. Walkerdine (1984) has suggested that these ideas were significantly developed in response to particular readings of Piaget's theories of child development that emphasized the notion of 'stages of development' and 'readiness for learning'. As Murphy (1996, p. 11) has put it:

> Central to this pedagogy was the belief that a child's development towards scientific rationality emerges spontaneously as she explores and 'plays' with the environment.

In the past, knowledge was often viewed as an established body of facts, skills and attitudes that can, and should, be taught to children as soon as they were capable of mastering it. This view was articulated by the right-wing pressure groups that contributed to the Education Reform Act and was reflected in the subject specification and much of the content of the National Curriculum. But curriculum does not necessarily determine pedagogy and the historical association of an emphasis on the teaching of 'facts' and the use of didactic pedagogies is unfortunate. The popular distinction that has been made between 'play' and 'work' trivializes the issues. In fact, the continuum that is assumed to exist between the didacticism considered essential to a 'banking' (Freire) approach to education, on the one hand, and the *laissez-faire* adoption of the more romantic notions of early childhood on the other may be quite spurious. But as the Rumbold report (DES, 1990, p. 14) suggested:

> For the early years educator – how children are encouraged to learn – is as important as, and inseparable from, the content – what they learn. We believe that this principle must underlie all curriculum planning . . . Educators should

guard against pressures which might lead them to over-concentration on formal teaching and upon the attainment of a specific set of targets.

In order to understand the different approaches adopted in the different settings in the pre-school sector a short description of the 'big-picture' of pre-school education and care in the UK might be helpful.

In 1996 the Audit Commission stressed the diversity prevalent in pre-school provision that included: maintained nursery education (within the school system); reception classes in maintained primary schools; private schools; private day nurseries; playgroups (often part of the voluntary sector); local authority day nurseries; family centres and childminders.

Services have been characterized by unevenness in access, effectiveness, quality and costs (Audit Commission, 1996, p. 30). The voluntary sector has half-day parent-run playgroups which cater for the largest number of children under four. Within the state sector education departments provide free, full-day and half-day nursery provision, whilst social services contribute to full-time care programmes in daycare centres and combined nurseries. These different settings are now administered by education departments at both the local and national level. However, the deep historical 'split' between 'care' and 'education' created divisions which are likely to continue for some time, in spite of recent national initiatives to set-up Early Years Development Partnerships in each local authority.

The 'patchwork' of diverse forms of provision has been matched with an equally diverse workforce (Sylva et al., 1992; Siraj-Blatchford, 1995). Traditionally, the initial training of those who work in the education and care sectors has differed. A small percentage of teachers can be found, mainly in the nursery sector and normally attached to primary schools. These teachers have had three or four years of higher education. Those trained for the care sector have normally had only two years of mainly childcare training in further education. In addition, the voluntary sector carers and childminders receive local training based on programmes devised by their national organizations. Different early childhood 'educators', therefore, hold differing perceptions of the nature of early childhood, play, educational assessment and of how all of these elements are integrated in an early childhood curriculum and pedagogy.

The Government, partly in response to the growing critique, and in an effort to 'standardize' the education that young children receive, is now introducing a set of learning goals which all providers have to meet if they are funded to educate four year olds. (There is nothing similar for under-fours although this might change if a Foundaton Stage for 3–5 year olds is established.) These learning goals for children as they reach statutory school age 5–5.4 years (or 'Desirable Outcomes for Children's Learning') were published in *Nursery Education Scheme: The Next Steps* (SCAA, 1996) which outlined Government plans 'to provide, over time, a nursery education place of good quality for all four year olds whose parents wish to take it up' (SCAA, 1996, p. 3). Participating institutions have also been required to provide information about 'the extent to which the quality of provision is appropriate to the desirable out-comes in each area of learning' (SCAA, 1996, p. 3). All provision for four year olds is now inspected by the Office for Standards in Education (OFSTED) and the inspection reports outline how well settings support children's progress towards these Desirable Learning Outcomes.

As previously argued, however, changes in curriculum have only an indi-rect effect upon pedagogy and the teacher's choice of 'teaching style' (Galton, 1989). The particular collection of techniques that teachers favour will be determined by a whole range of factors, including their previous experience and training, their individual personality, their conception of childhood and learning, as well as the particular contexts in which they work, the accom-modation and resources that are available and the influence of co-workers. Even in the case of schools providing the National Curriculum, there is con-siderable variation in the pedagogic principles employed by different teachers.

THE INFLUENCE OF THE DESIRABLE LEARNING OUTCOMES

The Desirable Learning Outcomes (DLOs) describe six areas of learning which facilitate children's transition onto the National Curriculum at age five. They are: Personal and Social Development; Language and Literacy; Mathematics; Knowledge and Understanding of the World; Physical Development and Creative Development. At this early stage of implementa-tion it seems that early childhood educators have reacted to these Outcomes differently, depending on the kind of provision they work in and according to their training (Moriarty and Siraj-Blatchford, 1998a). Educators claim lit-tle has changed in many settings where a tradition of acceptance of the edu-cational role remains. The situation has been complicated by changes in admissions whereby increasing numbers of four year olds have been enter-ing reception classes, leaving other pre-school settings predominately cater-ing for three year olds. It also appears that, in some settings, the DLOs are being implemented in an over formal, even didactic, manner (Moriarty and Siraj-Blatchford, 1998b). Where these didactic tendencies are being reported, the evidence suggests that they may represent little more than an initial reac-tion to anxieties regarding the terms of inspection by OFSTED. Educators who have been given no pedagogic guidance, when faced with the need to cover new curriculum content, have often fallen back upon direct teaching. If pedagogic confusion is such a common response to curriculum change then in future we will need to provide pedagogic guidance alongside curriculum initiatives. The failure of the DLOs to provide any guidance on process or pedagogic priorities has already been criticized by pre-school specialists. The consultation on the DLOs may now take this into account in any revisions to the document. However, the first consultation period has been based on even more rigid early learning goals and the proposal that we adopt a Foundation Stage for children 3–5.

CONSENSUS ON THE IMPORTANCE ATTACHED TO 'PLAY'

Early childhood pedagogical practices in the UK continue to vary a great deal but there is one major area of consensus in provision. Virtually every form of early childhood pedagogy (and alternative provisions) are based on some form of play. Play is considered to be efficacious for one or more of the following reasons:

- it motivates children and enhances learning
- it provides a context for exploration and experiment
- it is the child's 'work'
- it is 'developmentally appropriate'.

Perhaps the oldest and most powerful justification for the emphasis on play has come from research in biology (or zoology) which claims that many animals have evolved a distinct period of childhood for the specific purposes of learning through play (Smith and Cowie, 1991). There is, amongst early childhood educators, a widespread consensus regarding the importance of play. This has not led to pedagogic uniformity, however, largely because there are wide differences of opinion and variation in understanding regarding the degree of influence that adults should have over the play curriculum (Bennett *et al.*, 1997). Unsurprisingly given their history (poor and very different levels of training which have persisted over the last century) pre-school educators have found it difficult to articulate their practices convincingly.

Since the 1980s one approach, influenced significantly by the translation and adaptation of Vygotskian theories of learning, has been increasingly influential. The 'social constructivist' perspectives have drawn attention to the importance of experience and instruction, to the nature of the social context in which learning takes place and to the support that needs to be provided for the child by more knowledgeable adults and peers. The search for quality in early childhood services, including conditions for effective practice, continues to be the subject of a great deal of academic study in the UK and overseas (Sylva *et al.*, 1996). But the terms of the debate have been largely determined by the pedagogic techniques considered most relevant by the researchers involved which, in turn, have been shaped by the learning theories to which they have subscribed.

TEACHING TECHNIQUES AND DEVELOPMENTALLY APPROPRIATE PRACTICE (DAP)

Social constructivist principles have been promoted worldwide through the institutionalization of what has come to be termed 'Developmentally Appropriate Practice' (DAP) (Bredekamp and Copple, 1997; Hurst and Joseph, 1998). In the United States, as Dunn and Kontos (1997) have suggested, DAP has been promoted by the National Association for the Education of Young Children (NAEYC) and their publications tend to

represent 'a record of the consensus thinking' on the subject of early childhood pedagogy. But despite a consensus of opinion in the UK as well as in
the US, research in the US suggests that only 20–30 per cent of US settings
are putting the ideas into practice (Dunn and Kontos, 1997) and there is little cause to think the situation is different in the UK. Given the strength of
the consensus, it is useful to consider the pedagogic techniques considered
most relevant to 'good practice' in the DAP literature and tradition.

The NAEYC provides extensive guidance for practitioners both in their
publications (e.g. Bredekamp and Copple, 1997) and in their extensive web
presence.[1] The central declared aim of the DAP initiative has been 'to enhance
development and learning' and to achieve this through providing an optimal
balance between children's self-initiated learning and the adult guidance or
support offered to them.

Teachers provide children with opportunities to make meaningful choices
and time to explore their world through active involvement. Teachers offer
children the choice of participating in a small-group or a solitary activity.
They assist and guide children who are not yet able to use and enjoy child-
choice activity periods and they provide opportunities for the practice of
skills in a self-chosen activity (NAEYC, 1996).

DAP encourages teachers to use a variety of ways of flexibly grouping
children for the purposes of instruction, supporting collaboration and building a sense of community. Children have opportunities to work individually,
in small groups, and with the whole group.

In considering the pedagogic 'techniques' considered especially relevant to
early childhood education we can usefully distinguish between those techniques concerned with the management of the environment and those concerned with interactions. Both are emphasized in DAP. In a play centred
curriculum the availability and 'positioning' of both material and human
resources is often considered crucial:

> The positioning of equipment to encourage interactions between children of
> mixed abilities can have a positive effect on children's learning. Bennett and Cass
> (1989) suggested that placing children of mixed age and/or mixed ability in small
> groups could enhance their learning.
>
> (MacNaughton and Williams, 1998, p. 173)

Adults may position themselves strategically in a setting so as to maximize
their interaction with the children and even in the 'most free' of free play
settings resources can be allocated to encourage interaction between children.
Specific equipment and materials can also be positioned to gain and maintain children's attention, and materials (including some of the children's own
work) can be displayed to show that they are especially valued. The displays
and resources available to the children are, ideally, changed regularly in order
to provide a broad range of learning experiences and/or the most stimulating

---

[1](http://www.naeyc.org)

learning environment. The introduction of a new piece of equipment or idea at a key moment in a child's play can significantly enhance their experience:

> A child is playing with Lego bricks. The teacher asks her what she is doing. She says 'making a tower . . . it keeps falling down.' The teacher points to the standard lamp in the home corner and asks 'Why doesn't that fall down?' The child answers 'it has a big bit on the bottom'. The teacher suggests that she might try fixing the tower to a base.
>
> (Siraj-Blatchford and MacLeod-Brudenell, 1999)

In most pre-school settings some part of the child's day will be spent with their peers, singing songs and rhymes, dancing and playing big group games, sitting listening to a story or participating in other structured listening and talking activities (for example, recalling their 'news' or the events of the weekend). Adults may read, discuss, play musical instruments and sing and dance with the children. If they are to ensure a safe environment, adults also need to provide instructions and necessary information for the group. Planned activities may encourage the children to develop a variety of physical, intellectual or craft skills. Adults can support children in (for example) solving puzzles, designing and making play structures or environments, developing collaborative fantasy play.

Most of the day, however, will usually be spent in individual or small group play. The interactive techniques available to the adults in these contexts are numerous. In supporting a child's painting activity, for example, adults may demonstrate a particular technique or find themselves broadening a child's experience by describing some experience, object or environment that the child has never known. They may question children and direct their attention to things that they might otherwise miss. Adults can also provide valuable role models – particularly influential where other positive models are unavailable in the home or family environment (for example, of women confident with handling technology or of a male carer).

> To sustain an individual child's effort or engagement in purposeful activities, teachers select from a range of strategies, including but not limited to modelling, demonstrating specific skills, and providing information, focused attention, physical proximity, verbal encouragement, reinforcement and other behavioral procedures, as well as additional structure and modification of equipment or schedules as needed.
>
> (NAEYC, 1996)

Adults can also provide constructive criticism and reinforce positive behaviours and learning outcomes. They can encourage and help children struggling with a task. They can also 'scaffold' children's learning by directing a child's attention to some new aspect of a situation, or help them manage a task more effectively by breaking it down into a sequence of smaller tasks, or by helping a child to sequence activities in the right order (Smith, 1994).

Another technique widely considered to be crucial in most of the more structured educational settings is systematic observation and the recording or documentation of children's performance and behaviour. Teachers can use both their general knowledge of child development and learning and their specific knowledge of the children in their care to identify the range of activities, materials, and learning experiences that are appropriate for a group or individual child. This knowledge is used in conjunction with knowledge of the cultural backgrounds and experience, and the strengths, needs and interests of individual children:

> Teachers continually observe children's spontaneous play and interaction with the physical environment and with other children to learn about their interests, abilities, and developmental progress. On the basis of this information, teachers plan experiences that enhance children's learning and development.
>
> (NAEYC, 1996).

A limited range of most of the above techniques are employed in most UK early childhood settings. As previously suggested, they have all been promoted in guidelines provided by early years educators favouring DAP, and in many other approaches, but the knowledge and understanding of these vary among individual early years educators for the reasons previously given. The quality and content of training is highly variable but efforts are being made in many areas of the country to provide in service (INSET) support. In the last few years a very significant provider in this respect has been the Effective Early Learning (EEL) Research project.

PROMOTING DAP: THE EFFECTIVE EARLY LEARNING (EEL) PROJECT

The EEL project provides a professional development programme that is involved in 'evaluating and developing quality in early childhood settings' (Pascal and Bertram, 1995, p. 1). The programme is based on a collaborative action research model and informed by what the directors of the project refer to as the 'Pascal/Bertram Quality Evaluation Framework'. For Pascal and Bertram (1997), effective learning demands that an essentially symbiotic relationship be developed between the child and the adult. Drawing upon work carried out by Laevers (1995) in Belgium, they refer to the importance of the 'involvement' of the child and the 'engagement' of the teacher. An involved child is one who has focused their attention, is persistent, and who is intrinsically motivated, rarely distracted, fascinated and absorbed by his or her activity. An engaged adult is one who shows sensitivity and stimulation yet grants enough autonomy for children to make their own judgements and express their own ideas.

The learning relationship is considered symbiotic by Pascal and Bertram (1997, p. 135) because:

> not only does the adults' style of engagement directly affect the children's levels of involvement, but the children's involvement affects the adult's style of engagement.

As Pascal and Bertram recognize, involvement and engagement do not operate in an affective vacuum. Both the 'learning disposition' of the child and the 'professional well being' of the teacher provide significant conditions for learning. Pascal and Bertram apply the model to measure 'quality' provision in their collaborative action research. As a behavioural concept, 'involvement' clearly does provide an indicator of the kind of learning conditions described by Piaget (1995) and Vygotsky (1978). But Laevers originally derived the notion of 'engagement' from Rogers (1983) whose influence has been greater in the areas of counselling and therapy than in education. As a basis for the development of a pedagogic research instrument, engagement has benefits but also some drawbacks.

- Its exclusive focus of attention on adult engagement distracts attention from the influence of peers who may be encouraged to scaffold each others' learning.
- It effectively excludes the possibility of recognizing the value of direct instruction for some areas of teaching, despite its widespread practice in the early years (for example, in teaching songs and rhymes or giving instructions in safety, hygiene and toiletting).
- In prioritizing process, it provides no basis for assessing the content of the engagement (for example, to what extent the teacher's intervention may be considered 'worthwhile') or whether the 'correct' information is imparted.

There are other instruments and guidance which measure quality and can be used for self-evaluation within settings such as the Early Childhood Environment Rating Scale (ECERS) and the Quality in Diversity framework. However, the EEL intervention has proven to be the most favoured approach by early years educators.

THE INFLUENCE OF ESTABLISHED THEORIES OF LEARNING

One criticism of DAP has been associated with its allegedly uncritical application of 'developmental stage theory' in determining the early years curriculum and the suggestion that any particular set of classroom or nursery practices could be defined as objectively appropriate for all children at a certain stage of their development (Spodek and Saracho, 1991, p. 24; New, 1994). A second line of criticism concerns the idea of 'developmental appropriateness' itself. This sees the child as moving along a biologically-determined and common sequence of developmental stages.

The more extreme 'child-centred' or 'care' approaches to early childhood provision have been referred to earlier. These approaches have been defended in the past by reference to a crude application of constructivist learning theory. The tenets of this theory, that children actively construct their world through the natural processes of play and discovery learning, are taken to the lengths of evoking the notion of the child as a 'lone scientist'. The approach has also been (mistakenly) attributed to Piaget (see Bennett *et al.*, 1997, pp. 2–4).

Piaget's constructivism, however, was more sophisticated. He described a learning mechanism which involved the child in the active elaboration of their own mental structures as they assimilated and accommodated new experiences. But, crucially for Piaget, this learning machine was 'fuelled' by the effect of 'interest' and it was triggered by the recognition of some 'disequilibrium' between the child's new phenomenon or experience and their prior knowledge and skill. The child's interest in the new phenomenon or experience might be the spontaneous result of their natural curiosity but it would also be influenced by the adults and peers around them. Piaget argued, therefore, that the child's intellectual adaptation was as much an adaptation to the social environment as it was an adaptation to their physical and material environment. This provided a potentially strong foundation for early years educational practice as it accounted simultaneously for learning and for motivation.

Unfortunately, this latter part of Piaget's theory, which provides an account of the role of social factors in early childhood development, has been largely neglected (DeVries, 1997). Yet Piaget argued that adult-child and peer relations influence every aspect of development and that affective and personality development are intimately related to intellectual and moral development. Perhaps most importantly, Piaget argued that reciprocity in peer relations provides the foundations for perspective taking and for decentring. This suggests that collaborative play is exceptionally important for children. According to DeVries, Piaget proposed ways in which co-operative social interaction between children and between children and adults function to promote cognitive, affective and moral development. As DeVries (1997, p. 16) says:

> If Piaget was correct, then we need to reconsider the structure and methods of our schools from the point of view of long-term effects on children's socio-moral, affective and intellectual development.

Given the failure of many educationalists to recognize the full extent of Piaget's contribution, we are largely indebted to Vygotsky for the foundations of our theories of teaching 'as assisted performance' (Tharp and Gallimore, 1991). Vygotsky defined what he referred to as the 'zone of proximal development', that is the distance between the actual developmental level as determined by individual problem solving and the level of potential development as determined through problem solving under adult guidance or in collaboration with more capable peers (Vygotsky, 1978, p. 86). The notion has now been popularly extended beyond problem solving to encompass performance in other areas of competence. The aims of teaching, from this perspective, are to assist children within this zone, and to provide the support and encouragement they require to perform successfully in areas that would otherwise be beyond them. The key challenge for educators becomes one of defining the limits of the zone, matching or 'tuning' the support, or of 'scaffolding' the learning (Wood, 1988), to a point just beyond each child's current seeming capabilities. According to this account, any assistance provided that lies within the children's existing capability is wasted, while assistance beyond the extremity of the zone will be meaningless and potentially damaging to the child's self-confidence. All efforts need to be made firmly *within* the 'zone of proximal development'.

As DeVries has argued, a great deal of work remains to be done to integrate Piagetian and Vygotskian theory. There can be little doubt, however, that it would be a worthwhile project. The academic understanding of learning underpinning current UK trends in early childhood education (Siraj-Blatchford, 1998) are predominantly based on principles of social constructivism drawn from both Vygotsky and Piaget but also conditioned by a cautious scepticism regarding any alleged essential or natural limitations to children's intellectual development. What this means in practice is that, whilst most theorists accept Piaget's account of 'intellectual adaptation' as the most convincing model that has yet been put forward to account for children's educational development, they now follow McGarrigal and Donaldson (1974) in rejecting the curriculum prescription that is implied by the acritical acceptance of crude notions of either the 'essential child' or of 'developmental stages'.

EFFECTIVE PRE-SCHOOL PRACTICES: THE EVIDENCE FROM RESEARCH

The quality of early childhood institutional programmes have been, and continue to be, the subject of a great deal of academic study in the UK and elswhere (Sylva *et al.*, 1996). Schweinhart *et al.*, (1993, p. 17) provide the following summary of the main characteristics of effective programmes, staffing and administration that have been identified:

- Effective programs use explicitly stated, developmentally appropriate active-learning curricula that support children's self-initiated learning activities.
- Effective teaching staff have been trained in early childhood education and do not change jobs often.
- Effective administrators provide systematic in service training on site and supervisory support for their staff's curriculum implementation.
- Effective programs maintain classes of fewer than 20 three to five year-olds for every pair of teaching adults.
- Staff treat parents as partners and engage in extensive outreach with monthly visits to learn from parents and to help them understand the curriculum and their children's development.

Research findings from the longitudinal study in New Zealand, *Competent*

Children (Wylie, 1998) show that, by age six, the children in the study gained higher or lower educational outcomes depending on such factors as: age at which children started ECE (before three had greater positive impact); quality of staff interactions with children and the extent to which children were allowed to complete activities. The educational achievement of children in this study will be followed for some years to come.

Longitudinal studies from America have demonstrated that social and motivational elements of pre-school programmes are as important as educational and academic outcomes. In some ways these have been demonstrated to be more important. Programmes such as High/Scope (which I shall describe later in the chapter) produced greater social outcomes which benefited both the individuals concerned and society in general. This success is attributed to the process of teaching and learning in the High/Scope programme which emphasizes interaction, reasoning, reflection and responsibility for self-learning. Whilst the focus of this chapter is academic learning, these studies highlight the importance of considering the wider social benefits to society.

Other studies have shown that 'formal' approaches to teaching young children are counterproductive (Schweinhart and Weikart, 1997; Nabuco and Sylva, 1996). They can hinder young children's learning by generating higher anxiety and lower self-esteem. These studies compare different types of programmes in ECE, such as High/Scope with a formal programme and a free-play programme. The results show that, where children are encouraged to take initiative for their own learning, the outcomes are higher all-round than for those programmes which emphasize teacher-directed activities. These findings have direct implications for the way we plan for four-year-olds in reception classes in the UK. Sylva (1997, p. 2), drawing together this evidence and arguing for more emphasis on pedagogies which emphasize self-initiated learning and social development, stated:

> The new emphasis on social development will require a new, sophisticated pedagogy (including assessment) to prepare children for group work in primary classrooms and participation as adults in the community.

ALTERNATIVE ECE PROGRAMMES

Having reviewed the major pedagogic issues and identified some of the challenges that early years education currently faces, I will now consider the opportunities and limitations to be afforded by adopting some of the most commonly promoted ECE programmes for early years education. Five alternative models have been selected: Reggio Emilia (Italy), High/Scope (USA), Movimento da Escola Moderna (Portugal), Te Whariki (New Zealand) and Quality in Diversity (UK). Many others might have been included (such as Montessori or Steiner). Each model could easily be analysed in terms of their curriculum but it is the pedagogic implications which will be considered here. However, these five programmes have all been subject to the increased attention on early years writing and practice in recent years. The diversity of the approaches offered is also considered to provide a basis for developing an analytical framework in our consideration of future developments. But to begin with, we need an overview of each of the alternative programmes:

Reggio Emilia

Reggio Emilia is a district in Northern Italy where, over the last thirty-five years, the municipality has developed an extensive network of early childhood services for children from birth to six, providing for over a third of children under three and nearly all children aged three to six. The city has become world-famous for the pedagogical work in these services, attracting many visitors from all over the world – although only recently beginning to attract visitors and interest from the UK (for further reading on Reggio Emilia see Moss *et al.*, 1999; Edwards *et al.*, 1993 and Gura, 1997). Providers of the early childhood services in Reggio understand the young child to be a co-constructor of knowledge and identity, a unique, complex and individual subject, engaging with and making sense of the world from birth, but always doing this in relationship with both adults and other children.

Reggio pre-schools develop close relationships between staff and parents and they employ some important 'pedagogical tools'. These 'tools' include: the pedagogical documentation procedure, thematic work, the role of specialist staff (such as 'atelierista' (resident artist) and 'pedagogista' – or child development specialist) and the time built into the pedagogues' working week to analyse, debate and reflect on their pedagogical practice. Each pre-school consists of three classrooms (one each for three year olds, four year olds and five year olds) and an art studio. Two co-teachers and a resident art specialist, who all play an integral role in the children's learning, are assigned to each room. A pedagogista co-ordinates the work of educators from several schools.

'Documentation' procedures are considered important for the children's learning and are focused on children's experiences and thoughts that may arise in the course of their work. Children are encouraged to express their understanding through symbolic representation such as drawing, sculpture or writing. These are then discussed and displayed and the displays form an important part of the documentation.

High/Scope

The High/Scope approach, which has gained considerable popularity in the UK, is based on the practice of Sara Smilansky. Weikart *et al.* (1971), working in the USA in the early 1970s, developed Smilansky's approach into what they termed the Cognitive Orientated Curriculum. The High/Scope approach in early years education starts from the Piagetian principle that 'children learn actively and construct their own knowledge' (Macleod, 1989, p. 33) and that this knowledge comes from their personal interaction with the world. These principles of social constructivism result in a curriculum that emphasizes children learning through direct experience with real objects and from applying logical thinking to this experience. An explicitly DAP model, the daily routines consist of the cycle of 'plan, do and review'. During planning, children decide what activity they will engage in for the session. Once the 'do' part of the routine is complete, the children recall what they have done during review time. The children's progress is assessed around 58 key experiences, which are grouped around the eight categories of active learning, language, experiencing and representing, classification, seriation, number, spatial relations and time (Hohmann et al., 1979). The setting is organized to provide the High/Scope experience and is divided into interest areas to promote active learning and specific kinds of play. The materials are sufficiently accessible to allow the children independence. The adult's role is to participate as a partner in the children's activities and there is an emphasis on positive interaction strategies, allowing children to share control and form authentic relationships with other children. The adult supports the children's learning and extends it by helping them to find solutions to problems. The approach claims to develop learning dispositions of independence, questioning and reasoning in the child as the foundations of other subsequent learning.

The High/Scope programme has been reviewed regularly through the study of a cohort of 123 African Americans born in poverty and identified as being at high risk of failing in school. When these children were aged three and four they were randomly divided into three groups. One group received a 'traditional' pre-school programme based on formal instruction. Another group followed a High/Scope programme and the last group had no programme. At the age of twenty-seven, the participants were interviewed and other data were analysed. The High/Scope group was found to have had fewer arrests, had a higher economic status, had performed better academically and had a greater commitment to marriage (Schweinhart et al., 1993). The evidence suggests, therefore, that a pedagogy that enables children to construct their own understandings may lead to positive outcomes in the long term.

The Movimento da Escola Moderna (MEM) Curriculum

The MEM curriculum was initially heavily influenced by Frinet, the French educationalist whose work centred around the use of a printing press and community education. Following their Frinetian foundations, MEM settings made frequent use of printing as a means of 'amplifying communication through space and time'. More recently, with the introduction of personal computers (Nabuco, 1997) and the growing influence of Vygotsky, the emphasis has remained on literacy and democracy but the practices have altered. The MEM was first introduced in Portuguese pre-school settings in the 1960s. According to Niza (1991) the educational aims of MEM are three-fold:

- an initiation into democratic life
- the re-institution of values and social meanings
- the co-operative reconstruction of culture.

The learning focus within MEM is on the group rather than on either the teacher or individual children. Communication, co-operation and negotiation are considered central in supporting the child's social, intellectual and moral development. The children are introduced to empowering 'instruments' and institutional routines that include the compilation of attendance charts and classroom diaries, attendance and involvement in council meetings.

Whilst in most other pre-school programmes the teacher takes full responsibility for the organization of the learning environment and activities, in MEM the children themselves are provided with the support that they need to make their own decisions. The children are encouraged to reflect upon and evaluate their experiences and to make collective decisions regarding their future activities in the 'co-operative council'. According to Folque (1995), 'didactic tricks' and simulations are rejected in favour of using the 'real' instruments of learning applied in wider society. In terms of science, for example, scientific investigation is encouraged as early as possible (see Siraj-Blatchford and MacLeod-Brundenell, in press). What Niza (1993) refers to as an 'epistemological homology' between teaching-learning and development is applied across the curriculum.

Te Whariki: The Woven Mat

In New Zealand, the metaphor (taken from the Maori language) of Te Whariki (woven mat) has been used to describe a curriculum framework in which each early years centre weaves its own curriculum and creates their own pattern from features and contexts unique to them, their children and their community (Carr and May, 1993). The curriculum framework includes four principles: empowerment; holistic development; family and community; and relationships. In addition there are five strands: well-being; belonging; contribution; communication; and exploration. Goals give clear directions for learning programmes and describe learning outcomes which identify the knowledge, skills and attitudes children should have the opportunity to develop. Over 130 outcomes are identified.

Te Whariki early years settings, therefore, in conjunction with their local community, develop statements on their practices and the philosophies that underpin their pedagogy. The Te Whariki document refers to the principles relating learning 'to the wider world and of providing the flexibility to respond to different conditions, different needs, and the expectations of local communities' (NZ, Ministry of Education, 1996, p. 43). Additionally, each early years setting is required continually to assess itself and the quality of its provision, according to its own values and context. This is termed 'a continuing dialogue' to be engaged in with the people involved in the provision and with the local community, so that it can encourage particular challenges and activities and . . . 'provide for the cognitive, social, emotional, and physical development of the children' (p. 29). Many of the pedagogical implications in Te Whariki are embedded and may be open to different interpretation. This is partly intentional in order to accommodate differences in local contexts.

Quality in Diversity in Early Learning (QDEL)

The Quality in Diversity framework has been formulated by working groups and a project team convened by the Early Childhood Education Forum (ECEF) in the UK over the last four years. The framework represents a major collaboration between representatives of all of the major national organizations concerned with the care and education of young children. Grounded in principles drawn from Te Whariki, it emphasizes the need to achieve quality provision for children of 'different abilities, dispositions, aptitudes and needs', in a range of settings that cater for the diverse needs of a multi-cultural, multi-lingual and multi-faith society. The strength of the framework will be in providing an auditing tool in the development of practice. One of its declared intentions has been to support practitioners in making comparisons between different approaches so that 'selected observations could be made to enable practitioners to identify and justify the diversity in their practice of quality' (ECEF, 1998, p. 8).

The framework provides guidance on three main elements: Foundations, Goals and Entitlements. While the Foundations and Goals relate most closely to policy and curriculum practice, the area of Entitlement relates most closely to pedagogy. The aim has been to describe the conditions considered essential for early learning and to define a basic entitlement to learning support.

The framework emphasizes parental partnership and (as in all of the other programmes considered here) play, which is considered crucial to early learning. There is also a clear recognition of the need for adults to *support and extend* children in their play. Children are considered to have an entitlement to have their learning *planned*, their *resources organized* and their *progress understood and recorded*. The importance of teachers *observing* children in their play and of *evaluating and adapting* what they do to maximize learning is emphasized. The 'practitioner's wheel' in Figure 2.1 represents the favoured pedagogic practice.

The concentric circles show the foundations of learning and around these are the 'practitioner's daily tasks'. The outer rim of the wheel shows the sources of information and evidence that the practitioners draw upon in their daily practice.

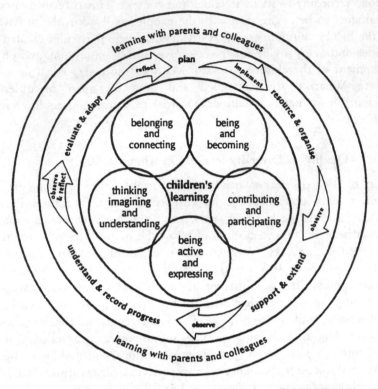

Early Childhood Education Forum

Fig. 2.1. The practioner's wheel (ECEF, 1998)

PEDAGOGICAL IMPLICATIONS IN THE UNITED KINGDOM

This chapter recognizes the strength to be found in variety and it is in this spirit that the following review of the five programmes is presented. No attempt is made to judge the programmes; they are all culturally specific and any such comparison would be foolish. However, the pedagogic emphases and strengths are drawn out.

The influence of Piaget can be seen in all five of the models; they all stress the importance of active learning and firsthand experience.

Reggio Emilia

As Katz and Chard (1989) have suggested, perhaps the greatest contribution of Reggio Emilia to early childhood education is their use of the documentation of children's experience as a standard element in classroom practice. Documentation typically includes samples of a child's work at several different stages of completion; photographs of work in progress; the comments of the teacher or other adults working with the children; transcriptions of children's discussions, comments, and explanations of intentions about the activity; and comments made by the parents.

Katz and Chard suggest these documentation processes contribute to quality provision in a number of ways, summarized as follows:

- Documentation provides a means by which children are encouraged to *reflect* upon their own work and that of their peers. They therefore, 'become even more curious, interested, and confident as they contemplate the meaning of what they have achieved' (Malaguzzi, 1993, p. 63). Documentation provides a means by which the children's ideas and work may be *validated*. When the children's efforts, intentions, and ideas are shown so clearly to be taken seriously this encourages them to approach their work with greater responsibly, energy and commitment.

- Documentation provides a basis for continuous planning based on the evaluation of work as it progresses. 'As the children undertake complex individual or small group collaborative tasks over a period of several days or weeks, the teachers examine the work each day and discuss with the children their ideas and the possibilities of new options for the following days. Planning decisions can be made on the basis of what individual or groups of children have found interesting, stimulating, puzzling, or challenging' (Katz and Chard, 1996). It provides a means of *communication with parents* which may often lead to them to become more involved in their child's learning and may even lead to parents re-examining the assumptions that they have made regarding their own role in the child's education (Malaguzzi, 1993, p. 64). Documentation also provides information for *practitioner research* and can serve to sharpen and focus the teachers' attention on the learning that is taking place within their setting.

High/Scope

High/Scope takes the emphasis on continuous planning and review that is found in Reggio Emilia a stage further, providing a more structured and institutionalized approach in the daily plan-do-review routines. The strong Vygotskian influence is demonstrated in the structured dialogue led by the teachers.

The Movimento da Escola Moderna (MEM)

The influence of Vygotsky and of Bruner in MEM are acknowledged and clear (Niza, 1991). The communication between children that is afforded by conferences, correspondence and the 'class journal' provides a crucial double function that was identified by Vygotsky. It has a cognitive and metacognitive function where the children are required to think about how they will express themselves and answer questions about their experiences. It also has a social function in presenting information for the benefit of the community. This Frinetian emphasis upon communication within MEM is echoed in the displays applied in Reggio Emilia and in the planning and evaluative dialogue in High/Scope. In each case it will provide similar benefits.

Te Whariki

The Te Whariki model suggests that an appropriate curriculum and pedagogy for young children will be determined by the needs of individual and specific groups of children, adults and communities. Social constructivism suggests that children learn best when they are being supported by adults or their peers in actively developing their individual and group capability. Research also suggests that children should be made aware of their learning and of the benefits to be gained from developing their experience in interaction with others. Here again we see clear parallels with the other programmes emphasizing the importance of parent and community involvement.

Quality in Diversity

In the Quality in Diversity model much of the specific pedagogic guidance is embedded, and little explicit reference is made to the quality of adult-child interactions. Some of the observations, however, provide hints regarding the specific adult roles favoured. At times it seems to be emphasizing a 'low profile' and at others a high degree of direction. At one point we hear of two adults who 'took little part' in managing an activity as 'the children were very much in control' (ECEF, 1998, p. 22). In another example of an activity the staff developed a whole series of supported investigations and other activities in response to questions that a group of children had asked about snails (p. 56).

CONCLUSIONS

One of the most interesting debates in recent early years educational research has been concerned with 'learning dispositions' and a good deal of the forgoing discussion of 'involvement' is closely related to this. When we talk about 'learning dispositions' we are talking about a child's 'natural tendency' or 'emotional attitude' to learning. Katz (1985) defines dispositions as 'relatively enduring habits of mind or characteristic ways of responding to experience' (p. 1). To take an example from Katz and Raths (1985), we might consider a child who has all of the skills required in being able to read but who habitually chooses, in the absence of rewards, not to do so. Such a child may be considered to be 'indisposed' to reading.

To be positively disposed towards something is, therefore, to be intrinsically motivated by it. As Katz and Raths suggest, dispositions should always be understood as 'habits of mind', rather than as 'mindless habits'. They constitute an important subject for educational research and, as Katz (1992) has also suggested, pedagogy can have a devastating effect upon a child's learning disposition. There is evidence to suggest, for example, that excessive early drill and practice in the teaching of reading will undermine a child's dispositions to be a reader. We know that young children are motivated when they wish to please the significant others in their lives and that the most significant others around them are adults. Adult behaviour, therefore, will be crucial in developing positive learning dispositions. Teachers in early childhood education need to be aware of their influence as role models.

Dweck (1991) has demonstrated that 'mastery' and 'helpless' orientations to learning in early childhood may be significantly related to school achievement. For Dweck, helpless children show a marked lack of persistence in the face of failure. They tend to see the problem in terms of their own incapacity to perform the task rather than seeing it as a matter of effort. They also have low expectations of success in future tasks (Dweck, 1991). These positive and negative dispositions need to be researched further. If we are to develop children's positive dispositions to learning we need to know more about the effects of specific pedagogic practices on different groups, and in different curriculum and institutional contexts. We also need to know more about how the children's toleration of pedagogic practices changes as they grow older.

Having identified the importance of learning to learn in the early years and the pedagogic strengths of both the commonly promoted DAP and alternative programme models, I shall now attempt to draw these together in providing a typology of the general pedagogic principles that are applied in early childhood provision.

It appears that, in addition to the techniques of pedagogic instruction and a balance of structured and self-initiated activity, early years teachers need to develop strategies associated with involvement and engagement. The kind of engagement considered here, however, is not so much the 'engagement of the teacher', as conceived by Pascal and Bertram, but rather an engagement in the Piagetian sense – of an intellectual engagement between the child and either another child or an adult. To engage with the child in this sense means to have identified or developed some common ground for discourse. Pascal and Bertram (1995) come close to this when they refer to interventions which are 'stimulating' or 'confusing/inappropriately' pitched. The problem is that, in their model, this aspect is not sufficiently emphasized and could be missed entirely. The co-construction emphasized in Reggio Emilia is particularly strong in this respect. However it is organized, the aim must always be to work from some common language or conceptual basis towards a development of that understanding. Three areas of pedagogy may be identified that are of equal importance to learning:

1. Instructional Techniques

Creating learning environments
  organizing materials/resources
  providing relevant/interesting and novel experiences
  providing opportunities for active exploration
  questioning
Direct instruction
  demonstrating
  describing
  answering questions
  directing the child's attention
  constructive criticism and reinforcement
Scaffolding
  directing attention to a new aspect of a situation
  helping the child to sequence activities
  managing complex tasks by breaking them down into manageable components

2. Encouraging involvement

The teacher may act as a role model, expressing his or her own interest and enthusiasm for the subject (as in High/Scope). They can also respond to the child's own interests (as in Quality in Diversity and MEM), encourage parents and community involvement (as in Reggio Emilia and Te Whariki) and encourage the children to recognize the 'validity' of what they are doing by communicating it beyond the classroom (as in both MEM and, in particular, Reggio Emilia). Whatever strategy is employed, the aim must be to achieve a high degree of intrinsic motivation in the activity in the short term and improved learning dispositions (such as perseverance) in the long term. The importance of longer term outcomes is often weak in the U.K. government documents.

3. Fostering engagement

Activities need to be matched to the child's capability. Knowledge of the child's current development is therefore crucial. The Reggio Emilia documentation, observation in Quality in Diversity, the dialogue in High/Scope and the communicative emphasis in MEM appear to be particularly strong in these respects.

It seems wise to be cautious about any kind of 'developmental' approaches that emphasize what it is that children 'ought to be able to do' at a particular age or stage. Given the variety of experiences that young children bring with them in the early years, these approaches are particularly inappropriate. Where they are adopted, those children who 'fail' to meet these criteria are often considered deficient in some way. Early years educators and teachers, therefore, would do better to construct an environment based on the view that children are active learners. Bruner's idea that anything can be taught to any child in an intellectually honest way seems especially relevant in this context (Bruner, 1986). The child's environment should create scope for the early years core curriculum, but it should be remembered that environment includes a very wide range of experience gained in interaction with more or less competent adults in the home, the media, older siblings and other children. We are all aware that, in their early years, children ask a great many questions that do not fit easily into subject compartments. This provides a major challenge for early years teachers who have a responsibility to develop positive educational dispositions, to encourage the child's inquiry and to show that society has a body of accumulated knowledge that is worth learning.

The major emphasis of early education has traditionally been cognitive and developmental psychology and research on early childhood and early childhood education have provided us with sophisticated accounts from these perspectives. Throughout the past century increasingly elaborate theories have been produced to describe the mechanics of learning. There is now a growing recognition of the importance of providing fuel for the learning organism. The fuels we are talking about are the learning dispositions that condition the child's interest in education, social commitment and citizenship.

Dweck's notions of 'helplessness' and 'mastery' are especially relevant in this respect. Teachers often feel 'helpless' in the face of what they see as the entirely 'natural' underachievement of some working class and ethnic minority children and parents. The same views were prevalent in the scientific and technological education of girls a decade ago. But attitudes have changed and girls are no longer living down to their teachers' and families' expectations; they are achieving on a par with, or better than, boys. This has implications for our practitioner training and for our work with parents. We should be able to achieve higher standards with all children if we change practitioners' expectations and support them in changing the expectations of their children. What is needed in place of the learned 'helplessness' of some practitioners and parents is their 'mastery' of how children learn within a framework of child development so that, if they appear to be failing with a child, they show resilience, patience and perseverance rather than giving up on them. In other words, a 'mastery' disposition to their pedagogy is needed.

This was illustrated by Munn and Schaffer (1993). The researchers, working in eight pre-school centres, set out to chart the development of literacy and numeracy in the years just before schooling by looking at the kinds of learning experiences the children were receiving. Their conclusions point to a key link with later achievement in the 'basics'. There was a clear distinction between pre-school centres where staff were 'reflective' and those where staff were 'unreflective'. Reflective staff were characterized by a dynamic understanding of children's learning and a positive attitude towards adult help. 'Unreflective' staff were characterized by a sense of powerlessness over children's learning and their ability to help. Munn and Schaffer conclude that there is an urgent need for in-service training which helps staff to focus on the positive role they can play in helping children learn.

In this chapter I have argued that three distinct areas of pedagogic influence may be identified (instruction, involvement and engagement). Early childhood educators should make an informed selection from the range of pedagogic techniques that have been developed and tested within the various early childhood educational programmes. Early childhood settings should draw upon other programmes but select those elements most appropriate for their particular needs and context. Whatever unique mix of techniques is adopted the aim must be to develop quality provision in each of the three areas of influence and to sustain high expectations.

Acknowledgements

I would like to thank Peter Moss, Peter Mortimore, Wendy Scott and John Siraj-Blatchford for helpful comments on an earlier version of this chapter.

REFERENCES

Audit Commission (1996) *Counting to Five: The Education of Children Under-five*, London: HMSO.

Bennett, N. and Cass, A. (1989) *From Special to Ordinary Schools: Case Studies in Integration*, London: Cassell.

Bennett, N., Wood, L. and Rogers, S. (1997) *Teaching through Play: Teachers' Thinking and Classroom Practice*, Buckingham: Open University Press.

Bredekamp, S. and Copple, A. (1997) (revised edition) (eds) *Developmentally Appropriate Practice in Early Childhood Programs*, Washington: National Association for the Education of Young Children.

Bruner, J. (1986) *Actual Minds-Possible Worlds*, Cambridge, Mass: Harvard Educational Press.

Carr, M. and May, H. (1993) Choosing a model: reflecting on the development and process of Te Whariki: national early childhood curriculum guidelines in New Zealand, *International Journal of Early Years Education*, 1(3): 7–21.

Chazan, M., Laing, A., Harper, G. (1987) *Teaching Five to Eight Year-Olds*, Oxford: Blackwell.

Department for Education and Science (1990) *Starting with Quality: A Report of the Committee of Inquiry into the Quality of Educational Experiences Offered to 3–4 Year Olds* (the Rumbold Report), London: HMSO.

DeVries, R. (1997) Piaget's Social Theory, *Educational Researcher*, 26(2) March.

Dunn, L. and Kontos, S. (1997) What have we learned about Developmentally Appropriate Practice? *Young Children*, 52(5): 4–13.

Dweck, C. (1991) Self-theories and goals: their role in motivation, personality, and development, in R.A. Dienstbier (ed.) *Perspectives on Motivation*, Nebraska Symposium on Motivation, 1990. Lincoln, NE: University of Nebraska Press.

Early Childhood Education Forum (ECEF) (1998) *Quality in Diversity in Early*

Learning: A Framework for Early Childhood Practitioners, London: National Children's Bureau.

Edwards, C., Gandini, L. and Forman, G. (1993) *The Hundred Languages of Children: The Reggio Emilia Approach to Early Childhood Education*, Norwood NJ: Ablex Publishing.

Folque, M.A. (1995) The influence of Vygotsky's work in the Modern School Movement Early childhood education curriculum model, unpublished paper.

Galton, M. (1989) *Teaching in the Primary School*, London: David Fulton.

Gura, P. (ed) (1997) *Reflections of Early Education and Care*. London: British Association for ECE.

Hohmann, M., Barnet, B. and Weikart, D.P. (1979) *Young Children in Action*, Ypsilanti: High/Scope Press.

Hurst, V. and Joseph, J. (1998) *Supporting Early Learning: The Way Forward*, Buckingham: Open University Press.

Katz, L.G. (1985) Dispositions in Early Childhood Education, *ERIC/EECE Bulletin* 18(2): 1–3.

Katz, L.G. (1992) What should young children be doing? *ERIC Digest*. Urbana, IL: ERIC, Clearinghouse on Elementary and Early Childhood Education, University of Illinois.

Katz, L.G. and Chard, S.C. (1989) *Engaging Children's Minds: The Project Approach*, Norwood, NJ: Ablex Publishing.

Katz, L.G. and Chard, S.C. (1996) The contribution of documentation to the quality of early childhood education, ERIC Database 0/PS/96/2 (http://ericeece.org/).

Katz, L.G. and Raths, J.D. (1985) Dispositions as goals for teacher education, *Teaching and Teacher Education* 1(4): 301–307.

Laevers, F. (1995) *An Exploration of the Concept of Involvement as an Indicator for Quality in Early Childhood Education*, Dundee: Scottish Consultative Council on the Curriculum.

Macleod, F. (ed) (1989) *The High/Scope Project*, Exeter: School of Education.

MacNaughton, G. and Williams, G. (1998) *Techniques for Teaching Young Children: Choices in Theory and Practice*, Melbourne: Longman.

Malaguzzi, L. (1993) History, Ideas and Basic Philosophy, in Edwards, C., Gandini, L. and Forman, G. *The Hundred Languages of Children: The Reggio Emilia approach to early childhood education*, Norwood NJ: Ablex Publishing.

McGarrigle, J. and Donaldson, M. (1974) Conservation accidents, *Cognition*, 3: 341–350.

Moriarty, V. and Siraj-Blatchford, I. (1998a) Early childhood educators' perceptions of the UK desirable outcomes for children's learning: a research study on the policy implications, *International Journal of Early Childhood Education*, 30(1): 56–64.

Moriarty, V. and Siraj-Blatchford, I. (1998b) *An Introduction to Curriculum for 3 to 5 Year-Olds*. Nottingham: Education Now.

Moss, P., Dahlberg, G. and Pence, A. (1999) *The Young Child in Civic Society: Reconceptualising Early Childhood Care and Development*, London: Falmer Press (in press).

Munn, P. and Schaffer, R. (1993) Literacy and numeracy events in social interactive contexts, *International Journal of Early Years Education*, 1(3): 61–80.

Murphy, P. (1996) Defining Pedagogy, in Murphy, P. and Gipps, C. *Equity in the Classroom: Towards Effective Pedagogy for Girls and Boys*, London: Falmer Press and UNESCO.

Nabuco, E. (1997) The effects of three early childhood curricula in Portugal on children's progress in the first year of primary school, unpublished PhD. thesis, Institute of Education, University of London.

Nabuco, E. and Sylva, K. (1996) The effects of three early childhood curricula on children's progress at primary school in Portugal, paper presented at the ISSBD conference in Quebec, Canada.

NAEYC (1996) Guidelines for decisions about developmentally appropriate practice, Position Statement, July, (www.naeyc.org).

New, R. (1994) Culture, child development and developmentally appropriate practices: teachers as collaborative researchers, in Mallory, B. and New, R. (eds.) *Diversity and Developmentally Appropriate Practices*, New York: Teachers College Press.

New Zealand: Ministry of Education (1996) *Te Whariki: Early Childhood Curriculum*, Wellington, NZ: Learning Media Ltd.

Niza, S. (1991) O sentido do acto pedagogico: uma prespectiva pedagogica de desenvolvimento funcional (The meaning of pedagogical action: a functional developmental perspective), unpublished paper.

Niza, S. (1993) O modelo curricular de educacao pre-escolar da escola moderna Portuguesa (The modern school movement early childhood education curriculum model), unpublished paper.

Pascal, C. and Bertram, A. (1995) *Evaluating and Developing Quality in Early Childhood Settings: A Professional Development Programme*, Worcester: Amber Publishing Co. Ltd.

Pascal, C. and Bertram, A. (1997) A conceptual framework for evaluating effectiveness in early childhood settings, in *Researching Early Childhood 3, Settings in Interaction*, Goteborg University, Early Childhood Research and Development Centre.

Piaget, J. (1995) (1st edn, 1928) *Sociological Studies*, New York: Routledge.

Rogers, C. (1983) *Freedom to Learn*, Columbus: Merrill.

School Curriculum and Assessment Authority (SCAA) (1996) *Nursery Education: Desirable Outcomes for Children's Learning on Entering Compulsory Education* London: SCAA and DfEE.

Schweinhart, L.J., Barnes, H.V. and Weikart, D.P. (1993) *Significant Benefits: The High/Scope Perry Preschool Study through Age 27*, Michigan: High/Scope Educational Research Foundation.

Schweinhart, L.J. and Weikart, D.P. (1997) The High/Scope preschool curriculum comparison through age 23, in *Early Childhood Research Quarterly*, 12: 117–143.

Siraj-Blatchford, I. (1995) Combined nursery centres: bridging the gap between care and education, in Gammage, P. and Meighan, J. *The Early Years: The Way Forward*, Nottingham: Education Now Books.

Siraj-Blatchford, I. (ed.) (1998) *A Curriculum Development Handbook for Early Childhood Educators*, Stoke-on-Trent: Trentham Books.

Siraj-Blatchford, J. and MacLeod- Brudenell, I. (1999) *Supporting Science, Design and Technology in the Early Years*, Buckingham: Open University Press (in press).

Smith, P. and Cowie, H. (1991) (2nd edition) *Understanding Children's Development*, Oxford: Blackwell.

Smith, P. (1994) Play and the uses of play, in Moyles, J. (ed.) *The Excellence of Play*, Buckingham: Open University Press.

Spodek, B. and Saracho, O. (eds) (1991) *Issues in Early Childhood Curriculum*, New York: Teachers College Press.

Sylva, K. (1997) Developing the primary school curriculum: the next steps, paper presented to SCAA conference, 9/10 June.

Sylva, K., Siraj-Blatchford, I., Johnson, S. (1992), The impact of the UK National Curriculum on pre-school practice. Some top-down processes at work, in *International Journal of Early Childhood*, 24: 41–51.

Sylva, K., Melhuish, E., Sammons, P. and Siraj-Blatchford, I. (1996) The effective provision for pre-school education project, unpublished report, London, Institute of Education.

Tharp, R. and Gallimore, R. (1991) A theory of teaching as assisted performance, in Light, P., Sheldon, S. and Woodhead, M. (eds.) (1991) *Learning to Think*, London: Routledge.

Vygotsky, L. (1978) *Mind in Society: The Development of Higher Psychological Processes*, Cole, M., John-Steiner, V., Schribner, S. and Souberman, E. (eds. and trans.). Cambridge Mass: Harvard University Press.

Walkerdine, V. (1984) Developmental psychology and the child-centred pedagogy, in Henriques, J., Holloway, W., Unwin, C., Venn, C. and Walkerdine, V. (eds) *Changing the Subject: Psychology, Social Regulation and Subjectivity*, London: Methuen.

Weikart, D., Rogers, L., Adcock, C. and McClelland, D. (1971) *The Cognitively Oriented Curriculum: A framework for pre-school teachers*, Urbana IL: University of Illinois.

Wood, D (1988) *How Children Think and Learn: The Social Contexts of Cognitive Development*, Oxford: Blackwell.

Wylie, C. (1998) *Six Years Old and Competent: The Second Stage of the Competent Children Project – a summary of the main findings*, Wellington: New Zealand Council for Educational Research.

3

Primary School Learners

Caroline Gipps and Barbara MacGilchrist

Over the last ten years in England and Wales the political and media spotlight has focused attention on primary education. Drawing on international comparisons of academic achievement in core areas of learning, especially literacy and numeracy, concerns have been raised about the apparently poor standards achieved by pupils in the UK at the end of primary schooling. As a result of these concerns, policy-makers have sought to define the content and range of a national primary curriculum and have endeavoured to develop ways of assessing pupils' progress and marking levels of attainment at ages seven and eleven. More recently, however, pedagogy – how primary children are best taught – has become a key consideration. Previous notions of 'good primary practice', particularly so called 'child-centred' approaches to teaching, have been challenged. A 'back-to-basics' campaign has gathered momentum and this has resulted in unprecedented government intervention in the form of prescribing how teachers should teach children to become literate and numerate. A new national curriculum for teacher training has been introduced and a set of competencies (that all new primary teachers are thought to need) has been defined and incorporated in new legislation.

The timing of this book, therefore, is particularly significant because there is a danger of one orthodoxy being replaced by another, in the absence of an explicit theory of teaching and learning in the primary years. There is a danger that primary pedagogy will be reduced to a narrow set of competencies on the assumption that once teachers have acquired, and learnt to use, these effective learning will ensue.

We will argue that this simplified view of primary pedagogy ignores the complex nature of teaching and its relationship with, and impact on, learning. We take the view that teachers can, and will, be more effective if they possess an understanding of the multi-dimensional nature of pedagogy and the multiple purposes it needs to serve. In the sections which follow we explore the complex relationship between pedagogy and learning and identify some significant factors that primary practitioners need to understand in order to maximize their effectiveness in the classroom.

To do this, we draw together some of the key findings from a range of different types of research studies because we believe that all of them have something to contribute to our understanding of the topic. We argue that, to become more effective, teachers need to develop a much more sophisticated understanding about learning and the impact that their beliefs and attitudes about learning and learners can have on what – and how – they teach in the classroom. As Michael Fullan (1991) has put it, school improvement, and therefore pupil improvement, 'depends on what teachers do and think. It's as simple and as complex as that' (p. 117). Part of our intention in this chapter is to explore what it is that influences, often implicitly, what teachers think, and therefore do, in their everyday interactions with children.

In our – inevitably selective – review of the research literature, beginning with theories about how children learn, we identify some of the key implications for pedagogy and illustrate these in practice by drawing on two recent studies of effective primary teachers in action. We argue that teachers themselves need to exhibit the characteristics of effective learners if they are to continue to improve their own pedagogy so as to maximize their impact on the learning of the pupils they teach.

THEORIES ABOUT LEARNING

'Contemporary cognitive psychology has built on the very old idea that things are easier to learn if they make sense' (Shepard, 1991, p. 8). Isolated facts, if learnt, quickly disappear from the memory because they have no meaning and do not fit into the learner's conceptual map. Knowledge learnt in this way is of limited use because it is difficult for it to be applied, generalized or retrieved. 'Meaning makes learning easier, because the learner knows where to put things in her mental framework, and meaning makes knowledge useful because likely purposes and applications are already part of the understanding' (Shepard, 1992, p. 319).

A significant shift has occurred over the last fifteen years in our understanding of how learning takes place. Recent work in cognitive and constructivist psychology shows learning in terms of networks with connections in many directions; not as an external map that is transposed directly into the student's head. Rather it appears to be part of an organic process of reorganizing and restructuring as the student learns, suggesting that learning is a process of knowledge construction (von Glasersfeld, 1987; Driver *et al.*, 1985). Learning occurs not by recording information but by interpreting it, so that teaching is seen not as direct transfer of knowledge but as an intervention in an ongoing knowledge-construction process (Resnick, 1989). Thus in *constructivist* learning theory students learn by actively making sense of new knowledge, making meaning from it, and mapping it in to their existing knowledge map or schema. Piagetian constructivists analyse learning within the individual giving priority to pupils' sensory-motor and conceptual activity. *Social constructivists* recognize the social nature of much learning (Driver *et al.*, 1994) and focus on an individual acquiring knowledge-in-social-action.

Information-processing models of learning tend to have three elements, two of which overlap with constructivist models: a first stage in which, through selective attention, certain aspects of the environment are filtered for conscious processing; a second, in which active mental engagement with the new input occurs so as to make personal sense of it, using selectively recalled prior learning in the process; finally a structuring of the resultant learning in such a way that it can be stored usefully in the long-term memory (Atkins et al., 1992). Thus, as with constructivist models, knowledge is seen as an entity, something cohesive and holistic which then provides a scaffolding for later learning.

A different view of learning, the *sociocultural*, is described by Wertsch (1991, p. 6) thus:

> The basic goal of a sociocultural approach to mind is to create an account of human mental processes that recognizes the essential relationship between these processes and their cultural, historical and institutional settings.

Socioculturalists, like constructivists, assume human agency in the process of coming to know. Socioculturalists, however, argue that meaning derived from interactions is not exclusively a product of one person. They view the individual as being engaged in relational activities with others. Building on Vygotsky's (1978) arguments about the importance of interaction with 'more knowledgeable others' and the role of society in providing a framework for the child's learning, sociocultural theorists see learning as essentially a social activity. As Bruner and Haste (1987) put it:

> 'through . . . social life, the child acquires a framework for interpreting experience and learns how to negotiate meaning in a manner congruent with the requirements of the culture. "Making sense" is a social process; it is an activity that is always situated in a cultural and historical context' and '. . . the child's development depends upon her using, so to speak, the tool kit of the culture to express the powers of mind'.

Given these different views, most constructivist and sociocultural theorists approach research on learning in different ways and disagree over whether the mind, i.e. learning, or coming to know, 'is located in the head or in the individual-in-social-action' (Cobb, 1994, p. 13). The two schools do, however, have two elements in common: they both emphasize the crucial role of activity in learning, and both focus on the processes of learning.

Research also indicates that good learners tend to have good metacognitive strategies (Bruner, 1996). Metacognition is a general term which refers to a second-order form of thinking: thinking about learning. It includes a variety of self-awareness processes to help plan, monitor, orchestrate and control one's own learning. Such learners monitor their learning using particular strategies which hinge on self-questioning in order to get the purpose of learning clear, searching for connections and conflicts with what is already known, and judging whether understanding of the material is sufficient for the task. An essential aspect of metacognition is that learners monitor or regulate their own learning, and that self-assessment or self-evaluation are crucial components of learning. If pupils are to become competent assessors of their own work then they need sustained experience in ways of questioning and improving the quality of their work, and supported experience in self-assessment which includes understanding what counts as the expected standard as well as the criteria on which they will be assessed (Sadler, 1989). We return to this key aspect of pedagogy in a later section. In Pollard's (1990) social-constructivist model of the teaching/learning process, he stresses the importance of the teacher as a 'reflective agent' with a role which is dependent on the sensitive and accurate assessment of a child's needs. This places a premium on formative teacher assessment of pupil understanding.

What do we take from this research that is helpful in our thinking about learning, and what does it tell us about teaching? What strikes the strongest chord with us is the emphasis on thinking and meaning-making. The learner has to be seen as active – by this we do not mean using discovery learning, but that the learner is encouraged to think about what he/she is learning, to make sense of it and to link it with other concepts, constructs or pieces of information. It helps for the learner to be aware of his/her own learning strategies – again an active process. Finally, the setting of learning and, crucially, the interactions between teacher and pupil, and between pupil and pupil, have important roles to play in the learning process.

TEACHERS' BELIEFS ABOUT LEARNING

Teachers' beliefs about learning, essentially how children's minds work, is increasingly being recognized as important. Teachers' views about how learning takes place, albeit implicit ones, affect the ways in which they design learning opportunities for their pupils. Evidence from a small study of primary teachers' beliefs about teaching and learning (Gipps et al., 1999) shows that teachers of Year 6 (Y6) children (10–11 year olds in the last year of English primary schools) have a teaching repertoire which is related to their views of how children learn. Working over time with a small sample (29 Y6 teachers) Gipps and colleagues found that these teachers' views about teaching and learning were complex and did not support clearly any one theory of learning. Seven teachers out of the 29 expressed the view that the best way to teach and ensure learning was to view knowledge as jointly constructed. Some teachers were quite passionate and emphatic about it, for example one felt he could 'throw himself' into it. Only three teachers out of the 29 felt they could wholeheartedly embrace the idea that 'children have to be active in their own learning and the teacher should be there to guide discovery'. Not one of the 29 teachers endorsed the approach: 'the teacher conveys information to children and that is how learning takes place' on its own. On the other hand few rejected the 'transmission' model outright; they limited it to certain purposes. In fact fifteen out of the sample of 29 expressed the view that all three approaches were appropriate and came into play at various times; a notion of fitness for purpose to which we would subscribe.

When these fifteen teachers were arguing that all three models of learning were in play, they reported different teaching modes for different circumstances. They described when they would become chiefly 'transmitters' of knowledge, when they would encourage children to discover for themselves, and when they felt they were 'constructing learning together'. These would change according to different subject areas, different children, and different age groups using different forms of pupil organization and school ethos.

That half the sample explicitly espoused the mixed-mode approach to teaching is interesting in the light of these teachers' more general comments on the effect of the national curriculum on their teaching practice. Although not one teacher believed that children learn solely from the transmission of facts, one quarter felt pushed into doing more of this because of the amount of work to be covered by the national curriculum or, in some cases, by the tests.

Their denial of the 'transmission' model as the only approach is interesting in the light of calls for a return to 'whole class teaching'. Class teaching does not, of course, necessarily imply a 'dead' or dull transmission of facts; far from it (Reynolds and Farrell, 1996). At its best it can involve every child in active learning, and in interacting with the material, which is a key feature of good quality learning. Too much passive class work, however, may lead to over-dependency on the teacher and only limited development of the self-monitoring or self-regulating strategies that we know are essential to becoming a good learner.

Bruner (1996, p. 53) has written about the conceptions that teachers have about the minds of learners:

> There are four dominant models of learners' minds that have held sway in our times. Each emphasizes different educational goals. These models are not only conceptions of mind that determine how we teach and 'educate', but are also conceptions about the relations between minds and cultures. Rethinking educational psychology requires that we examine each of these alternative conceptions of human development and re-evaluate their implications for learning and teaching.

Three of these four models are pertinent to this chapter; Bruner characterizes these as:

1. *Seeing children as imitative learners: the acquisition of 'know-how'.*
   Modelling is the basis of *apprenticeship*, leading the novice into the skilled ways of the expert. An underlying assumption is that the less skilled can be taught by showing, and that they have the ability to learn through imitation. Studies of expertise demonstrate that just learning how to perform skillfully does not get one to the same level of flexible skill as when one learns by a combination of practice and conceptual explanation.

2. *Seeing children as learning from didactic exposure: the acquisition of propositional knowledge.*

Didactic teaching usually is based on the notion that pupils should be presented with facts, principles, and rules of action which are to be learned, remembered, and then applied. Procedural knowledge, knowing how to, is assumed to follow automatically from knowing certain propositions about facts, theories and the like. Plainly there are contexts where knowledge can usefully be treated as 'objective' and given. In this view the assumption is that the child's mind is passive, a receptacle waiting to be filled. Active interpretation or construal does not enter the picture.

3. *Seeing children as thinkers: the development of intersubjective interchange.*

The new wave of research on 'other minds' is the manifestation of a more general modern effort to recognize the child's perspective in the process of learning. The teacher, in this view, is concerned with understanding what the child thinks and how she arrives at what she believes. 'Pedagogy is to help the child understand better, more powerfully, less one-sidedly.' Understanding is fostered through discussion and collaboration, with the child encouraged to express her own views better to achieve some meeting of minds with others who may have other views. Research on *metacognition* – what children think about learning and remembering and thinking (especially their own), and how 'thinking about' one's own cognitive operations affects one's own mental procedures, has contributed to this focus.

(Bruner, *op cit.*, pp. 53–61)

Bruner concludes:

Modern pedagogy is moving increasingly to the view that the child should be aware of her own thought processes, and that it is crucial for the pedagogical theorist and teacher alike to help her to become more metacognitive – to be as aware of how she goes about her learning and thinking as she is about the subject matter she is studying. Achieving skill and accumulating knowledge are not enough. The learner can be helped to achieve full mastery by reflecting as well upon how she is going about her job and how her approach can be improved. Equipping her with a good theory of mind – or a theory of mental functioning – is one part of helping her to do so.

(ibid., p. 64)

Recent research on the brain and learning (Hart, 1983; Jensen, 1994; Sylvester, 1995) supports Bruner's definition of pedagogy. It confirms the importance of metacognition; it also emphasizes the importance of early education. The first ten years of childhood are known to be highly significant in the development of the brain's capacity to learn (Dryden and Voss, 1994; Hannaford, 1995).

Other research stresses the need for children to be provided with a supportive but challenging multi-sensory environment in which they are given regular educative feedback and opportunities to review what they have learnt as well as opportunities to learn about, improve and extend, their current learning strategies (Smith, 1998). Smith also argues that 'brain research is now developing at an incremental, frightening pace . . . the formal education system in the UK is responding to this at a frighteningly slow pace' (p. 19).

We wish to argue that in order to prepare young children for the challenges and opportunities they will encounter in the twenty-first century, Bruner's description of modern pedagogy needs to be taken very seriously. A theme that recurs throughout this book is the importance of lifelong learning. For this to become a reality, primary teachers need to continue to learn how to develop *children as thinkers*. An essential part of this process will involve changing the beliefs teachers have, not just about learning, but also about the learners themselves.

TEACHERS' BELIEFS ABOUT LEARNERS

We argue that one of the hallmarks of effective teachers is the belief that all children can achieve. This belief manifests itself in a variety of ways in the classroom, the most common being through the high expectations teachers set for the children they are teaching. When drawing attention to some of the knowledge and skills teachers need to have in order to bring about effective learning, Mortimore (1993) identified the essential need for teachers to have psychological and sociological knowledge: 'Psychological knowledge so that they can understand how young minds operate and how young people cope with different cultural patterns and family traditions. Sociological knowledge of the way factors such as race, gender, class or religion operate to help or hinder successful teaching' (p. 296).

The research literature that has focused on the relationship between disadvantage and achievement and the extent to which schools can enhance the achievement of pupils whatever their background provides important sociological knowledge for teachers. Two common themes emerge from the literature. The first is that socio-economic inequality is a powerful determinant of differences in cognitive and educational attainment (Mortimore and Mortimore, 1986). Longitudinal studies support this finding (Douglas, 1964; Davie *et al.*, 1972). Social class, along with ethnic background, gender and disability, has been found to have a substantial influence on the life chances of young people (ILEA, 1983). The other common theme is that schools can and do make a difference, but that some schools are much more effective than others at counteracting the potentially damaging effects of disadvantage (Edmunds, 1979; Rutter *et al.*, 1979; Reynolds, 1982; Mortimore *et al.*, 1988; Smith and Tomlinson, 1989; Sammons *et al.*, 1995).

There have been numerous studies to identify the characteristics of highly successful schools (Sammons *et al.*, 1995). Whilst researchers are rightly cautious about identifying causal relationships, the review of the effectiveness literature by Sammons *et al.* (1995) has revealed a set of common features that can be found in effective schools. The majority of these concern the quality and nature of teaching and learning in classrooms along with the overall learning ethos of the school. Some draw attention in particular to the relationship between teachers' beliefs and attitudes and pupils' progress and achievement.

The idea of a self-fulfilling prophecy was first introduced by Merton (1968), and the well-known study by Rosenthal and Jacobson (1968) demonstrated how this concept can operate in the classroom. They showed that it was possible to influence teachers' expectations of certain pupils even though the information they had been given about those pupils was untrue. In their review of the literature Brophy and Good (1974) and Pilling and Pringle (1978) identify the power of teacher expectation in relation to pupils' learning.

In two studies of primary age pupils (Mortimore *et al.*, 1988; Tizard *et al.*, 1988), the importance of teacher expectations emerged. Tizard and colleagues focused on children aged four to seven in 33 inner London infant schools. The purpose of the research was to examine factors in the home and in the school that appeared to affect attainment and progress during the infant school years. Particular attention was paid to the different levels of attainment of boys and girls, and of white British children and black British children of Afro-Caribbean origin. The team found that there was a link between disadvantage and pupil progress and attainment. The literacy and numeracy knowledge and skills that children had acquired before they started school were found to be a strong predictor of attainment at age seven.

The study was able to identify those school factors that appear to exert a greater influence on progress than home background. The two most significant factors were the range of literacy and numeracy taught to the children and teachers' expectations. Whilst each of these factors was independently associated with progress, the team found that the school and class within it that the child attended proved to be an overriding factor in terms of the amount of progress made. A relationship was found between teacher expectations and the range of curriculum activities provided for children, especially in the areas of literacy and numeracy. The team reported that 'of the school-based measures we looked at, we found that teachers' expectations of children's curriculum coverage showed the strongest and most consistent association with school progress' (*op cit.*, p. 139). Where teachers had low expectations of children they provided a narrower curriculum offering.

The Junior School Project (Mortimore *et al.*, 1988) was a longitudinal study of a cohort of seven year old pupils in fifty London schools. The project drew together different aspects of disadvantage. Using sophisticated research techniques the team was able to account for what were called pupil and school 'givens'; for example, they were able to take account of pupil factors such as home language, family circumstances, age and sex, and school factors such as size and the stability of staffing. This enabled the team to focus on those factors over which the school had control, such as teaching methods, record keeping and curriculum leadership. They were able to examine which of these factors appear to have a positive impact on pupils' progress and achievement.

The research revealed significant differences in children's educational outcomes during the junior years. Age, social class, sex and race were each found to have an impact on cognitive achievement levels at age seven and eleven. For example, at age seven those children whose parents worked in non-manual jobs were nearly ten months further ahead in reading than pupils from unskilled manual homes. By the end of the third year the gap had widened. It was also found that with non-cognitive outcomes, such as behaviour and self-concept, there were differences according to age, social class, sex and race. Overall, however, it was found that it was the social class dimension that accounted for the main differences between groups of pupils.

It was the focus on progress that the pupils made over the four years of the study that demonstrated that some schools (and the teachers within them) were far more effective than others. With reading, for example, the average child in the most effective school increased his or her score on a ten point reading test by 25 points more than the average child attending the least effective school. The team found that schools which did better on one measure of academic progress tended to do better on others, and that effective schools tended to be effective for all pupils regardless of social class, ethnic group, sex or age.

High teacher expectations were a common characteristic of these schools. The team looked at ways in which expectations were transmitted in the classroom. They found, for example, that teachers had lower expectations of pupils from socio-economically disadvantaged backgrounds. Denbo's (1988) analysis of the research literature over a twenty year period supports the importance of teacher expectation. Denbo found that many studies demonstrated that both low and high teacher expectation greatly affected student performance. It has been demonstrated that if appropriate teaching styles and teaching expectations are used (Ofsted, 1993) then pupils can become positive about learning and improve their levels of achievement.

If, as described in the first part of this chapter, the learner is seen as an active partner in the learning process, then his/her motivational and emotional state becomes more relevant. One of the school outcomes studied by Mortimore *et al.* was the attitude of students towards themselves as learners. The team designed a measure of self-concept which revealed clear school differences. Some schools produced pupils who felt positive about themselves as learners regardless of their actual ability. Others produced pupils who were negative about themselves even though, according to their progress, they were performing well. Kuykendall (1989) argues that low teacher expectations have been shown to reduce the motivation of students to learn, and that 'perhaps the most damaging consequence of low teacher expectations is the erosion of academic self-image in students' (p. 18). Mortimore (1993) supports this view: 'for a pupil who is regularly taught by a teacher with low expectations, the experience can be demoralizing and too often leads to serious underachievement' (p. 295). Not unrelated to this, he draws attention to the need for teachers to provide good role models for pupils.

It is interesting that these findings mirror, in many respects, some of the studies about the brain and learning referred to earlier. Drawing on the work of LeDoux (1996), Goleman (1996) argues that emotions play a key role in cognitive development. He takes the view that emotional intelligence, as he calls it, is a vital capacity for learning. It involves, for example, motivation, the ability to persist and stay on task, control of impulse, regulation of mood and the capacity for keeping distress from swamping the ability to think. Not unrelatedly, Smith (1998) comments that many learners in the classroom avoid taking risks and prefer to stay in 'the comfort zone'. He reminds us that young learners will happily 'copy out in rough, copy it out in neat, draw a coloured border around it, highlight the key words in primary colour, draw you a picture' but that this 'rote, repetitive comfort zone activity is not where real learning takes place' (p. 43). He describes how studies of the brain indicate that 'the optimal conditions for learning include a positive, personal leaning attitude where challenge is high and anxiety and self-doubt is low' (p. 41). In her review of the literature on effective primary teaching, Gipps (1992) identified some important factors that mark out effective primary teaching. Amongst these is 'the importance of a good positive atmosphere in the classroom with plenty of encouragement and praise, high levels of expectations of all children and high levels of work-related talk and discussion' (p. 19). She came to the conclusion that, over and above what theories inform us about good teaching, theorists tell us that children are capable of more than we expect.

So, it seems clear that teachers *do* have beliefs about how children learn and that they need a teaching strategy able to negotiate a path among the rocks and hard places of context, content, child and learning. This resonates with the complexity of real classrooms. Furthermore, those teachers who see children as thinkers, and therefore capable of achieving more and more, are the ones who can enable children to view themselves as able to learn. This is a virtuous circle which needs to be encouraged.

LEARNERS' VIEWS ABOUT TEACHERS AND LEARNING

What do young learners think about teaching and learning? When pupils' opinions are sought about their learning and the most effective ways in which teachers can promote learning, pupils can be relied upon to stress the importance of teacher-pupil relationships (Rudduck *et al.*, 1996; MacGilchrist *et al.*, 1997).

In England comparatively little research has focused on primary pupils' views about learning, and their role in it, although a number of research studies have looked at the pupils' view of teachers and school. Wragg has asked pupils about what makes a good teacher (Wragg and Wood, 1984; Wragg, 1993) as has Woods (1990). In an evaluation of school improvement in a range of Scottish schools, the Improving School Effectiveness Project (ISEP) also asked primary pupils aged six and ten in Scotland about their experience of school (Thomas *et al.*, 1998). Blatchford (1996) has interviewed a sample of children at seven, eleven and sixteen on attitudes to school and school-based work. Pollard has been involved in a number of studies, the early ones looking at the child's view of the classroom and later ones at the curriculum and the assessment process in the ESRC funded PACE study (Pollard *et al.*, 1994; Pollard, 1996; Broadfoot and Pollard, 1996). Tunstall and Gipps, studying teacher feedback to young children in formative assessment, asked six and seven year old children about how the teacher helped them to improve their work (Tunstall and Gipps, 1996) and about what helped children to do well in various subjects/tasks (Gipps and Tunstall, 1998).

The findings are fairly consistent: children like teachers who are kind and helpful, fairly interesting and fun, and explain things well. Pollard (1990) found that it was the ratio of risk to enjoyment that determined how children felt about tasks, rather than the nature of the tasks themselves. What children liked best about their teacher varied across years and between genders but the issue of pupil autonomy kept emerging: pupils preferred not to be constantly controlled and directed (Pollard *et al.*, 1994). As they moved through the first two years of Key Stage 2 (Broadfoot and Pollard, 1996) the pupils became increasingly aware of teacher power and control and very aware of the extent to which their activities were evaluated by teachers. Their preferred orientation was 'pleasing the teacher' and they showed a growing preoccupation with avoiding failure (Broadfoot and Pollard, 1998). This finding poses a challenge for primary teachers as the impact of this kind of pedagogy appears to close down rather than open up learning opportunities.

THE TEACHER-LEARNER RELATIONSHIP

The previous section suggested that the relationship between teacher and pupil is crucial to the learning process. For information on the relationship between teacher and learner, research on classroom-based, informal, assessment is a useful source. Taylor *et al.* (1997) draw on the work of Habermas (1972, 1984) to develop the notion of *open discourse* in the communicative relationships of pupils and teachers. In open discourse, communication is oriented towards understanding and respecting the meaning perspectives of others.

> Open discourse gives rise to opportunities for students to (1) negotiate with the teacher about the nature of their learning activities (2) participate in the determination of assessment criteria and undertake self-assessment and peer-assessment (3) engage in collaborative and open-ended enquiry with fellow students and (4) participate in reconstructing the social norms of the classroom.
>
> (Taylor *et al.*, *op cit.*, p. 295)

Taylor and colleagues do not articulate how such a communicative climate might be established but have developed a questionnaire to evaluate the learning environment on five key dimensions including 'shared control' and 'student negotiation'.

Questioning, as we indicated earlier in the chapter, has a key role to play in pedagogy. Galton's work (1989) shows the importance of high levels of questioning and the need for the teacher to develop strategies which allow maximum levels of sustained interaction with all pupils, to enhance quality learning. However, it is also acknowledged that questioning in the classroom setting is not straightforward and that its success is partly dependent on the quality of the teacher-pupil relationship. First, where the teachers' questioning has been restricted to 'lower order skills', students may well see questions about understanding or application as unfair, illegitimate or even meaningless (Schoenfeld, 1985). And, as Rogoff argues, there are cultural differences in how individuals respond to questioning:

> For example, schooled people are familiar with an interview or a testing situation in which a high-status adult, who already knows the answer to a question, requests information from a lower-status person, such as a child. In some cultural settings, however, the appropriate behaviour may be to show respect to the questioner or to avoid being made a fool of by giving the obvious answer to a question that must be a trick question whose answer is not the obvious one (otherwise why would a knowledgeable person be asking it?).
>
> (Rogoff, 1990, p. 59)

Furthermore, much teacher questioning is 'closed' and pupils develop strategies to discover the answer the teacher wants before actually committing themselves to it (Edwards and Mercer, 1989; Pollard, 1985). In such a climate, attempts by the teacher to engage in detailed diagnostic questioning may be misinterpreted (Torrance, 1993). As Edwards and Mercer (1989) point out: 'Repeated questions imply wrong answers' (p. 45) and the pupil may change tack in order to give the 'correct' answer and stop the questioning process rather than become engaged in an interactive process with the teacher. The point here is that opening up of questioning by the teacher can be seen as sharing power and control, and indeed what counts as acceptable knowledge, with the pupils (Gipps, 1999).

Black and Wiliam (1998) argue that the 'opening moves' of teachers and students in the negotiation of classroom contracts will be determined by their epistemological, psychological and pedagogical beliefs. When a teacher questions a student, the teacher's beliefs will influence both the questions asked and the way that answers are interpreted. In turn, the student's responses to questioning will depend on a host of other factors: whether the student believes ability to be incremental or fixed, for instance, will have a strong influence on how the student sees a question – as an opportunity to learn or as a threat to self-esteem (Dweck, 1986). Even where the student has a 'learning' as opposed to 'performance' orientation, the student's belief about what counts as 'academic work' (Doyle, 1988; Torrance and Pryor, 1998) will have a profound impact on the 'mindfulness' with which that student responds.

A key lesson emerging from this discussion is the need to understand the learner's view. In relation to informal assessment, this includes his/her expectations and assumptions about the classroom culture alongside his/her interpretation of the demands of the task and the criteria for success (Aikenhead, 1997). Sadler (1998), developing this line of argument, points out that teachers commonly bring to the classroom setting a more elaborate and extensive knowledge base than their students, a set of attitudes or dispositions towards teaching as an activity, skill in devising assessments, a deep knowledge of criteria and standards appropriate to the assessment task, evaluative skill in making judgements about student performance, and expertise in framing feedback statements. Sadler (1998) argues that we need to be mindful of the balance of these resources because:

> ultimately the intention of most educational systems is to help students not only grow in knowledge and expertise, but also to become progressively independent of the teacher for lifelong learning. Hence if teacher-supplied feedback is to give way to self assessment and self monitoring, some of what the teacher brings to the assessment act must itself become part of the curriculum for the student, not an accidental or inconsequential adjunct to it . . . The attitude of the teacher towards helping students is also crucial, but is to a large extent beyond the control of the learner. (Sadler, *op cit p.,* 82)

Smith's (1998) model of accelerated learning illustrates, in many respects, how Sadler's ideas can be put into practice in the classroom. He uses the findings of brain research to offer a means whereby teachers can raise pupil motivation and achievement in a planned, structured but flexible way. The structured approach to teaching 'is based on an understanding of how we learn rather than an expedient preoccupation with what we learn' (p. 23). Smith argues that 'attention to process and appropriate process interventions shifts thinking away from content and "coverage" ' (p. 24).

If we are serious about bringing the student in to some ownership of the learning and assessment process (and hence into self-evaluation and metacognition) it means teachers sharing power with students – rather than exerting power over them. This requires teachers to reconstruct their relationships as, in both learning and assessment, they shift responsibility to the students. This does *not* mean the teacher giving up responsibility for student learning and progress; far from it. It means, however, that the teacher takes on the added responsibility of involving the learner more as a partner and doing so explicitly. In other words, training their pupils so that they develop lifelong learning skills.

Bruner argues that we need to move on from an impoverished conception of teaching 'in which a single, presumably omniscient teacher explicitly tells or shows presumably unknowing learners something they presumably know nothing about' (Bruner, 1996, p. 20). Bruner talks instead of developing the classroom as a community:

> of mutual learners, with the teacher orchestrating the proceedings. *Note that, contrary to traditional critics, such subcommunities do not reduce the teacher's*

role nor his or her 'authority'. Rather, the teacher takes on the additional function of encouraging others to share it. Just as the omniscient narrator has dis
appeared from modern fiction, so will the omniscient teacher disappear from
the classroom of the future.

(Bruner, ibid., pp. 21–22, our emphasis)

This brings us full circle back to the lessons of learning theory: the teacher
in developing her pedagogical practice must see the pupil as an active agent
and a partner in learning, and encourage her to be responsible for, and to
monitor, her own learning.

MacGilchrist *et al.* (1997) suggest that effective teaching and learning
involves a *pact* between the teacher and the learner. They draw attention to
the interdependence of the teacher and learner (Figure 3.1). They describe in
diagrammatic form what the learner and the teacher each bring to the situation and, in turn, identify what they both need to bring to ensure that effective teaching and learning is brought about. In many respects, this sums up
some of the important psychological and sociological aspects of teaching we
have described in this chapter. A key implication of all this is that teachers
need to review on a regular basis their beliefs and attitudes about learners
and learning, challenge constantly the expectations they have of their pupils
as well as seeking to understand and enhance the motivation of those they
are teaching.

EFFECTIVE TEACHERS IN ACTION

What does effective pedagogy look like in practice? Recent research on effective teaching at primary level, conducted for the Teacher Training Agency
(TTA), gives us some insights. What follows is a description of the findings
of two studies of primary teachers at work in the classroom. These studies
were carried out for the TTA during 1995–97, and we quote from them
extensively. The first is that by Askew, Brown and colleagues at King's
College on effective teachers of numeracy (Askew *et al.*, 1997). These primary teachers were identified from a sample of 90 teachers and 2,000 pupils
on the basis of their pupils' test score gains over the school year. The
researchers investigated their teaching styles and approaches as well as their
beliefs about:

The nature of numeracy. This includes teachers' beliefs about:

• the nature of numeracy;
• expectations of learning outcomes.

Pupils and how they learn to become numerate. Included here are beliefs
about:

• whether or not some pupils are naturally more mathematical;
• the type of experiences that best bring about learning;

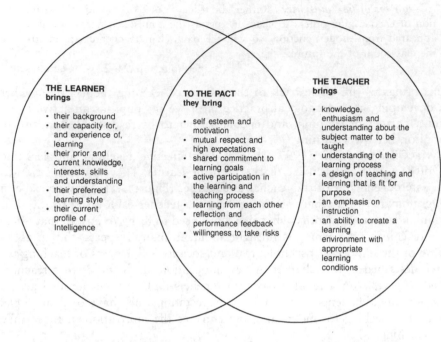

Fig. 3.1 The teaching and learning PACT – the interdependence of the teacher and learner
© 1997 B. MacGilchrist, K. Myers and J. Reed (p. 52)

- the role of the pupils in lessons.

How best to teach pupils to become numerate. These are related to beliefs about teaching numeracy in terms of:

- perception of the teachers' role in lessons;
- the influence of the 'accepted' wisdom of 'good' primary practice.

Askew and colleagues found that highly effective teachers of numeracy:

- had a coherent set of beliefs that included believing that being numerate involves using strategies which are both efficient and effective, and rests on the development of a rich network of connections between different mathematical ideas.

They used teaching approaches which:

- connected different areas of mathematics;
- encouraged pupils to describe their methods and their reasoning, and used these for developing understanding and establishing connections;

- emphasized the importance of using mental, written or electronic methods of calculation which were the most efficient for the problem in hand.

They believed that all pupils are able to become numerate and used teaching approaches which:

- ensured that all pupils were being challenged and stretched, not just those who were more able;
- built upon pupils' own mental strategies for calculating, and helped them to become more efficient.

They also believed in the importance of dialogue and shared imagery so that teachers gained better understanding of pupils' thinking and pupils gained access to the teachers' knowledge.

These teachers used teaching approaches which:

- encouraged discussion, in whole classes, small groups, or with individual pupils.
- used systematic assessment and recording methods to monitor pupils' progress and record their strategies for calculation, to inform planning and teaching.

Less effective teachers either used little assessment or used it as a check that taught methods had been learned. The researchers believe that the mathematical and pedagogical purposes behind particular classroom practices were as important as the practices themselves in determining effectiveness (Askew *et al.*, 1997, pp. 1–3).

This research identified three 'teaching orientations' which the researchers characterized as: connectionist, transmission and discovery. The most effective teachers were connectionist and believed in the value of getting children to think and talk about what they were learning, and to make connections among different areas of mathematics and different ideas in the same area of mathematics.

The importance of this research is that it links effective learning in the pupils (as evidenced by measured progress) with teachers' practice and beliefs about learning. Essentially, these teachers were operating on a constructivist model of learning, requiring the pupils to be active in their learning and to make sense of the information being learned.

The second study, on effective teachers of literacy, was carried out by Wray and colleagues at Exeter and Plymouth (Medwell *et al.*, 1998). The researchers surveyed the effective teaching of literacy and subsequently worked with a sample of 228 teachers identified by peers and by reading test results as effective. They also carried out detailed investigations involving classroom observations and interviews with 26 of these teachers and ten 'controls'. The researchers found that effective teachers of literacy:

- generally placed a high priority on meaning in their teaching of literacy, centring much teaching around 'shared texts' as a means of making the connections between word, sentence and text explicit to the children;
- taught the conventions of reading and writing in a systematic and structured way but also in a way that made clear to pupils the reasons for their importance;
- placed emphasis on establishing clear and purposeful contexts for reading and writing;
- tended to emphasize the functions of the language features they were teaching, e.g. learning the rules of grammar would help improve their writing;
- had strong and coherent beliefs about teaching literacy, which guided their selection of teaching materials and approaches;
- had well-developed systems for monitoring and assessment, using their findings in subsequent planning.

'The lessons of these teachers were conducted at a brisk pace. They regularly refocused children's attention on the task at hand and used clear time frames to keep children on task. They also tended to conclude their lessons by reviewing, with the whole class, what the children had done during the lesson. Lessons which ended with the teacher simply saying "We'll finish this tomorrow" were much more common among the validation [or control] teachers.

The effective teachers also used modelling extensively. They regularly demonstrated reading and writing to their classes in a variety of ways, often accompanying these demonstrations by verbal explanations of what they were doing. In this way they were able to make available to the children their thinking as they engaged in literacy . . . because of their concern to contextualize their teaching of language features within shared text experiences, made explicit connections for [their] pupils between the text, sentence and word levels of language study' (Medwell *et al.*, 1998, p. 78).

As with effective teachers of numeracy, these effective teachers placed a high priority on meaning and on making connections, in this case between reading and writing. Again, the value of this study is that it links teachers' practice and beliefs about learning, and thus their pedagogy, with the effective progress of the pupils.

CONCLUSION

There are some significant connections and similarities between the findings of the educational research we have cited and cognitive research on the functioning of the brain. Both paradigms emphasize that learning is an active process and can be enhanced or inhibited depending on the range and type of learning opportunities provided, particularly in the early years. Both draw attention to two types of learning: assimilating and integrating new knowledge in a way that ensures that it makes sense to the learner and becomes part of her long-term memory and is usable in a range of contexts; and thinking about learning in order to develop and maximize learning skills.

In England the current focus in primary education is on the first type of learning, namely on the academic content of the curriculum, in particular literacy and numeracy, and on how best this should be taught. It goes without saying that this is an essential aspect of school learning and we agree entirely, for example, that young children need to become literate and numerate as soon as possible. The two TTA-funded studies cited in the previous section provided exemplars of how effective teachers can successfully engage pupils in this process. We wish to argue however, that attention needs to be paid *simultaneously* to the second type of learning, because, without this, the education system is in danger of failing young people in the long term. Ensuring that the primary children of today become the flexible, adaptable, lifelong learners of the future, able to cope with the challenges and opportunities of the uncertain world they will face in the twenty-first century, will not happen by chance; like the first type of learning it needs careful planning and requires a structured approach to its teaching.

In order to develop a primary pedagogy which encourages effective learning we need primary teachers who not only have good subject knowledge and classroom management skills but who also have a good understanding of how children learn and are able to use this understanding to inform the teaching strategies they employ.

More attention needs to be paid to metacognition – the second type of learning which we have identified – and, therefore, to the practical strategies which teachers can use to encourage children to function effectively in thinking about learning. Important elements of pedagogy will include getting children to think about their own learning, teaching them how to evaluate their work and the effectiveness of their current strategies, and teaching them new learning strategies. Educationalists need to pay much more attention to the implications for pedagogy of the findings of research into the functioning and development of the brain to ensure that primary teachers maximize the brain's potential for learning in the primary years.

Primary teachers need to ensure that the classroom climate they create enables children to be both learners and thinkers. This will include creating an atmosphere in which it is acceptable to make mistakes and will require the type of relationship between the teacher and the learner described earlier, so that children develop from an early age a constructive attitude towards learning and a positive view about themselves as learners.

There is a key message that underlies these implications, namely that primary teachers need to ensure that they too are lifelong learners. They need to be given opportunities to model the active approaches to learning that we have advocated throughout this chapter. This will enable teachers to make explicit, and, if necessary, challenge, their beliefs about learning so that they can be as aware of how they go about their teaching as they are about the subject-matter to be taught.

REFERENCES

Aikenhead, C. (1997) A framework for reflecting on assessment and evaluation, in *Globalization of Science Education – Papers for the Seoul International Conference*. Seoul: Korean Educational Development Institute.

Askew, M., Brown, M., Rhodes, V., Johnson, D. and Wiliam, D. (1997) *Effective Teachers of Numeracy*, London: School of Education, King's College.

Atkins, M., Beattie, J. and Dockrell, B. (1992) *Assessment Issues in Higher Education*, Newcastle School of Education, University of Newcastle.

Black, P. and Wiliam, D. (1998) Assessment and classroom learning, *Assessment in Education*, 5(1): 7–73.

Blatchford, P. (1996) Pupils' views on school work and school from 7 to 16 years, *Research Papers in Education*, 11(3): 263–288.

Broadfoot, P. and Pollard, A. (1996) Continuity and change in English primary education, in P. Croll (ed.) *Teachers, Pupils and Primary Schooling: Continuity and Change*, London: Cassell.

Broadfoot, P. and Pollard, A. (1998) Categories, standards and instrumentalism: theorising the changing discourse of assessment policy in English primary education, paper presented to AERA Conference, San Diego.

Brophy, J. and Good, T. (1974) *Teacher/student Relationships: Cause and Consequences*, New York: Holt, Rinehart and Winston.

Bruner, J. (1996) *The Culture of Education*, Cambridge, Mass: Harvard University Press.

Bruner, J. and Haste, H. (1987) *Making Sense: The Child's Construction of the World*, New York: Routledge.

Cobb, P. (1994) Where is the mind?, *Educational Researcher*, 23(7): 13–20.

Davie, R., Butler, N. and Goldstein, H. (eds) (1972) *From Birth to Seven*, Harlow: Longman.

Denbo, S. (1988) *Improving Minority Student Achievement: Focus on the Classroom*, Washington, DC: Mid-Atlantic Equity Center Series.

Douglas, J. (1964) *The Home and School*, London: Macgibbon and Kee.

Doyle, W. (1988) Work in mathematics classes: the context of students' thinking during instruction, *Educational Psychologist*, 23(2): 167–180.

Driver, R., Guesne, E. and Tiberghien, A. (1985) *Children's Ideas in Science*, Milton Keynes: Open University.

Driver, R., Asoko, H., Leach, J., Mortimer, E. and Scott, P. (1994) Constructing scientific knowledge in the classroom, *Educational Researcher*, 23(7): 5–12.

Dryden, G. and Voss, J. (1994) *The Learning Revolution*, London: Accelerated Learning Systems.

Dweck, C. (1986) Motivational processes affecting learning, *American Psychologist*, (41): 1040–1048.

Edmunds, R. (1979) Effective schools for the urban poor, *Educational Leadership*, 37(3) 15–27.

Edwards, D. and Mercer, N. (1989) *Common Knowledge*, London: Routledge.

Fullan, M. (1991) *The New Meaning of Educational Change*, London: Cassell.

Galton, M. (1989) *Teaching in the Primary School*, London: David Fulton.

Gipps, C. (1992) *What We Know About Effective Primary Teaching*, London: Tufnell Press.

Gipps, C. (1999) Socio cultural aspects of assessment, in A. Irannejad and D. Pearson (eds.) *Review of Research in Education*, 24. American Educational Research Association (in press).

Gipps, C. McCallum, B., Brown, M. (1999) Primary teachers' beliefs about teaching and learning, *The Curriculum Journal*, (10)1: 123–134.

Gipps, C. and Tunstall, P. (1998) Effort, ability and the teacher: young children's explanations for success and failure, *Oxford Review of Education*, 24(2): 149–165.

Goleman, D. (1996) *Emotional Intelligence – Why it Matters More than IQ*, London: Bloomsbury.

Habermas, J. (1984) *A Theory of Communicative Action. Vol 1., Reason and the Rationalisation of Society*, Boston: Beacon Press.

Habermas, J. (1972) *Knowledge and Human Interests*, 2nd edn, London: Heinemann.

Hart, L.A. (1983) *The Human Brain and Human Learning*, New York: Addison Wesley Longman.

Hannaford, C. (1995) *Smart Moves: Why Learning Is Not All In Your Head*, New York: Great Ocean Publishers.

Inner London Education Authority (1983) Race, sex and class, *Achievement in Schools*, London: ILEA.

Jensen, E. (1994) *The Learning Brain*, San Diego: Turning Point.

Kuykendall, C. (1989) *Improving Black Student Achievement*, Washington, DC: The Mid-Atlantic Equity Center Series.

LeDoux, J. (1996) *Emotional Brain*, New York: Simon and Schuster.

MacGilchrist, B., Myers, K. and Reed, J. (1997) *The Intelligent School*, London: Paul Chapman.

Medwell, J., Wray, D., Poulson, L. and Fox, R. (1998) *Effective Teachers of Numeracy*, University of Exeter.

Merton, R. (1968) *The Self-Fulfilling Prophecy, Social Theory and Social Structure*, London: Collier MacMillan.

Mortimore, P. (1993) School effectiveness and the management of effective learning and teaching, *School Effectiveness and Improvement*, 4(4) 290–310.

Mortimore, P. and Mortimore J. (1986) Education and social class, in R. Rogers (ed.) *Education and Social Class*, Lewes: Falmer.

Mortimore, P., Sammons, P., Stoll, L., Lewis, D., and Ecob, R. (1988) *School Matters: The Junior Years*, Wells, Somerset: Open Books.

Office for Standards in Education (1993) *Access and Achievement in Urban Education*, London: HMSO.

Pilling, D. and Pringle, M.K. (1978) *Controversial Issues in Child Development*, London: Paul Elek.

Pollard, A. (1985) *The Social World of the Primary School*, London: Rinehart and Winston.

Pollard, A. (1990) Towards a sociology of learning in primary school, *British Journal of Sociology of Education*, 11(3).

Pollard, A., Broadfoot, P., Croll, P., Osborn, M. and Abbott, D. (1994) *Changing English Primary Schools? The Impact of the Education Reform Act at KS1*, London: Cassell.

Pollard, A. (1996) Playing the system: pupil perspectives of curriculum, assessment and pedagogy', in P. Croll (ed.) *Teachers, Pupils and Primary Schooling: Continuity and Change*, London: Cassell.

Resnick, L. (1989) Introduction to L. Resnick (ed.) *Knowing, Learning and Instruction: Essays in honour of R. Glaser*, New Jersey: Lawrence Erlbaum.

Reynolds, D. (1982) The search for effective schools, *School Organisation*, 2(3): 215–237.

Reynolds, D. and Farrell, S. (1996) *Worlds Apart? A Review of International Surveys of Educational Achievement involving England*, London: HMSO.

Rogoff, B. (1990) *Apprenticeship in Thinking: Cognitive development in social context*, Oxford: OUP.

Rosenthal, R. and Jacobson, L. (1968) *Pygmalion in the classroom: teacher expectation and pupils' intellectual development*, New York: Holt, Rinehart and Winston.

Rudduck, J., Chaplain, R. and Wallace, G. (1996) *School Improvement. What Can Pupils Tell Us?* London: David Fulton.

Rutter, M., Maughan, B., Mortimore, P. and Ouston, J. (1979) *Fifteen Thousand Hours; Secondary Schools and Their Effects on Children*, London: Open Books.

Sadler, R. (1989) Formative assessment and the design of instructional systems, *Instructional Science*, 18: 119–144.

Sadler, R. (1998) Formative assessment: revisiting the territory, *Assessment in Education*, 5 (1): 77–84.

Sammons, P., Hillman, J. and Mortimore, P. (1995) *Key Characteristics of Effective Schools: A Review of School Effectiveness Research*, research commissioned by Office for Standards in Education, London: Institute of Education and Office for Standards in Education.

Schoenfeld, A. (1985) *Mathematical Problem-solving*, New York: Academic Press.

Shepard, L. (1991) Psychometricians' beliefs about learning, *Educational Researcher*, 20: 8.

Shepard, L. (1992) What policy makers who mandate tests should know about the new psychology of intellectual ability and learning, in B. Gifford and M. O'Connor (eds.) *Changing Assessments: Alternative Views of Aptitude, Achievement and Instruction*, London: Kluwer.

Smith, A. (1998) *Accelerated Learning in Practice*, Stafford: Network Educational Press.

Smith, D. and Tomlinson, S. (1989) *The School Effect: A Study of Multi-Racial Comprehensives*, London: Policy Studies Institute.

Sylvester, R. (1995) *A Celebration of Neurons: An Educator's Guide to the Human Brain*, V.A.: ASCD.

Taylor, P., Fraser, B. and Fisher, D. (1997) Monitoring constructivist classroom learning environments, *International Journal of Educational Research*, 27(4): 293–301.

Thomas, S., Smees, R. and Boyd, B. (1998) Valuing pupils' views in Scottish schools, policy paper presented to the Scottish Office Employment and Industry Department, March 1998. To appear in *Education Research and Evaluation*.

Tizard, B., Blatchford, P., Burke, J., Farquhar, C. and Plewis, I. (1988) *Young Children at School in the Inner City*, New York: Lawrence Erlbaum.

Torrance, H. (1993) Formative assessment: some theoretical problems and empirical questions, *Cambridge Journal of Education*, 23: 333–343.

Torrance, H. and Pryor, J. (1998) *Investigating Formative Assessment: Teaching, learning and assessment in the classroom*, Buckingham: Open University Press.

Tunstall, P. and Gipps, C. (1996) How does your teacher help you make your work better?: Children's understanding of formative assessment, *The Curriculum Journal*, 7(2): 185–203.

von Glasersfeld, E. (1987) Learning as a constructive activity, in C. Janvier (ed.) *Problems of representation in the teaching and learning of mathematics*, Hillsdale: Lawrence Erlbaum.

Vygotsky, L. (1978) *Mind in Society*, London: Harvard University Press.

Wertsch, J.V. (1991) *Voices of the Mind: A Sociocultural Approach to Mediated Action*, Cambridge, Mass: Harvard University Press.

Woods, P. (1990) *The Happiest Days? How Pupils Cope with School*, London: Falmer Press.

Wragg, E. (1993) *Primary Teaching Skills*, London and New York: Routledge.

Wragg, E. and Wood, E.K. (1984) Teachers' first encounters with their classes, in Wragg, E. (ed), *Classroom Teaching Skills*, London: Croom Helm.

4

Pedagogy in the Secondary School

Susan Hallam and Judith Ireson

Teaching, in any phase of education, is influenced by prevailing social, political and economic circumstances, attitudes towards education, and beliefs about learning and teaching. Secondary schools, in their present form, were designed for the industrial age (Bayliss, 1998). They have been remarkably stable in their structure over the last 100 years and most changes made have been relatively superficial (Cuban, 1990; Sarason, 1990). The school day remains fairly inflexible; the process of teaching and learning is largely determined by the timetable and the structure of subject domains; children progress in age cohorts, often divided by ability; and summative learning outcomes are assessed by national examinations. For these reasons, the secondary years are arguably the most constrained of all phases of education.

Schools themselves further limit the extent to which the individual teacher has control over pedagogy. While the aims of education, the curriculum, assessment procedures, and financial resourcing are determined by external bodies, at the school level, policy – and through it ethos – is developed through a hierarchy of control which includes governors, the head teacher and heads of department. There is relatively little input from the classroom teacher. Issues central to the practice of pedagogy – resources, the physical working environment, the timetable, the ways that pupils are grouped and which pupils are taught by which teachers – are also determined through this hierarchy as are policies relating to behaviour and discipline. In addition, schools and the teachers working in them are assessed in relation to a set of external criteria laid down by Ofsted.

Although historically, the professional autonomy of teachers in the UK was largely taken for granted, this situation has gradually been changed over recent years. Within their classrooms, teachers are faced with many pre-determined constraints: aims and curricular objectives; a class of a particular year group, size and grouping structure (streamed, setted or of mixed ability) with unique interpersonal dynamics; a physical environment of a particular size and layout; specified resources and materials; a set length of lesson; and a commitment to an agreed amount of homework.

While teachers may have control over their own assessment procedures in the short term, in the longer term these are also determined by external agencies. Recent pressure for pupils to perform at high levels in national assessments ensures that these are the focus for pedagogy. The structure of formal feedback to pupils and parents (reports, parents' evenings) and procedures for further contact are also laid down by the school. Figure 4.1 diagrammatically illustrates these constraints. When these are taken into account the teacher has little real choice of teaching strategy. The curriculum and assessment procedures, which are operationalized in relation to specific learning aims, for particular pupils, at particular times largely determine the 'how' of teaching.

A further challenge for the teacher is that it is the pupils who have the task of learning. Teachers cannot learn for their pupils. Teachers teach. Pupils learn. It is this relationship which bedevils research on teaching and learning. Further, each pupil is a unique individual and has their own idiosyncratic knowledge base, preferred ways of learning, personality, motivations, interests, values, and social history. These factors contribute to the ways in which they undertake learning and need teaching. But pupils are not taught individually. Classes rarely have fewer than 25 pupils and often many more. This would seem to create an insoluble problem. How can one teacher promote learning in a group of individuals in ways that optimizes the learning of them all? Looked at in this way it is perhaps surprising that schools are as successful as they are.

Because we do not fully understand the relationship between the learning of the individual and the activities of the teacher, controversy about pedagogy is inevitable. Assessment of teachers and trainees tends to focus on the skills of the teacher. While there is reference to pupils and their engagement with the task, learning outcomes – often for practical reasons – tend not to be linked to the assessment of teaching. While engagement may be a prerequisite for learning, it is not always a sufficient condition to ensure that it happens.

The difficulty of capturing the tenuous relationship between teaching and learning has also meant that researchers have tended to focus on one or the other activity. Research, which takes learning as its starting point, has tended to stress the role of the teacher as the facilitator of individual learning and so has tended to focus on the pupil and their experience of learning. Research taking teaching as the focus has concentrated on the skills of the teacher in transmitting knowledge, giving clear explanations, and providing appropriate tasks. In the first model, the learner tends to be seen as active; in the second, as passive or as open to manipulation.

There are also many methodological challenges to researching the relationship between teaching and learning. Quantitative methods are problematic because of the difficulties of controlling the many confounding factors and of devising appropriate measures to assess the quality of teaching and learning. Qualitative methods are invaluable for illuminating the detailed interactions between teachers and learners during the learning process but,

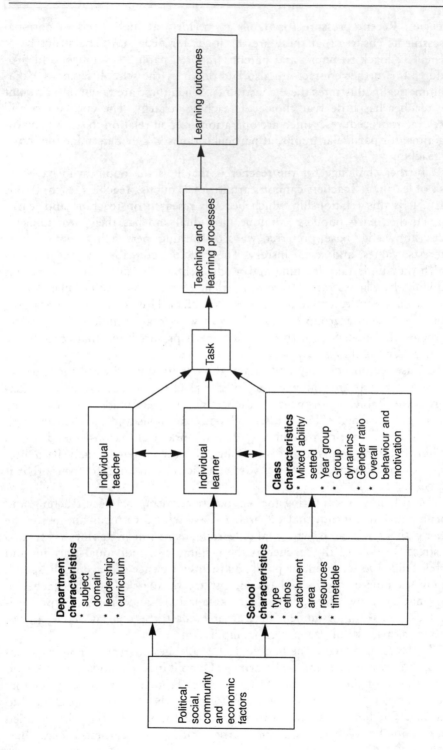

Fig. 4.1 Influences on secondary school learning

because of the nature of the data, tend to be undertaken only on a small scale. This inevitably raises questions about whether the findings can be generalized to other learning situations. As the aims of secondary education for the twenty-first century become more complex (including a new set of key skills) this will provide researchers with some difficult challenges as they attempt to elucidate the ways in which teaching and learning are related and the underlying processes involved.

Given these problems, where might we make a start in considering pedagogy in the secondary school? First, there is little doubt that the quality of teaching is important in promoting learning in secondary education. There is ever increasing evidence that schools do make a difference (Rutter *et al.*, 1979; Mortimore *et al.*, 1988; Reynolds, 1990, Sammons *et al.*, 1993, Mortimore, 1994), but no consistent effects have been found for a range of organizational factors, such as pupil grouping arrangements (Hallam and Toutounji, 1996; Ireson and Hallam, 1999) and class size (Blatchford and Mortimore, 1994). However, there is evidence of differences in performance between departments, in different years and for different groups of children (Nuttall *et al.*, 1989; Goldstein *et al.*, 1992; Sammons *et al.*, 1997). This suggests that it is what goes on in the classroom that is crucial to pupils' achievement. So what do we know about this central area of school life?

PEDAGOGY

As noted in Chapter 1, pedagogy is sometimes defined as the principles, practice or science of teaching. In secondary schools, subject knowledge, with a little 'on the job experience' was until recent times seen as sufficient training for teaching. If the systematic study and application of pedagogy is to be developed in the UK what might guide us in establishing its parameters in relation to secondary education? What should it include? What do we already know? What do we need to find out?

Table 4.1 sets out a possible framework. It is derived from Simon's (1995) assertion that the foundations of pedagogy must be based on the objectives or aims of teaching; the work of Uljens (1997) who has described four interrelated factors which must be considered in constructing what he calls school

Table 4.1 A pedagogy for secondary education

A pedagogy for secondary education may include:
Consideration of the aims of education and the values which underpin teaching
Knowledge of theories of learning
Knowledge of different conceptions of teaching
Knowledge of models of teaching and learning and of the dynamic interaction between student characteristics, the characteristics of the learning environment, task demands, the processes of learning and teaching and different kinds of learning
Understanding of how these can be operationalized in the classroom
Knowledge and skills for evaluating practice, research and theory relating to education.

didactics; what we know about learning itself; theories of learning; pedagogical practice; and educational theory. Each factor informs and interrelates
with every other. There is also a need for teachers to be able to evaluate the
theory and practice of teaching. The remainder of the chapter will focus on
the contents of Table 4.1, discussing the research evidence and issues arising
from it.

THE AIMS AND VALUES OF SECONDARY EDUCATION

The first requirement for developing an appropriate pedagogy is the recognition of the importance of establishing clear educational aims and a set of
values that underpin pedagogical processes. No discussion of effective
learning or teaching can take place without reference to its content. Debates
about effective pedagogy tend to become tacitly but nevertheless inextricably bound up with debates about what we should be aiming to teach. This
extends beyond the formal curriculum to include the learning of generic skills
and also what has been referred to as the hidden curriculum (Snyder, 1971).

So what are the current aims of education in England? The National
Curriculum determines the content of what is to be taught and defines specific learning objectives but does not set out overall aims for education. It
also makes little reference to generic skills such as metacognition, working
with others, communication, independent learning, creativity, problem solving, and critical thinking, although these may be implicit in the learning
objectives in some subject domains. Neither does the National Curriculum
make much reference to the values within which the curriculum is embedded and therefore the ways it should be taught to promote such values. As
the relationship between teacher and students is one of unequal power and
much learning occurs by observation, pupils inevitably learn about ways of
behaving and interacting with others from the example set by the teacher.
The lack of a clear value system set out within the curriculum to guide teachers is therefore an important omission (Gutierrez et al., 1995).

In defining the aims of education it may also be advisable to take account
of pupils' motivation as, without this, learning cannot take place. Recent
research suggests that pupils in the UK tend to have relatively utilitarian
views of school. Pupils see the main functions of education as helping them
to do well in examinations, acquire qualifications and life skills and ultimately be employed. They wish to be supported by schools in achieving these
aims (University of North London Truancy Unit, 1994; Keys and Fernandes,
1993). The possible increase in disaffection from school in recent years may
suggest that not all pupils feel they are receiving this support. Those who
truant tend to see lessons as irrelevant, unenjoyable, or too difficult. Some
50 per cent of pupils report being bored in some lessons, while 10 per cent
suggest this is the case in all or most lessons (Keys and Fernandes, 1993).
For a small proportion of pupils, school is seen as a waste of time. The dis-
proportionate amount of time which many teachers seem to spend in relation

to classroom control would also suggest that there may be a much greater proportion of pupils who are not committed to the current curriculum and pedagogical methods.

LEARNING AND THEORIES OF LEARNING

Learning appears to be a natural process for human beings (Newell, 1990). Despite this, our understanding of learning processes continues to be incomplete. Human beings seem to be able to learn in a range of circumstances and often in spite of all kinds of obstacles. Underpinning most modern theories of learning in the western world are ideas first introduced by the Greeks. Plato proposed the notion that we are born with knowledge which then unfolds as we mature. A generation later Aristotle proposed that experience was the basis of learning. In 1781, Kant, in his *Critique of Pure Reason*, tried to resolve the tensions between these positions and suggested that while experience was important for learning there must be structures underpinning it. He suggested that these were rules for producing abstract mental representations, which he called schemata. These ideas about the way that knowledge is constructed are now widely accepted in educational thinking. However, much learning also occurs at a relatively superficial and automatic level. Many of our emotional and physical responses are learned without recourse to conscious cognitive processing and where cognitive engagement is required, it can be undertaken at a low level without the student acquiring deep understanding. This often occurs because the learner is insufficiently motivated to expend the necessary effort.

Historically, each learning theory has influenced educational practice, although there appears to be no straightforward relationship between theory, policy and practice. The social and political climate at any time seems as important, if not more so, in determining the impact of theory and research on practice. The rationalist position has implicitly underpinned thinking on child centred education, the focus being on the child developing their naturally occurring talents (Froebel, 1912; Isaacs, 1932), and the psychometric tradition. The extensive development of intelligence testing in the UK (Burt, 1921; Vernon, 1956) and its use in selecting children for particular types of education inhibited research on learning and teaching because of the underlying assumption that learning is determined by ability, rather than by effort or the quality of teaching. This assumption continues to influence much current policy and practice, perhaps because the ideas are so embedded in our culture through the class system (Galton, 1892). Pupils continue to be grouped by ability (see Hallam and Toutounji, 1996) and modern theories of intelligence which offer alternative conceptions (Gardner, 1983; Ceci, 1990; Sternberg, 1988b) have not gained wholehearted acceptance in the educational community or beyond it.

In the 1970s, particularly in the USA, research focused on aptitude-treatment interactions (ATI) which attempted to establish the optimum types of instruction for pupils of different abilities (Snow, 1987). Within this framework research in the UK explored the relationship between personality and academic achievement (Entwistle, 1972). However, as the degree of complexity of individual differences became more apparent, researchers in intelligence began to pursue an information processing approach (Gardner *et al.*, 1995) and stressed the importance of strategy use (Sternberg, 1988b) and the situated aspects of intelligence (Ceci, 1990). Doubts were also cast on the consistency of personality and behaviour in different learning situations (Mischel, 1968) and ATI research disappeared.

The experiential view of the development of knowledge, as suggested by Aristotle, is particularly prominent in the behaviourist tradition and still exerts a powerful influence on secondary schools. Behaviourist policies are advocated as a means of improving behaviour (Wheldall and Glynn, 1989), through assertive discipline techniques (Ellis and Karr-Kidwell, 1997) and in learning programmes such as Mastery Learning (Block, 1971; Bloom, 1971), Personalised Systems of Instruction (PSI) (Keller, 1968), in computerized learning and, particularly, in work with children with Special Educational Needs.

Constructivism has an equally long history; from Kant, through the work of Bartlett (1932) on memory and Piaget's theory of intellectual development (Piaget, 1950; Piaget and Inhelder, 1958) both of which have been particularly influential in primary and science education in the UK. The work of Kelly (1955) has influenced thinking about constructive alternativism, leading to modern techniques in handling behaviour problems. Social constructivism, as embodied in the work of Vygotsky (1962, 1978), sees culture as important in accounting for human action and cognition within social practices (Lave, 1988; Saljo, 1996). In education this has led to a strong emphasis on the importance of the context of learning (Tharp and Gallimore, 1988), the notion of cognitive apprenticeship and the ability of children to learn in communities with adults (Chaiklin and Lave, 1993; Rogoff, 1990).

Phenomenographic research also fits within the constructivist framework that takes into account the pupils' experience of learning (Marton and Booth, 1997). This approach aims to identify the qualitatively different ways in which individuals experience and understand the world and systematically describes them in terms of deep or surface approaches to learning. While work in this tradition continues (Marton and Booth, 1997) and is highly influential in Scandinavia, another strand has adopted a different methodological perspective and uses questionnaires to assess students' approaches to learning (Biggs and Moore, 1993; Entwistle and Ramsden, 1983). This methodology has enabled researchers to develop models relating students' approaches to a range of other factors.

Recently, there has been a move away from simply theorizing about learning in secondary education, and attempts have been made to develop multidimensional models which take account of the dynamic interplay of a range of factors which affect and, in turn, are affected by learning outcomes. Such a model will be outlined and discussed later in this chapter. There has also been a much greater recognition of the active role of the learner (Kolb, 1984; Biggs and Moore, 1993) and the importance of emotion and motivation.

The ease with which emotional responses can be conditioned through the association of two events in time (Watson and Raynor, 1920) has been recognized often to be maladaptive in school. Many pupils are prevented from academic learning because of their own emotional responses and their vain attempts to cope with them (Boekaerts, 1993; Midgely *et al.*, 1996).

In contrast to the relative ease with which emotional responses can be acquired, academic learning, at the very least, requires time and engagement. These might therefore provide a suitable starting point for the consideration of the qualities of effective teaching. It might be conceptualized as providing the pupil with time or opportunity to learn and as engaging the pupil with learning. How these two elements might be achieved may vary depending on the subject domain, the particular task, the individual pupil, his or her class, and the immediate working environment. A particular challenge for the teacher is how to engage pupils who are in the same class when they exhibit markedly different individual characteristics.

CONCEPTIONS OF TEACHING

We believe that effective teaching can only be considered in relation to effective learning. This raises the question of how learning and teaching are generally conceptualized. Research has shown that academic learning can be defined as a quantitative increase in knowledge; memorizing; the acquisition for subsequent utilization of facts and methods; the abstraction of meaning; and an interpretative process aimed at understanding reality (Saljo, 1979). Much secondary school learning can be understood in relation to the lower three levels.

Are there parallels between conceptions of teaching and learning? Certainly, teaching has been seen in many different ways. It has been seen on a continuum from the transmission of knowledge at one end to the facilitation of learning (Kember, 1997) at the other, broadly mirroring conceptions of learning. However, teaching in the secondary school serves functions other than those that are purely academic. It may be for this reason that there are many ways of viewing it, for instance, as clinical problem solving (Kagan, 1988); a cognitive skill (Leinhardt and Greeno, 1986); work (Marshall, 1988); craft knowledge (Leinhardt, 1990); management (Biggs and Telfer, 1987); improvised conversation (Yinger, 1994); apprenticeship (Pratt, 1992); transaction (Barnes, 1976); guided participation (Rogoff, 1990); or as the practice of a community of learners (Rogoff *et al.*, 1996). Fenstermacher and Soltis (1986) further distinguish between: the executive approach; the therapist approach; and the liberationist approach, while Joyce *et al.* (1997) outline four models of learning: information processing; social; personal; and behavioural and cybernetic, each of which, they argue, can inform teaching.

What are we to make of this plethora of ideas? There seems to be little consensus about the nature of teaching. In addition, teaching has been viewed as a science, a complex skill which can be learned or as artistry (Hopkins *et al.*, 1994). This latter conception is often adopted to justify providing the minimum of training for teachers, the assumption being that teaching cannot be acquired but is a gift. This is a misunderstanding of the basis of artistry. Artists are experts in their field. High levels of expertise are acquired through the acquisition of extensive knowledge and much practice of relevant skills. During practice the skills become automated. This means that they can be carried out with minimal conscious cognitive effort allowing attention to be focused on higher order processes (Underwood and Bright, 1996). In teaching, this develops through the gradual acquisition of a complex knowledge structure.

This structure is made up of sets of actions (physical and cognitive) known as schema. These become increasingly organized and extensive links are made between them (Leinhardt and Greeno, 1986; Berliner, 1986; Swanson *et al.*, 1990). They also occur at different levels of generality. Because they have become automated they enable the teacher consciously to monitor activity in the classroom and automatically to deal with a range of situations as they arise. Concurrently with undertaking an activity an expert teacher also acquires and takes note of information which may be generated incidentally.

This information can be saved, revised and used in future situations (Leinhardt and Greeno, 1986). Experienced teachers build up a complex network of schema which incorporate the subject matter, how it is to be taught, how to manage the class and a deep knowledge base with which they learn to deal effectively with highly specific matters, such as explanations to suit a range of learners. Expert teachers focus primarily on the pupils and usually adopt a combination of activities either sequentially or concurrently to deal with one or more goals simultaneously taking account of the current conditions at the time (Brown and McIntyre, 1993). Teaching, like most expert skills relies on knowing 'how to do the right thing at the right time' (Dorner and Scholkopf, 1991).

Because these processes have become automated, expert teachers are often unable to make their skills explicit (Berliner, 1986; Schon, 1983). The terms scripts and scenes have been adopted to describe how these automated skills are operationalized. Berliner (1986) describes one script, 'grooving' where, when faced with a new class, the expert teacher sets a task or tasks that have to be undertaken in a particular way. This establishes their authority. 'Grooved' students are then easier to manage. To the observer, the demonstration of such skills appears as artistry with the teacher able to improvise and to adapt to relevant conditions. This has been described as the wisdom of practice (Leinhardt, 1990; Shulman, 1986). Inexperienced teachers are unable to respond in this way, lacking the knowledge about the difficulties pupils will experience and how they can assist them (Borko and Livingston, 1989).

The flexibility which is exhibited by expert teachers may explain the lack of a single, simple conception of teaching. Expert teachers are able to adopt a range of strategies which are fit for particular learning aims and circumstances. In any single lesson they may transmit knowledge and facilitate learning by stimulating interest, explaining, instructing, managing, discussing, guiding, counselling, and supporting. Teachers' decisions about what will be appropriate in a particular situation have to take account of a range of interacting factors, which will now be explored using a multi-dimensional model of teaching and learning as a framework.

MODELS OF TEACHING AND LEARNING

The first model of school learning was proposed by Carroll (1963). He suggested that the degree of learning was a function of the time actually spent learning divided by the time needed for learning. This suggests that the learner will succeed in a learning task if s/he is given opportunity and allowed sufficient time to engage actively with the task until mastery is achieved. Perseverance is also required, i.e. continuing to work when conditions are not optimal or feedback is negative. The time needed for learning is determined by: aptitude for learning a particular task (itself dependent on prior learning or the traits or characteristics of the learner); ability to understand instruction (verbal ability); and the quality of that instruction (the organization and presentation of teaching materials). Carroll's (1963) model has had a considerable influence on research relating to school learning (e.g. Cooley and Leinhardt, 1975; Bloom, 1976; Harnischfeger and Wiley, 1976; Bennett, 1978; Haertel et al., 1983; Carroll, 1989) and has highlighted the importance of time, effort and motivation in determining achievement.

Most current models of school achievement have their basis in Carroll's ideas (Biggs and Moore, 1993; Creemers, 1994) and take account of the characteristics of the learner; the learning environment; the process of learning itself; learning outcomes and how these feed back into the next learning situation (Biggs and Moore, 1993). Studies testing these models tend to confirm the multidimensional influences of a wide range of variables on learning (e.g. Fraser, 1989). While these models have been invaluable in providing an appropriate framework for understanding learning and in particular its relationship with assessment (Biggs and Moore, 1993) they have not been particularly helpful in elucidating the teaching-learning relationship as it operates in school classrooms. The quality of instruction, part of the model outlined by Carroll, and its relationship with learning is still problematic.

Figure 4.2 sets out a model of teaching and learning which attempts to address this problem. It is embedded within the wider framework set out in Figure 4.1. The model is concerned with those factors affecting the process of teaching and learning and the interrelationships between them. It is dynamic. Change in one part of the model affects other parts, for instance,

learning changes learners. During a learning experience the individual under-
goes change which means that the characteristics which they bring to any
subsequent learning experience will be different. As learning is undertaken,
levels of expertise and prior knowledge, learning approaches and styles, and
metacognition may all change. Self-esteem and future motivation can also be
affected as feedback in relation to learning outcomes occurs. Similarly, as
teaching is evaluated in relation to pupils' learning, teachers' expectations,
beliefs, knowledge of teaching strategies and their fitness for purpose will
change as will their self-efficacy in relation to teaching. Over time, there will
also be changes in student/teacher perceptions of each other.

Elements within the model can also be considered as relevant to more than
one of its facets. For instance, the quality of teaching might be seen in relation to teacher characteristics or as contributing to the process of teaching
and learning. The model can also be viewed over different time scales: in an
immediate classroom situation or over a longer-term series of interactions
between teacher and learner. What is to be learned is central to the model.
Learning tasks are set by the teacher in relation to curriculum requirements
and their knowledge of particular pupils. Tasks and their purposes may be
interpreted differently by pupils and teachers.

The process of teaching and learning depends on the implementation by
pupils and teacher of person and task oriented strategies. The match between
these and their relative successes will determine learning outcomes which may
be qualitative, quantitative, affective or related to national assessment criteria. Immediate information about progress on a task will feed back into the
process while longer term, summative assessment feeds back to both teacher
and learner and thus changes the characteristics they bring to future learning situations. Where learning outcomes are perceived as positive by both
parties, the increase in the self-esteem of both is likely to influence future
student/teacher perceptions positively, leading to better motivated teaching
and learning. Where this is not the case, a negative downward spiral may
develop, with each party blaming the other for failure. The next sections will
consider the model in greater detail.

LEARNER CHARACTERISTICS

There is a considerable literature on individual differences between learners
and the direct and indirect ways that these can affect learning outcomes. It
is beyond the scope of this chapter to consider them in depth but we know
that prior knowledge (Voss, 1978); age and developmental factors (Berk,
1997); abilities, (Sternberg, 1988b; Gardner, 1993; Ceci, 1990), which may
be the manifestations of prior knowledge; conceptions of learning (Saljo,
1979); metacognition (Wang et al., 1990) cognitive and learning styles
(Riding and Rayner, 1998); approaches to learning (Entwistle, 1988; Biggs
and Moore, 1993); motivation (Biggs and Moore, 1993); effort (Brookhart,

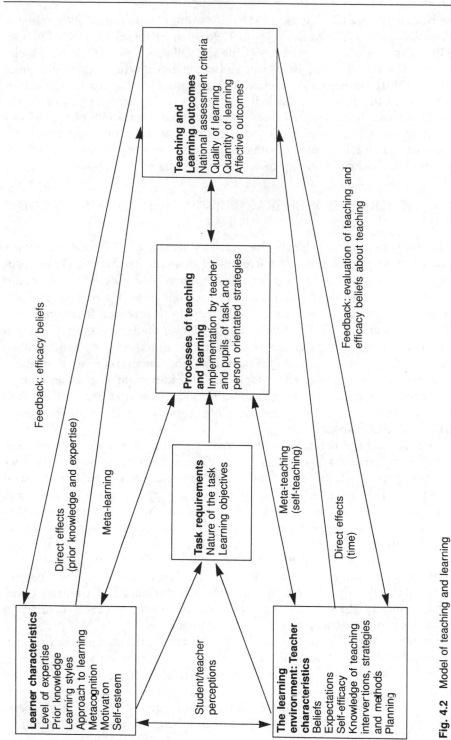

Fig. 4.2 Model of teaching and learning

1998); well-being (Boekaerts, 1993); self-esteem (Scott *et al.*, 1996); self-effi-cacy (Bandura, 1977; Midgely *et al.*, 1996); gender (Halpern, 1992; Elwood, 1995; Fan *et al.*, 1997); ethnicity (Gillborn, 1990; Kellner, 1998); and social economic status (Kumar, 1993) can all have effects on the learning outcomes of individual students. In practice it is not possible for teachers to tailor teaching to the needs of each individual child taking account of this degree of difference. However, if teachers are aware of the ways in which these dif-ferences can affect learning, they can ensure that, over time, the tasks that they set, the teaching methods that they adopt and the materials that they use provide sufficient variety to facilitate learning in all pupils.

TEACHERS, THEIR CHARACTERISTICS AND PERCEPTIONS OF PUPILS

There is considerable evidence that teachers' beliefs and expectations have a crucial effect on the learning outcomes of their pupils. Argyris (1976) pro-poses that teachers hold what he calls 'espoused' theories – those underly-ing professional practice and 'theories-in-use' that guide professional practice. What teachers 'think', influences 'what they do' (Clark and Peterson, 1986; Carlgren *et al.*, 1994). It is important, therefore, that teachers understand a substantial body of knowledge about learning and a range of issues related to it such as the nature of intelligence or the importance of motivation. Teachers' expectations of their pupils are also important in relation to rais-ing achievement (Mortimore *et al.*, 1995; Gottfredson *et al.*, 1995; Jussim *et. al.*, 1998), although the effect does not seem to operate in all classrooms all of the time (Rogers, 1990).

Where teachers' perceptions of effective teaching have been explored, they tend to be related to goodness of fit. They are most satisfied when they observe pupils' behaviour that indicates appropriate engagement with learn-ing tasks. This relies on making assessments of pupils' needs (Cooper and McIntyre, 1996). While it is easy to criticize teachers for their tendency to stereotype pupils, a generalized typing of ability or academic knowledge plays an important part in the decisions they make about their teaching approaches. They need to find ways of simplifying the complex task of man-aging the learning skills of all the pupils in their classrooms. Their percep-tion of ability differences tends to be uni-dimensional and stable (Cooper and McIntyre, 1996) but, given that issues of intelligence are generally not addressed in their training, this is not surprising.

Similarly, teachers tend to have elaborate belief systems relating to estab-lishing control over their students particularly in inner city schools (Turner, 1993). This suggests that for teachers to optimize learning they need to have a greater awareness of the complexities of individual differences, the impor-tance of their perceptions and expectations of pupils on learning outcomes and the ways in which pupils view them and their behaviour (Woods, 1990).

Positive interactions between teachers and pupils are important in facilitating learning. Teachers' self-efficacy as teachers is also an important predictor of pupil learning outcomes (Tschannen-Moran *et al.*, 1998).

TASK REQUIREMENTS

The National Curriculum specifies the nature and purpose of most tasks for each subject at secondary level. However, learning objectives and goals can be defined in abstract ways which can be applied across curriculum content. Teaching methods which fit these purposes can then be applied to achieve these goals. Bloom *et al.* (1956) provided an early framework outlining knowledge; comprehension; application; analysis; synthesis; and evaluation. Gagne (1970) derived from the learning objectives outlined in 'The Conditions of Learning' a series of instructional events to be undertaken by the teacher to assist the learner. These later provided the foundations for the development of the field of instructional design. This approach has been very influential, particularly in the USA, although it has been criticized for its narrow focus and the difficulties of pursuing several goals simultaneously within its framework. However, working backwards from goals to the requirements of instructional events is one of the most effective and widely employed techniques for achieving certain types of learning objectives (Gagne and Merrill, 1990).

Increasingly, transferable generic skills – which it is expected will be required for future employment – are being specified as learning objectives. For instance, adaptability, creativity, communication and social skills, problem solving, organization, time management, being able to work independently, metacognition and the use of information technology are being identified as important as are personal competencies which develop citizenship (Bayliss, 1998). Such educational aims are important for developing the motivation and skills required for learning through life and are likely to become more important in the future.

THE PROCESSES OF TEACHING AND LEARNING

In discussing issues relating to learning, we argued that academic learning required time and engagement on the part of the learner. In the school environment this means that the teacher has to ensure that these conditions are met. To achieve this the teacher must be able to manage the classroom environment and have pedagogical knowledge relating to their own subject and a range of learning outcomes including generic skills.

Managing the classroom environment

The literature on teacher effectiveness suggests that effective teachers operate in a holistic way, drawing on a range of skills and their observations of a particular class at a particular time (Kyriacou, 1991). There has been a number of reviews of what constitutes effective teaching and the characteristics of the effective teacher (e.g. Brophy and Good, 1986; Creemers, 1994; Tabberer, 1994; Joyce *et al.*, 1997; Wittrock, 1986). Mortimore (1994) also suggests a range of necessary teacher skills, organizing, analysis, synthesis, presentational, assessment, management and evaluative.

International studies of teacher effectiveness have explored differences in classroom management, maintaining order, student practice, questioning skills, teaching methods, and classroom climate. The evidence suggests that teachers either display all of the effective behaviours or they do not (Creemers, 1997). Despite considerable rhetoric regarding the efficacy of different teaching styles, teachers' behaviour is too complex to be classified as traditional or progressive (Galton *et al.*, 1980; Mortimore *et al.*, 1988) and, even within particular subjects, the relationship between styles and learning outcomes remains unclear (Barnes *et al.*, 1987).

According to Doyle (1986), classrooms are complex settings with multiple dimensions operating simultaneously, immediately and unpredictably. The variety of possible interactions between teachers and pupils is enormous. Teachers need to learn how to manage this environment in a positive way (Brookover *et al.*, 1979; Mortimore *at al.*, 1988; Scheerens, 1992). Research has consistently shown that neutral and warm environments have a strong relationship with achievement, while a negative atmosphere can affect pupils' progress negatively (Soar and Soar, 1979). Woods (1990), reviewing the literature on pupils' affective reactions to school, describes how the teacher has to ensure that pupils are maintained 'on task' in order to promote learning. To achieve this, teachers have to be adept at making the work interesting and varied, giving attention to individuals, using humour and converting work to play. Furthermore, as pupils get older they also wish to be treated with respect (Rudduck *et al.*, 1996; Keys and Fernandes, 1993), with their rights and responsibilities acknowledged (Powell, 1980).

While creating the appropriate environment for learning is important, this must not be to the detriment of focusing on academic work (Brophy and Good, 1986). Effective teachers tend to be business-like, task oriented, interacting primarily on a teacher-student basis, operating their classrooms as learning environments, and spending most time on academic activities (Brophy and Good, 1986). The least effective are too concerned with personal relationships and affective outcomes or are disillusioned and bitter, dislike their students and concentrate on discipline and authority issues. Teachers whose pupils achieve the best scores assume personal responsibility for their teaching and the learning of their pupils, feel efficacious, have an internal locus of control, tend to organize their classrooms and plan proactively on a daily basis, and display 'a can do' attitude (Tabberer, 1994).

There is considerable consensus regarding the generic skills that teachers require in relation to the management of the classroom (e.g. Brophy and Good, 1986; Porter and Brophy, 1988). It appears important that teachers pay attention to the quantity and pace of instruction, giving information, questioning the students, handling seatwork and homework and also take account of the learning context. They also need to have clear intentions and convey these to their pupils (Tabberer, 1994; Bruner, 1996; MacGilchrist *et al.*, 1997).

Teachers routinize many operations in order to reduce the complexity of classroom activity (Creemers and Tillema, 1988). This enables them to focus their attention on dealing with those events which may disrupt learning. This constant monitoring has become known as 'withitness' (Kounin, 1970). Teachers can adopt a range of strategies to manage the classroom (Marland, 1993) but often prefer whole class teaching because it reduces the level of complexity (Creemers and Tillema, 1988). While training can prepare teachers for many aspects of classroom management, to develop expert skills requires considerable practice.

Teaching methods for different subject domains

In England, teaching expertise is currently centred around the curriculum content for each subject domain (Cooper and McIntyre, 1996). Much teacher training is devoted to enabling teachers to 'deliver' the curriculum. Also there is a tendency, within current assessment procedures, for content coverage to determine achievement more directly than the particular teacher behaviours used to teach it (Wright and Nuthall, 1970; Hughes, 1973). Despite this, there is relatively little research on the ways that effective teaching differs in relation to different subject domains or topics within subjects. Stodolsky and Grossman (1995a, 1995b) have explored teachers' perceptions of different subject domains and the evidence from research on grouping pupils by ability suggests that teachers perceive their subjects as depending on different levels of prior or sequential learning (Hallam and Toutounji, 1996). Maths and foreign languages tend to be perceived as requiring considerable sequencing while English and humanities much less so. Within subject domains there are also wide differences in the teaching and learning requirements of different topics. For instance, helping children to compose requires very different teaching strategies to teaching them to learn to read music.

Much of the research on teacher effectiveness has centred on pupil achievement in tasks where there are measurable outcomes in terms of increases in knowledge, e.g. mathematics. Findings which suggest that pupils may achieve more when a teacher carefully organizes and sequences the curriculum; clearly explains and illustrates what pupils are to learn; frequently asks direct and specific questions to monitor progress and check understanding; gives prompts and feedback to ensure success; corrects mistakes and allows pupils to use a skill until it is over learned or automatic (Doyle, 1987) may apply to the learning of some tasks but may not be appropriate where learning outcomes are open ended, for instance, where creativity or problem solving are involved.

These findings suggest that knowledge of pedagogical skills forms a crucial part of teachers' expertise. While trainee teachers at secondary level have acquired content knowledge at undergraduate level prior to their training, this needs to be transformed for the purposes of teaching (Wilson *et al.*, 1987; Shulman, 1987). This transformation involves four sub-processes: critical interpretation; consideration of alternative ways of representing the subject matter (teachers should possess a repertoire that consists of metaphors, analogies, illustrations, activities, assignments and examples); adaptation of teaching to take account of the student population; and tailoring the materials to the specific students in each class. Evaluation and reflection can then lead to changes in knowledge and subsequent plans (Wilson *et al.*, 1987). Over time teachers appear to acquire something akin to a map of their discipline which guides their teaching based on their knowledge of the subject, how they perceive it and issues which it addresses (Gudmundsdottir, 1991). Armstrong (1994) has suggested ways of teaching which map onto Gardner's (1993) theory of intelligence but they are relatively superficial, tending to describe general activities related to subject domains rather than relating teaching to the learning of specific topics or outcomes.

Strategies for teaching particular learning objectives

There is no clear dividing line between pedagogical knowledge for particular subjects and more general teaching strategies. Sometimes teachers, in planning their teaching, draw on knowledge of general teaching skills and apply them to the topic (Marks, 1990; Pendry, 1994). Much of the research on teaching has focused on the attainment of clearly defined single instructional objectives within an instructional framework. Gagne (1970) set out a series of 'events' which are designed to promote learning.

These events include activating motivation; informing the learner of the objective; directing attention; stimulating recall; providing learner guidance; enhancing retention; promoting the transfer of learning; eliciting performance; and providing feedback. Gagne's work has provided a powerful model for instructional design, although the learning objectives to which it can be applied are narrow and only one can be addressed at a time. This poses some difficulties as, in any one lesson, multiple objectives may be required (Gagne and Merrill, 1990). However, the model has considerable intuitive appeal and has been highly influential. Its central tenet, that design begins with the identification of the goals of learning, is crucial for thinking about teaching and can be applied to a range of learning outcomes.

Within Gagne's framework there has been considerable research examining how specific aspects of the instructional process might be optimized (Clark *et al.*, 1979; Smith and Land, 1981). One focus has been questioning. Wragg (1984), for instance, stressed the value of higher order questioning in which students are encouraged to think and reason. Tobin (1987) studied teacher 'wait time' and the quality of questioning and found that longer wait times were especially important when instruction was concerned with higher cognitive level objectives and that a mix of questions at different cognitive levels produced the highest achievement. Recent work has explored the relationship between questioning and discipline (Carlsen, 1997). Brophy and Good (1986) in their review provide a very clear account of research relating to optimum instruction including the pacing of lessons and the questioning of students.

There is also a developing literature on the use of discussion (Cowie and Rudduck, 1990; Cooper, 1993; Dillon, 1994); Socratic teaching techniques (McClelland, 1993); whole class teaching (Croll, 1998); games, simulations and role play (van Ments, 1990); computer assisted learning (Kulik and Bangert-Drowns, 1990); the use of information technology (Gbomita, 1997; also see Chapter 10); peer teaching (Topping, 1992) and evidence which supports mastery learning, abroad (Creemers, 1994; Slavin, 1987) and in the UK (Arblaster et al., 1991; Parkinson et al., 1983), co-operative group work (Slavin, 1995; Gillies and Ashman, 1997) and individualized systems of learning (Bangert et al., 1983; Hughes, 1993). What is lacking is a systematic examination of the learning objectives which these various techniques are best placed to meet.

Promoting generic skills

While consideration of the development of generic or key skills at secondary school level is a relatively recent phenomenon in the UK, there is already a considerable body of evidence relating to the promotion of, for instance, creativity (Sternberg, 1988a; Fryer, 1996); working with others (Slavin, 1995); critical thinking (Costello, 1997); problem based learning (Boud, 1985), and metacognition (Wang et al., 1990). However, some of this research has been undertaken in other phases of education and much work remains to be done.

The interface between teacher and learner

A number of writers have proposed models which suggest how the activities of teacher and learner might be related, through didactics (Uljens, 1997); the interdependence of teacher and learner through a learning PACT (MacGilchrist et al., 1997); and through conversational frameworks, originating in the work of Pask (1976) as proposed by Francis (1992). Francis (1994) suggests that learners and teachers have 'different voices' with respect to learning and hear each other through a confusing filter. This is compounded by the classroom situation in which teachers have practical difficulty in dealing with individual pupils (Bennett et al., 1984; Black and Dockrell, 1984).

Francis's model (see figure 4.3) suggests that work on a task requires action which provides feedback to the learner and teacher. Learners and teachers are capable of evaluating this feedback and reproducing this evaluated infor-

mation for later use. If there is more than one possible way of acting on the
task the learner has to make a choice in the light of an appraisal of the current situation and earlier evaluated feedback information. The teacher may
be able to help here, having greater knowledge of more possibilities and
effects than the learner. For the teacher to assist the individual learner both
need to demonstrate their understandings of how a task should be done and
why it should be done that way. This suggests the necessity of teachers hearing learners' voices and provides a useful framework for exploring under
what conditions they might not be heard. Deficiencies in a learning conversation would effectively block a teacher's attention to the student's voice with
respect to that learning. Francis points out the problems of attending to learners as individuals in classroom contexts but suggests that teachers can attend
very closely to each individual for some of the time and suggests that this
will improve teaching for all. These relationships are set out in Figure 4.3.
Research needs to address how this learning conversation can be developed
in the classroom to promote learning.

TEACHING AND LEARNING OUTCOMES, ASSESSMENT AND FEEDBACK

In much formal education, assessment drives teaching and learning (Elton
and Laurillard, 1979). This is particularly the case in secondary education
in nations where teaching is focused on raising national examination performance. To ensure focus on the attainment of particular learning outcomes
it is necessary formally to assess them. Teaching and learning are most effective where they are 'constructively aligned' with assessment procedures
(Biggs, 1996). If, over time, generic skills come to be considered as an important outcome of learning, it will be necessary to find appropriate ways of
formally assessing them in order to ensure that they are taken seriously. This
may prove difficult. Learning has a range of outcomes, qualitative, quantitative and affective, which may or may not be formally assessed, which nevertheless through the process of 'backwash' affect future learning (Biggs and
Moore, 1993). It is particularly important that the affective outcomes of
learning are considered. Negative attitudes towards learning inculcated during the school years can develop alienation from learning throughout life.
Teachers need to understand these processes and how formative assessment
and feedback can be used to promote learning in the classroom (Brophy and
Good, 1986; Black and Wiliam, 1998) and in relation to homework (Hallam
and Cowan, 1998). They also need to be aware of the importance of record
keeping in developing an understanding of pupils' needs (Mortimore et al.,
1988; Scheerens, 1992).

EVALUATION OF LEARNING AND TEACHING

Teaching methods can only be evaluated in relation to specific learning

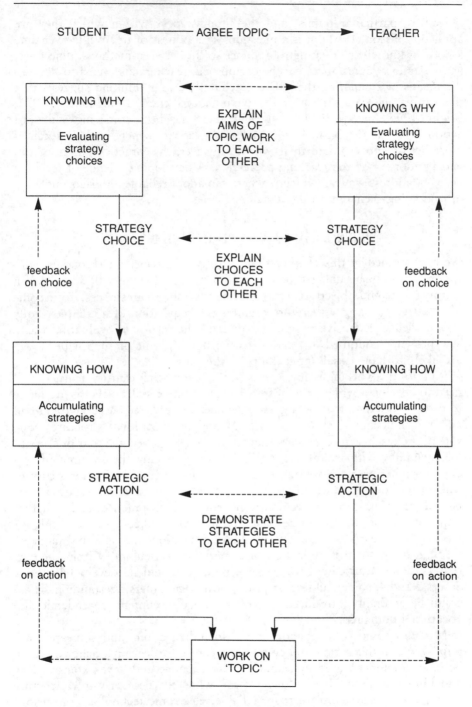

Fig. 4.3 The student-teacher conversation from Francis (1992)

objectives, particular pupils, and the circumstances within which they are applied (Ohlsson, 1991). It is a question of 'goodness of fit'. While over time a body of knowledge relating to goodness of fit between methods, objectives, learners and circumstances can be established, teachers also need to develop the means of evaluating their own teaching. Current thinking suggests that this can be achieved through reflective practice (Schon, 1983; Batten, 1993; Bright, 1995; Silcock, 1994), although there has been some move toward action research (McNiff, 1994; McKernan, 1996) which enables teachers more actively to evaluate their work. However, this practice has not been widely adopted by the teaching profession. A developing science of teaching needs to address ways in which teachers can adopt reliable and rigorous ways of evaluating their day to day teaching.

PEDAGOGY NOW AND IN THE FUTURE

We have argued in this chapter that 'effective pedagogy' in secondary education can only be understood in relation to the goodness of fit, between learning aims and objectives, particular pupils and circumstances. To become an effective pedagogue therefore requires the acquisition of a complex body of knowledge, extensive practical skills and the means of evaluating them. The principles outlined in relation to the development of such a pedagogy are likely to have equal applicability in the future.

To fulfil the working requirements of the twenty-first century, learners will need to develop a wide range of transferable, generic skills. Schools are likely to be very different, placing a greater reliance on resource based learning and adopting much more flexible curricular and organizational structures. The role of the teacher in secondary education is likely to become that of a learning facilitator with overall responsibility for managing the learning of students together with the assistance of a range of helpers. The teacher's current role as the 'deliverer' of the curriculum is likely to be much reduced. The period of transition between current educational practice and what is required for the future will be controversial and is likely to be difficult for teachers and learners alike. In secondary education, it might be managed through the gradual introduction of a modular curriculum. Within the current National Curriculum framework, modules could be developed at Key Stages 3 and 4, some building on prior knowledge, others freestanding. These could be gradually introduced to cover a range of content in academic and vocational domains.

Modules could operate across ages (including adults and some primary pupils) within the setting of a community centre for learning. Schools would be open for longer, used by a much wider clientele and have extensive ICT and library facilities. In the longer term, when the necessary infrastructure is in place and systems are more reliable, electronic technology of various kinds may have the capability to provide educational provision to any learner in any geographical location. This flexibility should enable educational systems to evolve which will be able to cater for the, as yet, unknown, educational needs of the latter part of the twenty-first century.

REFERENCES

Arblaster, G.A., Butler, C., Taylor, A.L., Arnold, C. and Pitchford, M. (1991) Same-age tutoring, mastery learning and the mixed ability teaching of reading, *School Psychology International*, 12: 11–18.

Argyris, C. (1976) Theories of action that inhibit individual learning, *American Psychologist*, 3: 638–54.

Armstrong, T. (1994) *Multiple Intelligences in the Classroom*, Alexandria,Va: ASCD.

Bangert, R., Kulik, J. and Kulik, C. (1983) Individualized systems of instruction in secondary schools, *Review of Educational Research*, 53(2): 143–58.

Bandura, A. (1977) Self-efficacy: toward a unifying theory of behavioural change, *Psychological Review*, 84: 191–215.

Barnes, D. (1976) *From Communication to Curriculum*, Harmondsworth: Penguin Educational.

Barnes, D., Johnson, G., Jordan, S., Layton, D., Medway, P. and Yeomans, D. (1987) *The TVEI Curriculum 14–16: An interim report based on case studies in twelve schools*, Leeds: School of Education, University of Leeds.

Bartlett, F.C. (1932) *Remembering*, London: Cambridge University Press.

Batten, M. (1993) *Knowing How To Teach Well: Teachers Reflect on their Classroom Practice. ACER Research Monograph No. 44*, Hawthorn, VIC: Australian Council for Educational Research (ACER).

Bayliss, V. (1998) *Redefining School*, London: Royal Society for the Encouragement of Arts Manufactures and Commerce (RSA).

Bennett, N. (1978) Recent research on teaching: a dream, a belief, and a model, *British Journal of Educational Psychology*, 48: 127–47.

Bennett, N., Desforges, C., Cockburn, A. and Wilkinson, B. (1984) *The Quality of Pupil Learning Experiences*, London: Lawrence Erlbaum.

Berk, L.E. (1997) *Child Development* (4th edition) Boston, London: Allyn and Bacon.

Berliner, D.C. (1986) In pursuit of the expert pedagogue, *Educational Researcher*, 15(4): 5–13.

Biggs J.B. (1996) Enhancing teaching through constructive alignment, *Higher Education*, 32(3): 347–64.

Biggs, J.B. and Moore, P. (1993) *The Process of Learning* (3rd edition). London: Prentice Hall.

Biggs, J.B. and Telfer, R. (1987) *The Process of Learning* (2nd edition). Sydney: Prentice Hall of Australia.

Black, P. and Dockrell, W.B. (1984) *Criterion Referenced Assessment in the Classroom*, Edinburgh: The Scottish Council for Research in Education.

Black, P. and Wiliam, D. (1998) Assessment and classroom learning. *Assessment in Education*, 5(1): 7–74.

Blatchford, P., and Mortimore, P. (1994) The issue of class size for young children in schools: what can we learn from research, *Oxford Review of Education*, 20: 411–28.

Block, J.H. (1971) (ed.) *Mastery Learning*, New York: Holt, Rinehart & Winston.

Bloom, B.S. (1971) The affective consequences of mastery learning, in J.H. Block (ed.)

Mastery Learning, New York: Holt, Rinehart & Winston.

Bloom, B.S. (1976) *Human Characteristics and School Learning*, New York: Ballentine.

Bloom, B.S., Engelhart, M.D., Furst, E.J., Hill, W.H. and Krathwohl, D.R. (1956). *Taxonomy of Educational Objectives 1: Cognitive Domain*, New York: McKay.

Boekaerts, M. (1993) Being concerned with well-being and with learning, *Educational Psychologist*, 28(2): 149–67.

Borko, H. and Livingston, C. (1989) Cognition and improvisation: differences in mathematics instruction by expert and novice teachers, *American Educational Research Journal*, 26: 473–98.

Boud, D. (1985) *Problem Based Learning in Education for the Professions*, Sydney: Higher Education Research and Development Society for Australasia.

Bright, B. (1995) What is 'Reflective Practice'? *Curriculum*, 16(2): 69–81.

Brookhart, S. (1998) Determinants of student effort on schoolwork and school-based achievement, *The Journal of Educational Research*, 91(4): 201–208.

Brookover, W.B., Beady, C., Flood, P., Schweitzer, J. and Wisenbaker, J. (1979) *School Social Systems and Student Achievement: Schools can make a difference*, New York: Praeger.

Brophy, J. and Good, T.L. (1986) Teacher behaviour and student achievement, in C.M. Wittrock (ed.) *Handbook of Research on Teaching* (3rd edition). New York: Macmillan.

Brown, S. and McIntyre, D. (1993) *Making Sense of Teaching*, Buckingham: Open University Press.

Bruner, J.S. (1996) *The Culture of Education*, London: Harvard University Press.

Burt, C. (1921) *Mental and Scholastic Tests*, London: Staples Press.

Carlgren, I., Handal, G., and Vaage, S. (1994) *Teachers Minds and Actions: Research on Teachers Thinking and Practice*, London: Falmer Press.

Carlsen, W. (1997) Never ask a question if you don't know the answer: the tension in teaching between modelling scientific argument and maintaining law and order, *Journal of Classroom Interaction*, 32(2): 14–23.

Carroll, J.B. (1963) A model of school learning, *Teacher College Record*, 64: 723–33.

Carroll, J.B. (1989) The Carroll model: a 25-year retrospective and prospective view, *Educational Researcher, January/February*: 26–31.

Ceci, S.J. (1990) *On Intelligence . . . More or Less: A Bio-ecological Treatise on Intellectual Development*, Englewood Cliffs, NJ: Prentice Hall.

Chaiklin, S. and Lave, S. (1993) *Understanding Practice*, Cambridge: Cambridge University Press.

Clark, C., Cage, N., Marx, R., Peterson, P., Stayrook, N. and Winne, P. (1979) A factorial experiment on teacher structuring, soliciting and reacting, *Journal of Educational Psychology*, 71(4): 534–52.

Clark, C.M. and Peterson, P.L. (1986) Teachers thought processes, in S. Brown and D.McIntyre (eds.) (1993) *Making Sense of Teaching*, Buckingham: Open University Press.

Cooley, W.W. and Leinhardt, G. (1975) *The Application of a Model for Investigating Classroom Processes*, Pittsburgh: University of Pittsburgh, Learning Research and Development Center.

Cooper, H. (1993) Removing the scaffolding: a case study investigating how whole-class teaching can lead to effective peer group discussion without the teacher, *Curriculum Journal*, 4(3): 385–401.

Cooper, P. and McIntyre, D. (1996) *Effective Teaching and Learning: Teachers and Students Perspectives*, Buckingham: Open University Press.

Costello, P. (1997) Editorial: teaching critical thinking, *Curriculum*, 18(3): 115–116.

Cowie, H. and Rudduck, J. (1990) Learning through discussion, in N. Entwistle (ed.) *Handbook of Educational Ideas and Practices*, London: Routledge.

Creemers, B. (1994) *The Effective Classroom*, London: Cassell.

Creemers B. (1997) *Effective Schools and Effective Teachers: An International Perspective*, Warwick: Centre for Research in Elementary and Primary School Education, University of Warwick.

Creemers, B. and Tillema, H. (1988) The classroom as a social/emotional environment, *Journal of Classroom Interaction*, 23(2): 1–7.

Croll, P. (1998) *Whole Class Teaching*, London: David Fulton.

Cuban, L. (1990) A fundamental puzzle of school reform, in A. Leiberman (ed.) *Schools as Collaborative Structures: Creating the Future Now*, New York: Falmer Press.

Dillon, T. (1994) *Using Discussion in Classrooms*, Buckingham: Open University Press.

Dorner, D. and Scholkopf, J. (1991) Controlling complex systems, in K.A. Ericsson and J. Smith (eds.) *Toward a Theory of General Expertise: Prospects and Limits*, Cambridge: Cambridge University Press.

Doyle, W. (1986) Classroom organisation and management, in M.C. Wittrock (ed.) *Handbook of Research on Teaching* (3rd edition), New York: Macmillan.

Doyle, W. (1987) Research on teaching effects as a resource for improving instruction, in M. Wideen and I. Andrews (eds.) *Staff Development for School Improvement*, Lewes: Falmer Press.

Ellis, D. and Karr-Kidwell, P. (1997) A study of assertive discipline and recommendations for effective classroom management methods, *EDRS Availability: Microfiche [1 card(s)], Paper* (ED379207).

Elton, L.R. and Laurillard, D. (1979) Trends in student learning, *Studies in Higher Education*, 4: 87–102.

Elwood, J. (1995) Undermining gender stereotypes: examination and course work performance in the UK at 16, *Assessment in Education*, 2(3): 282–303.

Entwistle, N.J. (1972) Personality and academic attainment, *British Journal of Educational Psychology*, 42(2): 137–51.

Entwistle, N. (1988) *Styles of learning and teaching: an integrated outline of educational psychology*, London: David Fulton.

Entwistle, N. and Ramsden, P. (1983) *Understanding Student Learning*, London, Cassell.

Fan, X., Chen, M. and Matsumoto, A. (1997) Gender difference in mathematics achievement: findings from the National Educational Longitudinal Study of 1988, *The Journal of Experimental Education*, 65(3): 229–242.

Fenstermacher, G.E. and Soltis, L. (1986) *Approaches to Teaching*, New York: Teachers College Press.

Francis, H. (1992) *Individuality in Learning: A Staff Development Resource Book*, London: FEU/Institute of Education.

Francis, H. (1994) *Teachers Listening to Learners Voices. The Thirteenth Vernon-Wall Lecture*, Leicester: Education Section of the British Psychological Society.

Fraser, B. (1989) Research syntheses on school and instructional effectiveness, *International Journal of Educational Research*, 13(7): 707–18.

Froebel, F. (1912) *The Education of Man*, New York and London: Appleton.

Fryer, M. (1996) Creative teaching and learning. London: Paul Chapman Publishing.

Gagne, R.M. (1970) *The Conditions of Learning* (2nd edition), New York: Holt, Rinehart & Winston.

Gagne, R.M. and Merrill, M.D. (1990) Integrative goals for instructional design, *Educational Technology Research and Development*, 38(1), 23–30.

Galton, F. (1892) *Hereditary Genius: An Inquiry into its Laws and Consequences* (2nd edition), London: Watts and Co. (original work published 1869).

Galton, M., Simon, B. and Croll, P. (1980) *Inside the Primary Classroom*, London: Routledge and Kegan Paul.

Gardner, H. (1993) *Frames of Mind: The Theory of Multiple Intelligences*, New York: Basic Books.

Gardner, H., Kornhaber, M.L. and Wake, K.W. (1995) *Intelligence Multiple Perspectives*, New York: Harcourt Brace.

Gbomita, V. (1997) The adaptation of microcomputers for instruction: implications for emerging instructional media implementation, *British Journal of Educational Technology*, 28(2): 87–101.

Gillborn, D. (1990) *Race, Ethnicity and Education: Teaching and Learning in Multi-ethnic Schools*, London: Unwin Hyman.

Gillies, R. and Ashman, A. (1997) The effects of training in cooperative learning on differential student behavior and achievement, *Journal of Classroom Interaction*, 32(1): 1–10.

Goldstein, H., Rasbash, J., Yang, H., Woodhouse, G., Pan, H., Nuttall, D. and Thomas, S. (1992) Multilevel models for comparing schools, *Multilevel modelling newsletter*, 4(2):, 5–6. London: University of London, Institute of Education.

Gottfredson, D., Marciniak, E., Birdseye, A., and Gottfredson, G. (1995) Increasing teacher expectations for student achievement, *Journal of Educational Research*, 88 (3): 155–63.

Gudmundsdottir, S. (1991) Pedagogical models of subject matter, in J. Brophy (ed.) *Advances in Research on Teaching, Volume 2*, London: JAI Press.

Gutierrez, K., Rymes, B. and Larson, J. (1995) Script, counter script, and underlie in the classroom: James Brown versus Brown v. Board of Education, *Harvard Educational Review*, 65(3): 445–71.

Haertel, G.D., Walberg, H.J. and Weinstein, T. (1983) Psychological models of educational performance: a theoretical synthesis of constructs, *Review of Educational Research*, 53(1): 75–91.

Hallam, S. and Cowan, R. (1998) What do we know about homework? A literature review, paper presented at the Conference of the British Educational Research Association, Belfast, August 27–30th.

Hallam, S. and Toutounji, I. (1996) *What Do We Know about the Grouping of Pupils by Ability? A Research Review*, London: Institute of Education, University of London.

Halpern, D.F. (1992) *Sex Differences in Cognitive Abilities*, Hillsdale, NJ: LEA.

Harnischfeger, A. and Wiley, D.E. (1976) The teaching-learning process in elementary schools: a synoptic view, *Curriculum Inquiry*, 6: 5–43.

Hopkins, D., Ainscow, M. and West, M. (1994) *School Improvement in an Era of Change*, London: Cassell.

Hughes, D. (1973) An experimental investigation of the effects of pupil responding and teacher reacting on pupil achievement, *American Educational Research*

Journal, 10(1): 21–37.

Hughes, M. (1993) *Flexible Learning: Evidence Examined*, Stafford: Network Educational Press Ltd.

Ireson, J. and Hallam, S. (1999) Raising standards: is ability grouping the answer? *Oxford Review of Education*).

Isaacs, S.S. (1932) *The Children We Teach: Seven to Eleven Years*, London: University of London Press.

Joyce, B., Calhoun, E., and Hopkins, D. (1997) *Models of Learning – Tools for Teaching*, Buckingham: Open University Press.

Jussim, L. Smith, A., Madon, S., and Palumbo, P. (1998) Teacher expectations, in J. Brophy (ed.) *Advances in Research on Teaching, Volume 7*, Greenwich, Connecticut: JAI Press.

Kagan, D. (1988) Teaching as clinical problem solving: a critical examination of the analogy and its implications, *Review of Educational Research*, 58: 482–505.

Keller, F.S. (1968) Goodbye teacher . . . , *Journal of Applied Behavioural Analysis*, 1: 79–89.

Kellner, D. (1998) 'Multiple literacies and critical pedagogy in a multicultural society', *Educational Theory*, 48(1): 103–122.

Kelly, K.A. (1955) *A Theory of Personality: The Psychology of Personal Constructs*, New York, London: W. W. Norton.

Kember, D. (1997) A reconceptualisation of research into university academics conceptions of teaching, *Learning and Instruction*, 7(3): 255–75.

Keys, W. and Fernandes, C. (1993) *What Do Students Think about School? Research into Factors Associated with Positive and Negative Attitudes towards School and Education*, Slough: NFER.

Kolb, D.A. (1984) *Experiential Learning*, Englewood Cliffs: Prentice Hall.

Kounin, J. (1970) *Discipline and Group Management in Classrooms*, New York: Holt, Rinehart & Winston.

Kulik, J. and Bangert-Drowns, R. (1990) Computer-assisted learning, in N. Entwistle (ed.) *Handbook of Educational Ideas and Practices*, London: Routledge.

Kumar, V. (1993) *Poverty and Inequality in the UK: The Effects on Children*, London: National Childrens Bureau.

Kyriacou, C. (1991) *Essential Teaching Skills*, Oxford: Blackwell.

Lave, J. (1988) *Cognition in Practice: Mind, Mathematics, and Culture in Everyday Life*, Cambridge: Cambridge University Press.

Leinhardt, G. (1990) Capturing craft knowledge in teaching, *Educational Researcher*, 19(2): 18–25.

Leinhardt, G. and Greeno, J.G. (1986) The cognitive skill of teaching, *Journal of Educational Psychology*, 78: 75–95.

MacGilchrist, B., Myers, K. and Reed, J. (1997) *The Intelligent School*, London: Paul Chapman.

Marks, R. (1990) Pedagogical content knowledge: from a mathematical case to a modified conception, *Journal of Teacher Education*, 41(3): 3–11.

Marland, M. (1993) *The Craft of the Classroom: A Survival Guide to Classroom Management in the Secondary School* (2nd edn). Oxford: Heinemann.

Marshall, H.H. (1988) Work or learning: Implications of classroom metaphors, *Educational Researcher*, 17(9): 9–16.

Marton, F. and Booth, S. (1997) *Learning and Awareness*, Mahweh, New Jersey: LEA.

McClelland, J. (ed.) (1993) *Socratic Education*, Hull: University of Hull, Institute of Education.

McKernan, J. (1996) *Curriculum Action Research: A Handbook of Methods and Resources for the Reflective Practitioner*, London: Kogan Page.

McNiff, J. (1994) *Teaching and Learning: An Action Research Approach*, London: Routledge.

Midgley, C., Arunkumar, R., and Urdan, T. (1996) 'If I do well tomorrow, there's a reason': predictors of adolescents' use of academic self-handicapping strategies, *Journal of Educational Psychology*, 88(3): 423–34.

Mischel, W. (1968) *Personality and Assessment*, New York: Wiley.

Mortimore, P. (1994) School effectiveness and the management of effective learning and teaching, *School Effectiveness and School Improvement*, 4(4): 290–310.

Mortimore, P., Sammons, P., Stoll, L., Lewis, D. and Ecob, R. (1988) *School Matters*, Wells: Open Books.

Mortimore, P., Sammons, P., Stoll, L., Lewis, D. and Ecob, R. (1995) Teacher expectations, in B. Moon and A.S. Mayes *Teaching and Learning in the Secondary School*, London: Routledge/Open University.

Newell, A. (1990) *Unified Theories of Cognition*, Cambridge: Cambridge University Press.

Nuttall, D., Goldstein, H., Prosser, R. and Rasbash, J. (1989) Differential school effectiveness, *International Journal of Educational Research*, 13(7): 769–76.

Ohlsson, S. (1991) System hacking meets learning theory: reflections on the goals and standards of research in artificial intelligence and education, *Journal of Artificial Intelligence in Education*, 2(3): 5–18.

Parkinson, B.L., Mitchell, R.F. and Johnston, R.M. (1983) Mastery learning in modern languages – a case study, *PLET*, 20(1): 43–53.

Pask, G. (1976) Conversational techniques in the study and practice of education, *British Journal of Educational Psychology*, 46: 12–25.

Pendry, A. (1994) The pre-lesson pedagogical decision making of history student-teachers during their internship year, PhD thesis, University of Oxford.

Piaget, J. (1950) *The Psychology of Intelligence*, London: Routledge & Kegan Paul.

Piaget, J. and Inhelder, B. (1958) *The Growth of Logical Thinking from Childhood to Adolescence*, New York: Basic Books.

Porter, A.C. and Brophy, J. (1988) Synthesis of research on good teaching: insights from the work of the Institute for Research on Teaching, *Educational Leadership*, 46: 74–85.

Powell, M. (1980) The beginning teacher evaluation study: a brief history of a major research project, in C. Denham and A. Lieberman (eds.) *Time to Learn*, Washington, DC: National Institute of Education.

Pratt, D. (1992) Conceptions of teaching, *Adult Education Quarterly*, 42: 203–20.

Reynolds, D. (1990) An introduction to managing school effectiveness, *School Organisation*, 10(2&3): 163–5.

Riding, R. and Rayner, S. (1998) *Cognitive Styles and Learning Strategies*, London: David Fulton.

Rogers, C. (1990) Teachers expectations and pupils achievements, in N. Entwistle (ed.) *Handbook of Educational Ideas and Practices*, London: Routledge

Rogoff, B. (1990) *Apprenticeship in Thinking: Cognitive Development in Social Context*, New York: Oxford University Press.

Rogoff, B., Matusov, E., and White, C. (1996) Models of teaching and learning:

participation in a community of learners, in D.R. Olson and N. Torrance (eds.) *The Handbook of Education and Human Development*, Oxford: Blackwell.

Rudduck, J., Chaplain, R. and Wallace, G. (eds.) (1996) *School Improvement: What Can Pupils Tell Us?* London: David Fulton.

Rutter, M., Maughan, B., Mortimore, P. and Ouston, J. (1979) *Fifteen Thousand Hours*, London: Open Books.

Saljo, R. (1979) *Learning in the Learners' Perspective. 1. Some Commonsense Conceptions*, reports from the Department of Education, Goteberg University, No 76.

Saljo, R. (1996) *Learning and Discourse: A Sociocultural Perspective*, the sixteenth Vernon-Wall Lecture, Leicester: Education Section, British Psychological Society.

Sammons, P., Nuttall, D.L. and Cuttance, P. (1993) Differential school effectiveness: results from a reanalysis of the Inner London Education Authoritys Junior School Project data, *British Educational Research Journal*, 19(4): 381–405.

Sammons, P., Thomas, S. and Mortimore, P. (1997) *Forging Links: Effective Schools and Effective Departments*. London: Paul Chapman Publishing.

Sarason, S. (1990) *The Predictable Failure of Educational Reform: Can We Change Before Its Too Late?* San Francisco: Jossey-Bass.

Scheerens J. (1992) *Effective Schooling: Research, Theory and Practice,* London: Cassell.

Schon, D. (1983) *The Reflective Practitioner*, New York: Basic Books.

Scott. C., Murray, G., Mertens, C. and Dustin, E. (1996) Student self-esteem and the school system: perceptions and implications, *Journal of Educational Research*, 89(5): 286–93.

Shulman, L. (1986) Those who understand: knowledge growth in teaching, *Educational Researcher*, 15(2): 4–21.

Shulman, L. (1987) Knowledge and teaching: foundations of the new reforms, *Harvard Educational Review*, 57(1): 1–22.

Silcock, P. (1994) The process of reflective teaching, *British Journal of Educational Studies*, 42(3): 273–85.

Simon, B. (1995) Why no pedagogy in England?, in B. Moon and A.Shelton Mayes (eds.), *Teaching and Learning in the Secondary School*, London and New York: Routledge/Open University.

Slavin, R.E. (1987) Mastery learning reconsidered, *Review of Educational Research*, 57: 175–213.

Slavin, R.E. (1995) *Cooperative Learning: Theory, Research and Practice*, (2nd edition), Boston and London: Allyn and Bacon.

Smith, L. and Land, M. (1981) Low – inference verbal behaviours related to teacher clarity, *Journal of Classroom Interaction*, 17(1): 37–42.

Snow, R.E. (1987) Aptitude complexes, in R.E. Snow and M.J. Farr (eds.) *Aptitude, Learning and Instruction, Vol 3: Conative and Affective Process Analysis*, Hillsdale, New Jersey: LEA.

Snyder, B.R. (1971) *The Hidden Curriculum*, New York: Knopf.

Soar, R.S. and Soar, R.M. (1979) Emotional climate and management, in P. Peterson and H. Walberg (eds.) *Research on Teaching: Concepts, Findings and Implications*, Berkeley, CA: McCutchan.

Sternberg, R.J. (ed.) (1988a) *The Nature of Creativity*, Cambridge: Cambridge University Press.

Sternberg, R.J. (1988b) *The Triarchic Mind: A New Theory of Intelligence*, New York: Viking.

Stodolsky, S., and Grossman, P. (1995a) The impact of subject matter on curricular activity: an analysis of five academic subjects, *American Educational Research Journal*, 32(2): 227–49.

Stodolsky, S. and Grossman, P. (1995b) Subject-matter differences in secondary schools: connections to higher education, *New Directions for Teaching & Learning*, 64 (Winter): 71–8.

Swanson, H.L., O'Connor, J.E. and Cooney, J.B. (1990) An information processing analysis of expert and novice teachers problem solving, *American Educational Research Journal*, 27: 533–56.

Tabberer, R. (1994) *School and Teacher Effectiveness*, Slough: National Foundation for Educational Research.

Tharp, R.G. and Gallimore, R. (1988) *Rousing Minds to Life: Teaching, Learning and Schooling in Social Context*, Cambridge: Cambridge University Press.

Tobin, K. (1987) The role of wait time, *Review of Educational Research*, 57: 69–95.

Topping, K. (1992) Co-operative learning and peer tutoring, *The Psychologist*, 5: 151–57.

Tschannen-Moran, M., Hoy, A.W. and Hoy, W.K. (1998) Teacher efficacy: its meaning and measure, *Review of Educational Research*, 68(2), 202–48.

Turner, C. (1993) Teachers' perceptions of effective classroom management within an inner-city middle school, *EDRS Availability: Microfiche [1 card(s)] Paper* (ED368820).

Uljens, M. (1997) *School Didactics and Learning*, Hove: Psychology Press Ltd.

Underwood, G. and Bright, J.E.H. (1996) Cognition with and without awareness, in G. Underwood (ed.) *Implicit Cognition*, Oxford: Oxford University Press.

University of North London Truancy Unit, Truancy Research Project (1994) *Truancy in English Secondary Schools: A report for the DFE by the Truancy Research Project, 1991–92, University of North London Truancy Unit*, London: HMSO.

van Ments, M. (1990) Simulations, games and role play, in N. Entwistle (ed.) *Handbook of Educational Ideas and Practices*, London: Routledge.

Vernon, P.E. (1956) *The Measurement of Abilities*, London: London University Press.

Voss, J. (1978) Cognition and instruction: towards a cognitive theory of learning, in A.M. Lesgold, J.W. Pellegrine, S.D. Fokkema and R.Glaser (eds.) *Cognitive Psychology and Instruction*, New York: Plenum Press.

Vygotsky, L.S. (1962) *Thought and Language*, London: Wiley.

Vygotsky, L.S. (1978) *Mind in Society*, Cambridge, MA: MIT Press.

Wang, M.C. Haertel, G.D. and Walberg, H.J. (1990) What influences learning? A content analysis of review literature, *Journal of Educational Research*, 84(1): 30–43.

Watson, J.B. and Raynor, R. (1920) Conditioned emotional reactions, *Journal of Experimental Psychology*, 3: 1–14.

Wheldall, K., and Glynn, T. (1989) *Effective Classroom Learning*, Oxford: Blackwell.

Wilson, S., Shulman, L. and Rickett, A. (1987) 150 ways of knowing: representations of knowledge in teaching, in J. Calderhead (ed.) *Exploring Teachers Thinking*, London: Cassell.

Wittrock, M. (ed.) (1986) *Handbook of Research on Teaching* (3rd edition), New York: Macmillan.

Woods, P. (1990) *The Happiest Days? How Pupils Cope with School*, London: Falmer Press.

Wragg, E.C. (1984) *Classroom Teaching Skills*, London: Croom Helm.

Wright, C., and Nuthall, G. (1970) Relationships between teacher behaviours and pupil achievement in three experimental elementary science lessons, *American Educational Research Journal*, 7(4): 477–91.

Yinger, R.J. (1994) The conversation of practice, in R. Cliff, R. Houston and M. Pugach (eds.) *Encouraging Reflective Practice: An Examination of Issues and Exemplars*, New York: Teachers College Press.

5

Pedagogy in Further Education: New Contexts, New Theories and New Possibilities

Michael Young and Norman Lucas

Research on pedagogy and learning in further education (FE) mirrors the broader neglect of the sector by educational researchers and the university-based academic community more generally. Much of the debate about pedagogy has been dominated by adult educators in a search for a distinct professional identity which would distance them from pedagogy in schools (Brookfield, 1986). The concepts of 'andragogy' (Knowles, 1985) and 'conscientization' (Friere, 1972), developed by adult educators, have been of value in stressing certain distinctive features of adults as learners that need to be taken into account in developing pedagogy for the FE sector in which the majority of students are adults. However, with their tendency to encourage over-simplistic pedagogic dichotomies such as pedagogy/andragogy and banking/conscientization, they have been more successful as critiques of existing practice than as a basis for new strategies. Furthermore, they have failed to address not only the diversity of FE learners and the distinctive institutional contexts in which FE teachers find themselves, but also the changes that are occurring in the nature of work.

The chapter will concentrate on the new contexts that FE teachers find themselves in and the new demands being made on them. It will then go on to explore the implications of a number of new theories and ideas and argue that they point to a new approach to learning and pedagogy which provides a basis for responding to the new demands facing teachers in the FE sector. We begin by considering the increasing diversity of learners in FE and the shifts in the role of FE teachers as a result of changes in the economies and organization of work in industrial societies. We review the main FE traditions of pedagogy inherited from the past and argue that although each has an important element that needs to be retained in any new approach, they are either based on schooling models of pedagogy often inappropriate to the learning needs of many students in FE or on a one-sided rejection of schooling models that can only lead to FE students being excluded from acquiring any real knowledge base of their own. Furthermore, we argue that together and individually these approaches, though still widely prevalent, are an inadequate basis for responding to the new and likely future demands being made on the sector.

NEW CONTEXTS: THE DIVERSITY OF LEARNERS IN FE

In her introduction to her much publicized report for the Further Education Funding Council, *Learning Works* (FEFC, 1997), Helena Kennedy describes the diversity of FE as a large, fertile, least understood part of the 'learning tapestry'. Within this 'learning tapestry' there are 16–19 year olds, young adults and older adults returning to study, full and part-time students, evening class students, those on day release from training schemes or employment, students in workplaces as well as those in classrooms and, increasingly, students on-line through various networking arrangements. For many young people FE is both a first choice after 16 and a second chance for those who have not done well at school. For this reason the FE sector has a significantly higher proportion of students from ethnic minorities than would be expected from their distribution in the population as a whole. For adults FE is a means of gaining new skills, retraining or an avenue into higher education. The FE sector grew to 3.9 million students by 1996/7 and has undergone fundamental changes both in the diversity of students it provides for and the range of courses and qualifications that are offered. It caters for more adults than higher education and is the main provider of full-time and part-time study for 16–19 year olds. (Hodge, 1998).

Unlike schools and universities, colleges have a broad set of roles which reflects their unique interface with the world of work. They are expected to be at the centre of the government's flagship policies for the 'new deal', 'welfare to work' and 'lifelong learning'. They are likely to play a key role in the University for Industry's efforts to broaden adult access to learning, and to take a leadership role in regional development strategies to promote economic regeneration by developing partnerships with the private sector. It is useful, therefore, to remember that FE is not only a sector where very different pedagogic traditions confront each other but also one which acts as a bridge between school and university and between education and employment by providing people with new skills, knowledge and qualifications and allowing them progression along a wide range of pathways. Any discussion about pedagogy in FE must take account of the key feature of the sector – its diversity and the consequent fragmented nature of its pedagogic traditions.

The wide diversity of learner needs is the feature of the FE sector that most clearly distinguishes it from schools and universities. This is expressed in the range of types of programme that are found in FE and has become more marked since the Sixth Form colleges became part of the sector in 1993. Huddleston and Unwin (1997) identify five distinct curricular traditions, academic or 'general education' courses which include the General Certificate of

Secondary Education (GCSEs) and General Certificate of Education at Advanced Level (A levels) and, in rare cases, the International Baccalaureate; general vocational and prevocational qualifications such as the Business and Technical Education Council (BTEC) Certificates and Diplomas and the General National Vocational Qualification (GNVQs); job-specific Vocational National Qualifications (now largely NVQs); courses specifically designed for adults returning to study which range from access courses to those in basic literacy and numeracy skills; and finally the higher diploma and degree courses offered in a number of colleges.

Such a description of the FE curriculum in terms of these five traditions needs a number of explanations. First, the five traditions themselves are changing under pressures that we shall return to later in this chapter. Second, there is no neat fit between curriculum and pedagogy; this is partly as a result of borrowing between pedagogic approaches in integrated programmes such as those supported by the Technical and Vocational Education Initiative (TVEI) and partly because many staff teach on more than one type of programme. Third, there is a range of external pressures on colleges, largely as a result of the ways colleges are funded (Lucas, 1999), which are forcing teachers, whatever their subject area, to adopt more learner-centred and flexible pedagogies. Fourth, following the incorporation of colleges in 1993, the organization of teaching has changed with an increasing emphasis being given to 'cost effectiveness'. Fifth, the introduction of new information technologies is beginning to have an impact on teaching and learning strategies. Finally there are a number of broad economic and social changes that are having profound implications on FE because of its unique position linking education, training and the world of work. One example of this is the growth of 'franchising' as colleges offer growing numbers of programmes in the community and on employers' premises (Gravatt, 1997).

This chapter is concerned with the likely pedagogic outcomes of the new pressures on colleges that we have described. One possibility is that as a result of improving access, college programmes becoming more flexible, and increased efforts to accredit learning in workplaces, the numbers of modules, credits, qualifications, courses, diplomas and certificates expand many times. This might be described as the 'massification' of college output based increasingly on on-line provision of teaching and more automated forms of assessment.

The problem with such a scenario is that it is primarily a supply-side approach to improving education and training, geared to maximizing college outputs, and neglects three equally important factors if increases in output are also to lead to increases in quality. First, there is the issue of motivating those who have previously been reluctant to take advantage of learning opportunities. However flexible colleges make their provision and however many learning materials are available on-line, the task remains of motivating existing learners to continue to learn and convincing those who have become disaffected that learning is worth it for them. Second, supply cannot be separated from demand; improving access will only improve learning outcomes if there are parallel strategies for promoting demand for a more qualified workforce among employers. Third, even if improving the flexibility of provision by colleges could ensure greater access, the issue of the quality of the learning outcomes would remain. Would such an approach lead to the kind of learning that is needed in the twenty-first century? Would it encourage learners to be critical, innovative, enterprising and willing to collaborate and take risks in exploring new ideas? Would such an approach be the basis for a high-skilled competitive economy or would it be an extension of the 'low skill equilibrium' (Finegold and Soskice, 1990), albeit at a higher level of qualifications? Will such an approach lead to new forms of credentialism as more people get qualifications with less and less real value? It is possible that as more people get qualified as a result of making learning more accessible, knowledge becomes equated with information rather than understanding and the basic emancipatory purposes of learning are lost except for the few who reach the highest levels.

Many other questions remain unanswered; for example, will the increasing emphasis on targets and qualifications as a means of making schools and colleges more accountable turn them into 'results factories' rather than 'environments for learning'? It is arguable that the massification of educational provision based on improving access, making programmes more flexible and emphasizing outcomes underestimates the extent to which learning is not a simple combination of inputs and outputs. Furthermore, such an approach fails to take account of the fact that the learning demands of the future will not require just a quantitative expansion but a qualitative enhancement of the types of learning that are made available.

There is, however, an alternative possibility to the kind of massification of learning outputs of colleges we have described. It is at odds with immediate pressures for quantitative expansion but more consistent with the government's longer term strategic aims for lifelong learning that are expressed in the Green Paper *The Learning Age* (DfEE, 1998). It starts by being based on a model of a learning society in which learning is not primarily a separately measurable activity or outcome of which more is needed. Rather, learning becomes a social process integral to all activities in society whether or not they take place in a school or college. In such a scenario, colleges, instead of being marginal and always dependent on government, individuals or business for funds and legitimacy, become one of the sets of nerve centres or 'brains' of a learning society, with leadership roles in economic development, social and multicultural integration, and the reinvigoration of communities.

Which of these possibilities is the more likely depends on both government and the further education community itself, though it is the latter that we are primarily concerned with in this chapter. The FE community and others can put pressure on government to take a long term and strategic view of the means needed to enhance the quality and not just the quantity of learning. However, such pressures will have little credibility if the sector has not thought through its own approach to its professional specialism – pedagogy. Such an approach needs to avoid both defensive responses to change that see it as inevitably undermining traditional forms of professionalism and the uncritical acceptance of demands for greater flexibility and improving quantitative performance.

NEW CONTEXTS: TEACHING AND LEARNING IN FE

There is little research on the new skill needs of FE teachers or on the implications for colleges of any new approaches to pedagogy. There is evidence that since the incorporation of colleges in the early 1990s traditional organizational structures based on departments have been replaced by new forms of matrix-based management with teachers organized into project or course teams. More responsibility has been devolved to FE lecturers and there has been pressure on them to become more flexible and less tied to traditional subject or vocational identities. They are being required to contribute to a broader range of courses, to be involved in curriculum planning and often to take on new management responsibilities. They are increasingly expected to work collaboratively with other colleagues in providing measures of the performance of colleges and in establishing common quality assurance procedures and assessment methods (Guile and Lucas, 1996). In other words, not only are the learning needs of those entering FE becoming far more diverse, but new challenges are being posed to the traditional roles of FE teachers and how they approach pedagogic issues. These pressures are not only challenging existing ideas of pedagogy but also traditional concepts of professional responsibility.

With the shift away from formal teaching and the greater emphasis being placed on guided learning and tutorial support, the line between pedagogic and professional issues is becoming blurred. In earlier research on teachers in FE (Young *et al.*, 1995) we suggested that the pressures on FE teachers could be conceptualized in terms a series of shifts away from traditional notions of professionalism. We argued that the *insular* knowledge base that has characterized the teaching profession in the past was changing towards a more *connective* one and that this change could be represented in terms of five shifts, as follows:

- **from subject knowledge to curriculum knowledge**
  Most FE teachers remain vocational or subject specialists. However, their practice increasingly needs to be based on knowledge of how their specialism relates to other subject and vocational specialisms and of how generic (or 'key') skills can be developed through different subjects and vocational areas and through the college curriculum as a whole.
- **from teacher-centred to learner-centred pedagogic knowledge**
  This shift refers to teachers still having to focus on how to transmit their subject or vocational knowledge but also having to develop expertise

in assignment design, small group work, counselling and tutorial skills, and the use of IT and other resource-based learning facilities. FE teachers are increasingly having to be 'managers of learning', coaching students to become managers of their own learning.

- **from intra-professional knowledge to inter-professional knowledge**
This shift recognizes the blurring of roles of teachers and other educational professionals with specialist knowledge such as careers guidance or IT and the need for teachers to be able to relate their specialist knowledge and support students in gaining access to other forms of expertise.
- **from classroom knowledge to organizational knowledge**
This shift describes how FE teachers are increasingly having to learn to work in multi-specialist teams. They need not only teamwork and collaborative skills but sufficient knowledge of the college as an organization to enable them to link their college work with other local providers such schools and training partners.
- **from insular to connective knowledge**
This shift emphasizes the importance of teachers not only following the progression of their students while they are in college but as lifelong learners who draw on their college and work experience and plan their future. A connective role for FE teachers means a focus on learning outside and beyond college as much as the learning that is tied to specific courses.

The five shifts in the role and knowledge base of FE teachers outlined above give some indication of the new kinds of pressures that are impacting on teaching and learning in FE and the inadequacy, on their own, of the pedagogic traditions that have been associated with FE in the past. It is to these traditions that we turn in the next section.

PEDAGOGIC TRADITIONS IN FURTHER EDUCATION (FE)

Related to, but not synonymous with, the five curriculum traditions described earlier, a number of pedagogic traditions can be found in most FE colleges today. We realize that good innovatory practice can be found that crosses these traditions and the traditions we describe are rather general. However, our categorization illustrates both the strengths and weaknesses of the pedagogic resources available to the sector in developing its response to the new demands. Let us turn briefly to each of these traditions in turn.

The 'school' tradition of subject-based teaching

In a tradition which has often been associated in the past with general education departments of FE colleges, there has been a tendency to adopt a rather didactic, teacher or subject knowledge-centred approach to pedagogy. Such an approach is reflected in syllabi which assume that there is a straightforward relationship between a model of teaching as 'knowledge transmission' and a model of learning as the 'acquisition of knowledge'. At its crudest this assumption of knowledge moving from teacher to learner is what Friere (1972) evocatively called a 'banking' model. Policies geared to local institutional attainment targets can give legitimacy to such approaches. However, as we shall discuss in more detail later in this chapter, although the concept of 'knowledge transmission' refers to an important goal of any pedagogy it is only a very partial model of the actual process of learning. At most such ideas can be guides to the desired outcomes of pedagogy and learning.

The training and instruction tradition

This tradition is associated with the institution of apprenticeship and with the foundation of FE from Mechanics Institutes in the nineteenth century to the establishment of the technical colleges after the Second World War (Green and Lucas, 1998). It has tended to dismiss the need for teachers to have any specialist pedagogic knowledge, believing that expertise in a specific job is an adequate basis for transmitting job-specific skills. The aim of vocational education programmes in this tradition is to prepare people for employment, primarily through enabling them to copy the practice of a 'master craftsman'. The modern manifestation of this tradition are programmes geared to NVQs. NVQs, however, are distinguished from earlier approaches in that they represent an explicit attempt to identify skills needed in the workplace and use them as a basis for assessment criteria, thus hopefully bringing vocational education closer to the actual skills needed by an employee. The pedagogic role of the teacher is focused on assessing whether learners can demonstrate their workplace 'competence'. The criteria for defining competence tend to play down the need for the knowledge base that learners need if they are to reflect on their experience and understand the wider context within which their job is set. The NVQ approach to assessment and pedagogy is most adequate where the focus is on lower level skills which can be precisely specified; however, it does little to ensure that learners develop the complex skills needed in the workplaces which are emerging as we move into the twenty-first century.

The prevocational tradition

This tradition can be traced back to the work of the Further Education Unit in the early 1980s through qualifications such as Certificate of Prevocational Education, Diploma of Vocational Education and more recently GNVQs. As an approach to pedagogy it emphasizes that learning is a process and that learners must be active in applying their knowledge; it therefore stresses student guidance and support and limits the pedagogic role of the teacher to that of guide or facilitator. A key prevocational pedagogic instrument is the assignment with its emphasis on the active role of the learner. It was pioneered in CPVE programmes and formalized more recently in GNVQs. It is based on a rejection of the concept of knowledge transmission that is associated with the school tradition of subject teaching which by implication, it assumes, is only appropriate for the highest achievers. It arose in response to the disaffection of many school and FE students from academic models of general education and represents a direct criticism of and alternative to the over teacher-centred approaches typical of general education courses in FE.

The prevocational tradition seeks to emphasize the active involvement of students in their own learning and stresses the crucial importance of what the learner is 'doing'. Knowledge is not related to subjects but to applications; mathematics, for example, becomes the 'Application of Number' and English becomes 'Communication'. Pedagogy, within the prevocational tradition, is activity based and great emphasis is given supporting learners through guidance and setting targets. Such an approach has been described as a 'pedagogy of guidance' (Lucas, 1997) and can be seen as an oversimplified version of Dewey's (1963) famous but often misunderstood dictum for education as 'learning by doing'.

The prevocational tradition is not based on any explicit theory of learning of its own, because its assignment-based approach was largely a reaction to the rigidities of traditional academic approaches. As a result, it ends up by assuming that learning can be described as a set of individual processes or activities (e.g. gathering and evaluating evidence). By neglecting the knowledge acquisition aspect of any real learning, it makes it difficult for learners to acquire the basis for progressing to higher levels and of going beyond their existing situation. For all its welcome emphasis on active rather than passive learning, the prevocational tradition has only limited scope for stimulating the motivation of students to learn and for facing them with challenging ideas and questions about their previous knowledge. Although research provides evidence of considerable variation in the type of pedagogy used in GNVQs, there is always a danger that the emphasis on completing assignments and achieving outcomes can lead to little more than keeping students busy.

The experiential tradition

The experiential tradition is widely endorsed in adult education and gives priority to the learner's previous experience; it looks for ways of either formally recognizing or accrediting the learner's experience or using it as a basis for further learning. It starts from the justifiable criticism that subject-based general education and traditional vocational education approaches tend to neglect what learners bring to college programmes and this is a specific weakness in the case of adults who often have many skills that have not received formal recognition. As in the prevocational tradition referred to earlier, the teacher is limited to being friend, facilitator and coach.

The argument is taken to an extreme by the followers of Knowles (1985), who argues that any kind of pedagogy inevitably underplays the self-direction that has to be the principle basis of any adult learning. He replaces the concept of pedagogy with what he calls andragogy – an approach to learning which places at its centre the self directed adult learner. Friere's (1972) concept of conscientization has a similar focus on empowerment of the individual learner but is based on a more sophisticated political analysis of the broad context within which educational provision for adults is set. It stresses the importance of awakening a critical awareness among adults through dialogue and giving the space to them to develop their own ideas within their own social, political and economic contexts (Tight, 1996).

The problem with both of these approaches is that they convert a justifiable criticism of the weakness of schooling models into a complete alternative approach to teaching and learning which neglects certain basic features of any learning. It is not that a learner's prior experiences, often neglected in school approaches to pedagogy, are not important to enhancing learning; they are crucial for any learners beginning a course in an FE college. However, the informal experiential knowledge that people acquire in their pre-college experience can be only be a partial basis for a pedagogy. An uncritical celebration of experience can all too easily ignore the importance of providing learners with a knowledge base for reflecting on their experience and for understanding the complex workplace tasks that they are likely to face in the future.

Flexible learning

The final set of pedagogic practices that are becoming of increasing importance in FE can be described under the umbrella term *flexible learning*. Flexible learning refers to a range of strategies for improving access to learning and freeing learners from their dependence on teachers or fixed class hours. It includes learning workshops, resource-based learning, on-line access and all uses of information and communication technologies. These are relatively new developments which, because of the diversity of the learning needs of those entering FE colleges, have been taken further in FE than in any other sector of the education system, though they have been heavily influenced by the Open University.

The emphasis in this approach is on reducing the need for teachers and enabling learners to develop their own programmes by drawing on on-line and documentary resources. Recent research (Leney *et al.*, 1998) suggests that such an approach is often used as a way of off-setting the reduction of teaching hours rather than as arising from a new approach to learning. Furthermore, there is evidence that resource based approaches on their own, are not appropriate for many FE students who lack the motivation, confidence and learning skills to benefit from them. Indeed such students may need more not less teacher time if they are to take advantage of the potential flexibility of such approaches.

In this section of the chapter, we have commented on the weaknesses of the main pedagogic traditions found in FE. However, we would argue that they all share a more fundamental weakness that is not restricted to pedagogies associated with the FE sector. All the approaches to pedagogy and learning which we have discussed, whether based on 'learning from experience', 'learning by doing', learning as 'the acquisition of knowledge' or resourced-based learning are based on *individualistic* assumptions about the nature of learning.

Such assumptions reflect the dominance of psychology in learning theory and the interest of policy-makers in quantifying learning outcomes as a basis for making schools and colleges more accountable for their performance and outputs. Our argument is not to reject the value of trying to measure learning outcomes, or that it is wrong to view learning as the acquisition of knowledge or skill by individuals. It is that these are only partial perspectives on the process of learning itself. The partial nature of such individualistic assumptions is revealed when they are subject to conceptual critique (Lave, 1996) and through ethnographic research which sets out to describe the learning process in real life settings. The implications of such research for developing an alternative approach to learning and pedagogy in FE is discussed in the next section.

LEARNING AND PEDAGOGY IN FE: NEW PROBLEMS; NEW APPROACHES

The approach to learning adopted in this chapter draws on the symbolic interactionist tradition of research in sociology (Mead, 1934) and more recent work in cultural anthropology (Lave and Wenger, 1991), and argues that learning is first and foremost a social process that takes place in specific contexts. Four main principles for an approach to learning follow which draw on elements in each of the pedagogic traditions discussed in the previous section.

First, any learning involves the acquisition, transfer and production of new knowledge; it is not just reflection on past experience. Second, learning is not just a process of knowledge or skill 'transfer'. For learning to take place, learners need opportunities to reflect on their experience and to try out new ideas in practice. Third, learning, even when it appears to involve an activity as isolated as reading in a library, depends on the learner participating in a 'community of practice'; a community may be represented by the author and audience for a book or report; it may be within or between institutions, in or between communities or it may be a virtual community with a basis on the Internet or e-mail. Fourth, learning requires access to concepts and ideas that can provide frameworks for learners to reflect on practice, on subject or vocational knowledge and on their previous knowledge. It follows that for this approach, learning is inseparable from pedagogy, whether explicitly through the activities of teachers, instructors or mentors, or tacitly through the pedagogic models that are implicit in learning resources, assignments and tests.

These assumptions about learning and its link with pedagogy are not new, nor are they specific to the context in which FE teachers find themselves. Some will be referred to in other chapters of this book. However, we would argue that they have a particular significance in relation to the current demands being made on the FE sector, given the diversity of learning needs of those coming to colleges and the function of colleges as a bridge or transitional learning stage from school or adult life and as a basis for progression to a variety of destinations. These new demands being made on FE can be expressed as the need to find ways of:

- linking the learning of adults to their future employability as older notions of vocational preparation for specific jobs are no longer appropriate
- motivating young learners who have become disaffected from learning at school
- linking learning that takes place in different contexts (especially colleges and workplaces)
- realizing the learning potential of the new information technologies and other learning resources
- developing pedagogies that relate to the learning demands of leading-edge workplaces
- providing pathways for adults and younger learners to progress to higher education
- providing learning opportunities which are flexible enough to ensure both access to and motivation for lifelong learning.

Before returning to how FE might respond to this new 'pedagogic agenda', the next section elaborates the idea of *learning as a social process* that underpins the approach taken here, through a brief review of recent developments in learning theory. These developments can be found in a number of linked disciplines including cultural anthropology, social and educational psychology and educational philosophy.

RECENT DEVELOPMENTS IN LEARNING THEORY AND THEIR RELEVANCE FOR PEDAGOGY AND LEARNING IN FE

Our approach to learning is based on three new developments in learning: Theory-Situated Learning (Lave and Wenger, 1991), Activity Theory (Wertsch, 1981) and Ideas-Based Constructivism (Prawat, 1993). In summarizing these ideas, this section draws substantially on a paper by Guile and Young (1999) where a more detailed discussion of the idea of reflexive learning can be found. The concept of reflexive learning has three distinctive features.

First, it stresses how learning occurs within contexts but also between contexts. It thus avoids the weakness of approaches to learning as a 'situated process' in which the analysis tends to be bounded by specific contexts. Second, it goes beyond approaches such as 'learning by doing', 'learning as problem solving' and 'experiential learning' and asserts that access to ideas that enable people to conceptualize alternatives are crucial to learning. Third, it suggests that the new information and communication technologies are increasingly important to learning being reflexive as they can extend the idea of learning as participation in 'communities of practice' in particular settings to learning as participation in electronically distributed learning communities.

The starting point of our approach is the assumption that learning is a situated process that always takes place *in a context*. Context refers to the way that learning involves a process of social interaction and therefore takes place in a social context; it also refers to the fact that learning also takes place not just in contexts of interaction, but in the historical relationships that exist between people, their activity and the social world of which they are a part.

Learning as a situated process

Our starting point for this view of learning is Lave's (1993) argument that:

> psychological theories of learning which conceive of learning as a special mental process, ultimately impoverish and misrecognise it. (pp. 9–23)

The problem with the theories that Lave is referring to is that in treating models from either animal behaviour or information processing as if they described learning, they miss what is distinctive about human learning. In practical terms they can do little more than confirm the 'common sense' of policy-makers who want to distinguish good from bad teachers and the 'common sense' of teachers who experience 'good ' and 'bad' learners. Whereas making such distinctions is an inevitable if limited guide to making teachers more accountable and identifying the problems facing learners, it offers little in the way of prescriptions for an alternative pedagogy. Lave and Wenger's (1991) approach starts from the assumption that in everyday life learning is a 'situated process' and introduces the idea of 'legitimate peripheral participation' which proposes that people learn by participating in 'communities of practice'.

The pedagogic implications of such a perspective transcend both traditional academic and vocational divisions and those between college and workplace learning and point to the need to create opportunities for potential learners to participate in the full range of activities and roles associated with any body of expertise, skill or knowledge. Lave and Wenger develop Dewey's idea that learning occurs when people engage in specific activities, but stress that it is the community (which may be a small group, class or a whole institution) which learns as well as the individual. By reformulating the idea of transfer of learning as participating in a new 'community of practice', this approach throws light on one of the crucial issues on the FE learning agenda which underpins the role that colleges may play in promoting employability.

Two pedagogic issues follow: first, colleges need to create opportunities for learners to participate in new contexts. Second, employability becomes not just the acquisition of knowledge or skill in one context (the college) and applying it in another (the workplace); it has to be seen as a complex process of interaction and negotiation between lecturers and employers and may involve producing new knowledge as well as using existing knowledge in new contexts.

Such a perspective opens up quite new questions about the kind of knowledge that makes people employable. It is likely to involve the tacit knowledge that is embedded in 'communities' that people need to participate in as well as codified knowledge that can form a framework for further understanding (Gibbons et al., 1994). Whether a college is concerned with promoting their students' employability or with facilitating their progression to higher education, the issue is no longer just one of some knowledge or skills being more 'transferable' than others into the new context; it is also a question of developing a student's capability to cross boundaries and use knowledge in new contexts – what Engestrom refers to as developing their poly-contextual skills (Engestrom et al, 1995).

From situated learning to trans-situational learning

As suggested earlier, a weakness of symbolic interactionist and other ethnographic accounts of learning, despite their closeness to learning as experienced by learners, is that they cannot conceptualize how extra-contextual factors may shape learning that takes place in specific contexts. Activity Theory, with its origins in Vygotsky's (1978) psychology, provides a way of broadening the notion of context by suggesting that contexts can themselves be seen 'in context'. Engestrom (1991) in particular has used Activity Theory to conceptualize the relationship between the learning within a context and learning between contexts. For him, the starting point for learning is the contradictions that exist for the learner within particular contexts. In its starting point, therefore his approach has something in common with 'problem solving. However, the concept of 'problem solving' implies that the problems (and their solutions) originate in a context rather than sometimes from factors external to it. Guile and Young (1998) have found it useful to draw on Prawat's (1993) interpretation of Dewey to make clear the pedagogic implications of this distinction.

Prawat argues that for Dewey 'ideas' or subject-based knowledge were a critical component of problem-based learning. It follows that what we earlier referred to as reflexive learning involves being 'immersed' in ideas as well as in the world of experience as this provides the learner with a basis for making links between learning in specific contexts and ideas or practices which may have originated outside those contexts.

Engestrom has a much broader concept of 'contradiction' than is found in the problem-solving literature and one that is crucial for the development of pedagogy. He recognizes that learning often requires 'mediating resources' to help learners to postulate new relationships between context and practice (Engestrom, 1991; Engestrom et al., 1996). Engestrom develops his ideas by distinguishing between three types of learning, 'adaptive', 'investigative' and 'expansive', that are distinguished by the different relationships between learner and context that they presuppose. The three contexts he describes as 'discovery', 'investigation' and 'critique'. His typology of types of learning and contexts could be used by a college wishing to evaluate its own learning strategies as applied to both staff and students. The idea of expanded learning is dependent on the existence of adaptive and investigative learning. However, it goes beyond the context in which a learner is located and takes place when investigative learning is unable to deal with the problems that are being experienced by the learner and when the context within which the learning is located is itself challenged by the learner.

The typology of types of learning – as has been noted – has its origins in Vygotsky's (1978) Activity Theory which sees learning in terms of the relationships between the use and development of 'scientific' and 'spontaneous' concepts. Vygotsky uses 'scientific' in the sense of systematic knowledge rather limiting it to knowledge in the natural sciences. 'Spontaneous' concepts refer to people's 'common sense' or the ideas that emerge from everyday experience. In relation to the FE pedagogic traditions referred to earlier, the typology provides a framework for going beyond the didactic/experiential division that has dominated much vocational education and argues that any learning involves both.

CONCLUSIONS

This chapter began by arguing that the FE sector faces fundamental questions about its approaches to pedagogy. These questions, we argued, arise from a number of broad social and economic changes and how they interact with the unique circumstances of the FE sector with its wide diversity of learning needs and its location at the interface of education and work.

While not rejecting the element of value in each of the earlier approaches with their emphases on knowledge transmission, the activities of learners and the importance of learner experience, the chapter pointed to the inadequacies of each as a basis for developing a pedagogy for the future. It went on to suggest that within recent developments in learning theory there is a powerful set of ideas which could be the basis for an alternative approach that would rest on five fundamental assumptions:

• learning is a social process involving learners participating in 'communi-

ties of practice';
- learning is a situated not a generic process and always takes place in a context;
- contexts must not be seen as bounded but themselves mediated by wider contexts from the organizational to the global level;
- it is important to distinguish between different types of learning and their interdependence on each other;
- though a learner's previous experience must be taken account of, learning also involves being immersed in ideas that can provide the basis for reflection on that experience.

Each of these assumptions has enormous implications for pedagogy. However, they do not fit easily with traditional notions of accountability and they do not prescribe any simple or straightforward strategies for government to recommend. They do not imply a rejection of efforts to quantify learning outcomes; rather they emphasize the limitations of statistical comparisons and tables as a basis for such measures. This chapter recognizes that greater accountability is an important goal for the sector. However, the implications of our approach to learning is that new forms of accountability need to be developed that rely on a more rigorous professionalism within which teachers, in collaboration with users of FE, increasingly set and raise their own standards.

The approach to learning and pedagogy that we have proposed here calls into question any precise specification of learning outcomes. However, it also recognizes the limitations of experience on its own as a basis for enhancing learning and the importance of providing students with access to discipline-based, multi-disciplinary and other forms to systematic knowledge. In the situation facing the FE sector, where new kinds of work are demanding new forms of learning, the issue is not to identify the one best pedagogic technique but to clarify the different purposes of different types of learning and the different pedagogic strategies that may help realize them.

We stated at the beginning of this chapter that government, researchers and the FE sector itself all have to grasp their responsibilities, if FE is to fully realize its potential contribution to the future of this country. This chapter has pointed to an agenda for collaboration between researchers and practitioners. It is the responsibility of government to create the conditions for this to become a reality.

REFERENCES

Brookfield, S. (1986) *Understanding and Facilitating Adult Learning*, San Francisco: Jossey Bass.

Dewey, J. (1963) *Democracy and Education*, New York: The Free Press.

DfEE (1998) *The Learning Age: A Renaissance For A New Britain*, London: HMSO.

Engestrom, Y. (1991) Non scolae sed vitae discimus: towards overcoming the encapsulation of school learning, *Learning and Instruction*, Vol.1.

Engestrom, Y. (1995) *Training in Transition*, Geneva: ILO.

Engestrom, Y., Engestrom, R., Karkkainene, M. (1995) Polycontextuality and boundary crossing in expert cognition, *Learning and Instruction*, Vol 5.

Engestrom, Y., Viorkkunen, J., Helle, M., Pihlaja, J., Poketa, R. (1996) The change laboratory as a tool for transforming work, *Lifelong Learning in Europe*, Vol. 2.

Finegold, D. and Soskice, D. (1990) The failure of training in Britain: analysis and prescription, in D. Gleeson (ed.), *Training and Its Alternatives*, Milton Keynes: Open University Press.

Friere, P. (1972) *Pedagogy of the Oppressed* (translated by M. Ramer), Harmondsworth: Penguin.

FEFC (1997) *Learning Works: Widening Participation in Further Education Colleges*, Coventry: FEFC.

Gibbons, M., Limoges, C., Nowotyny, H., Schwartzman, S., Scott, P. and Trow, M. (1994) *The New Production of Knowledge*, London: Sage.

Gravatt, J. (1997) *Deepening the Divide: Further Education Franchising and the Diversion of Public Funds*, Praxis Paper No 6. London: Lewisham College.

Green, A. and Lucas, N. (1999) From obscurity to crisis: the FE sector in context, in A. Green and N. Lucas (eds.) *FE and Lifelong Learning: Realigning the Sector for the 21st Century*, London: Bedford Way Papers, Institute of Education, University of London.

Guile, D. and Lucas, N. (1996) Preparing for the future: the training and professional development of staff within the FE sector, *Journal of Teacher Development*, Vol. 5 No. 3.

Guile, D. and Young, M. (1998) *Learning Organisations and the Question of Learning*, London: Post-16 Education Centre, Institute of Education, University of London.

Hodge, M. (1998) Sixth Report of the House of Commons, Education and Employment Committee. Vol. 1. Report, 19th May, London: The Stationery Office.

Huddleston, P. and Unwin, L. (1997) *Teaching and Learning in Further Education: Diversity and Change*, London: Routledge.

Knowles, M. (1985) *Andragogy in Action: Applying Modern Principles of Adult Learning*, San Francisco: Jossey Bass.

Lave, J. (1996) The practice of learning, in S. Chaiklen and J. Lave (eds.), *Understanding Practice*, Cambridge: Cambridge Unversity Press.

Lave, J. and Wenger, E. (1996) *Situated Learning*, Cambridge: Cambridge Unversity Press.

Leney, T., Lucas, N., and Taubman, D. (1998) *Learning Funding: The Impact of FEFC Funding, Evidence from Twelve FE Colleges*, NATFHE, London: Post-16 Education Centre, Institute of Education, University of London.

Lucas, N. (1997) The 'Applied Route' at age 14 and beyond – implications for initial teacher education, in A. Hudson and D. Lambert (eds.) *Exploring Futures in Initial Teacher Education*, London: Bedford Way Papers, Institute of Education, University of London.

Lucas, N. (1999) Incorporated colleges: beyond the FEFC model, in A. Green and N. Lucas, *FE and Lifelong Learning: Realigning the Sector for the 21st Century*, London: Bedford Way Papers, Institute of Education, University of London.

Mead, G. H. (1934) *Mind, Self and Society*, Chicago: University of Chicago Press.

Prawat, R. (1993) The value of ideas, *Education Researcher*, Aug–Sept.

Tight, M. (1996) *Key Concepts in Adult Education and Training*, London: Routledge.

Vygotsky L.S. (1978) *Mind in Society*, Cambridge: Cambridge University Press.

Wertsch, J.V. (1981) *The Concept of Activity in Soviet Psychology*, Armonk: M.E. Sharpe.

Young, M., Lucas, N., Sharp, G. and Cunningham, B. (1995) *Teacher Education for the Further Education Sector: Training the Lecturer of the Future*, Association of Colleges, London: Post-16 Education Centre, Institute of Education, University of London.

6

Learners with Special Educational Needs

Jenny Corbett and Brahm Norwich

The term pedagogy, with its classical Greek origin, evokes something special and technical, perhaps even esoteric. That interest in teaching and teaching methods has been renewed recently under the label of pedagogy says much about the recycling of issues in the field of education and in the study of education. It also reveals the determining impact of the wider social context on education. In discussing pedagogy and special educational needs (SEN) in this chapter we need to address how pedagogy relates to other aspects of the educational process. What is the relationship between pedagogy and the curriculum, another term with esoteric connotations? Over the last two decades there has been considerable interest in the curriculum in the years leading up to the introduction of the National Curriculum ten years ago, and then with its implementation and revision in the mid-1990s. One perspective is that the curriculum is about what is to be learned, the content of learning and its organization into different areas and fields of learning for different stages and ages of learners. Curriculum questions relate at one end to wider philosophical questions about the aims of education and what is worth learning and why.

At the other end, curriculum questions are intimately connected with questions about ways of promoting learning, questions to do with ways and means, the how of teaching or what has come to be called pedagogy. But the relationship between curriculum and pedagogy is more inter-connected than this analysis indicates. There are different models of the curriculum which imply different assumptions about the nature and origins of what is to be learned, its specification and about the relationships between teachers and learners (Skilbeck, 1984). Curriculum is not simply about what is to be learned, so that pedagogy is not simply about how to teach this content. Some models of curriculum, which are sometimes known as process or constructivist models, assume that the content of learning cannot be specified in advance and therefore cannot be used to determine independently the best way of promoting learning. In a process model of the curriculum, the very ways of promoting learning come to define the content of learning, and therefore the curriculum.

In this chapter we discuss pedagogic issues relating to learners with special educational needs from this perspective of the inter-connections between pedagogy and curriculum. But as we will argue, pedagogic practices are also intimately connected with issues to do with the organization and grouping of learners in schools and classrooms. This point can be illustrated briefly by noting how the ability composition of a class and the numbers of learners in it can affect the kinds of teaching and classroom management methods used. One of our main points in this chapter is that pedagogic issues relevant to learners with special educational needs illustrate sharply these general points about inter-connections. Our second main point is that the SEN focus highlights a critically important aspect of general pedagogic questions, that pedagogy is centrally about the relevance of teaching to difference and diversity. Our intention in this chapter is to focus on issues relating to pedagogy and SEN which illustrate how SEN issues enhance our understanding of general pedagogic issues. An interest in teaching methods has been a central focus in the education of learners with SEN from the origins of special education in specialist kinds of teaching approaches and materials. So, there is a sense in which the current interest in pedagogy is nothing new in the field of special needs education. It could be said that special educators have always been developing and testing out new teaching approaches and materials, as those with difficulties and disabilities are so clearly dependent on the quality of teaching.

The current general interest in pedagogic practice derives from wider social and economic policies to raise educational standards. Much has been written about the global pressures to increase the skill levels of the population better to equip countries to compete in the global economy. Whether it is likely that government policies to raise general educational standards will increase economic growth is not the issue in this chapter. That educational standards have become such a central government priority is more relevant to our discussion, as this policy interest tends to bias the focus on pedagogy to general technical teaching prescriptions, such as the National Literacy framework (DfEE, 1998).

These prescriptions do not necessarily take account of the diversity of learners and the inter-connections between pedagogy, curriculum and the organization of education provision. What is under consideration here is the concept of effectiveness in teaching, which is associated with the renewed interest in pedagogy and has arisen as part of the movement seeking greater school effectiveness and improvement. We will be arguing that concepts of effective teaching need to take account of diversity. If we adopt and adapt the kind of inclusive language used in the SEN Green Paper (DfEE, 1997a) *Excellence for All* we would say that 'pedagogy is for all'.

In discussing pedagogy and learners with special educational needs we will be focusing our discussion on those with disabilities and difficulties in learning. That is because the field of SEN has traditionally been associated with this kind of exceptionality and so we will confine this chapter to this area.

But we are aware that there are many issues relating to provision and pedagogy which are common between this area of exceptionality and the areas of high ability and English as a second language. Pedagogic issues in these areas are also mainly about how to provide for these kinds and degrees of diversity within a common framework of curriculum, organization of learners and teaching methods. Much of what we will consider in this chapter, therefore, also relates to these other areas of diversity.

This chapter is organized in six sections. Following this introduction we discuss the continuing issue about whether teaching those with SEN requires specialist pedagogies or is just an extension of the same kinds of approaches used with those without SEN. A conceptual framework for considering different kinds of educational need is then presented as a way of making sense of common and distinct kinds of pedagogies. The next section covers key historical perspectives relating to the development of methods used with those with sensory impairments, the post-war focus on identifying deficits as the focus for remedial teaching and the growth of behavioural teaching methods in the 1970s and 1980s. In the fourth section we set out some examples of the current range of pedagogic practices in special and mainstream schools and discuss some contemporary issues relating to them. These different practices are discussed in terms of a conceptual model of the relationship between the specialization of schools, learner diversity and school differentiation as expressed in learner grouping and pedagogies. We then outline a model of different pedagogic approaches relevant to different kinds of curriculum goals for those with different difficulties and disabilities. In section five, we analyse the key issues about developing pedagogic practices which are needed in a more inclusive school system. We present the idea of a connective pedagogy which combines the importance of teaching which relates to individual learners while connecting individuals with their social context.

IS PEDAGOGY FOR SEN DIFFERENT OR MORE OF THE SAME?

In adopting an inclusive position on pedagogy we have to consider one of the continuing debates about providing for individual needs. Is teaching for pupils who have difficulties in learning *additional teaching of the same kind* as for those without difficulties or is it teaching which is *different in kind*? It may, of course, be that sometimes it is more of the same and sometimes a different kind of teaching. But either way we need to know when it is one or the other. There are special educators who deny that there is any need for different kinds of teaching, just the extension and refinement of similar kinds of teaching (for example, Solity and Bull, 1987).

This position denies that some children, the one-in-five assumed to have special educational needs, are different from other children in their learning needs. Support for this is derived from research studies which fail to show differences in learning characteristics between groups identified in terms of whether they are identified and labelled as having a learning difficulty or not

(Solity, 1993). What is at issue here is the wider and more general question of whether different teaching methods or pedagogies are more suited to some children and not others across the full range of abilities and attainments. This question has been studied in terms of aptitude – treatment interactions particularly in the USA (Corno and Snow, 1986). Research studies have examined whether more or less structured kinds of teaching result in greater learning gains for children differing in general characteristics, such as verbal abilities. Though there are continuing uncertainties about this research programme, a general conclusion from these US studies has been that greater mediation in teaching and teacher direction was more suited to lower ability learners in a range of curriculum subject areas. These studies have relevance to SEN pedagogy questions, particularly in relation to pupils with moderate learning difficulties (MLD), who merge into the group of lower ability learners. However, this type of study does not provide a research justification for different pedagogy between those with MLD labels and those designated as low attainers without a SEN designation. The implications of these aptitude-interaction studies is whether there should be differences in pedagogies between above average and below average learners.

The process of identifying pupils for special educational provision is not based on whether these pupils are judged to need different kinds of teaching on account of their disabilities or difficulties. Entitlement to additional or different provision in stages 1 to 3 of the SEN Code of Practice stages, or in stage 5 with a Statement of SEN, is based on attainment and progress levels. Access to special educational provision is therefore not dependent on demonstrating that differential pedagogies are needed. This is a very important point which underlies much of the uncertainty surrounding SEN resource allocation. There are two distinct though related levels of referring to education provision. The higher level relates to provision in terms of resources, placement and general curriculum and teaching approaches. This is the level where decisions are made about additional or different provision at one of the stages of the SEN Code of Practice including the stage of Statementing. The lower level relates to decisions about what and how to teach a particular individual child in a particular context. The two levels are distinct in the sense that the higher level decisions are about access and entitlement based on summative assessments, while the lower level decisions are about the planning of teaching based on formative assessments. But, though they are not easily related in practice, ideally decisions about access and entitlement to additional resources should follow decisions about individual pedagogic needs.

The Government's recent involvement in advising teachers on teaching methods has assumed a commonality of teaching methods across special and mainstream contexts. This is stated most starkly in the Green Paper in relation to pupils with specific learning difficulties (SpLD):

> As teachers become more adept at tackling reading difficulties, children with SpLd (such as dyslexia) should in all but exceptional circumstances be catered

for in mainstream schools without a statement. What is more, class-based strategies which help children with SpLD can help children with literacy difficulties caused by other factors.

(DfEE, 1997a, section 15–16 p. 14)

Although this is a logical position to take given the Green Paper's generally inclusive stance, it leaves unaddressed questions about the nature of pedagogy for pupils with difficulties in learning. To address these questions we propose a conceptual framework (Table 6.1) for understanding the relationships between educational needs and pedagogies which is relevant to pedagogic differentiation in SEN and in teaching generally.

A child with SEN might just need more of the same kind of pedagogy as others without a SEN. So, pedagogic needs might be common to all pupils irrespective of social, ethnic, gender and disability, reflecting that they all have *common* educational needs. This is the first aspect of the conceptual model. For example, in teaching reading to all children, some might need a different balance between phonological and whole word methods than others. These pedagogic differences can be seen as part of a common repertoire of pedagogic practices. This would be the view favoured by those supporting a strong inclusive position to the education of pupils with difficulties and disabilities (Solity and Bull, 1987; Ainscow, 1995).

But there are differences between children which might call for different styles of pedagogy. We believe that you cannot rule out in principle that some pupils with significant difficulties in learning can share certain distinctive characteristics and might respond better to *specific* kinds of pedagogy. Therefore, specific kinds of pedagogies are relevant to significant difficulties in learning. This is the second aspect of the conceptual model. For example, children with significant difficulties in phonological skills might benefit from intensive phonological training which is different from the phonological emphasis given as part of the common pedagogic style. But, these specific kinds of pedagogies might not replace the common ones. It is not a question

Table 6.1: Different kinds of educational needs and pedagogies

Educational needs	Pedagogies
1. Common to all	*1. Common to all* what is common to all drawing on a common variety of different teaching styles
2. Specific or distinct what is common to some but not others	*2. Specific to some, not others* specific to kinds of significant difficulties in learning
3. Individual what is unique to individual and different from all others	*3. Individual* reflecting person's individuality

of needing common pedagogies or different ones. It may be that a child needs the common kinds of pedagogy *and* additionally some specific kinds. Common and specific needs may be complementary needs. However, this may require more teaching time to combine the methods.

Common and specific pedagogies, however, may not take full account of pedagogically relevant differences between individuals who share certain distinctive learning characteristics. Pupils with difficulties in learning may need some pedagogic methods which suit their unique individual needs. This represents the third aspect of the conceptual model. It is a useful model because it acts to remind teachers of three related aspects of educational need, common, specific and unique individual needs which are not alternatives but may be complementary to each other. Pedagogy, therefore, also needs to be considered in terms of the relationships and balances between practices which are common to all, specific to some and not others and unique to individuals.

HISTORICAL PERSPECTIVES

It is also important to assess the impact of any pedagogy in relation to its stage of historical development. What might have been quite radical in the 1970s may be seen as redundant in the late 1990s. In the area of special education, it is salutary to recall that special schools for children with severe and multiple disabilities (in which sensory and physical disability was combined with learning disability) were a relatively recent addition to the educational system. Those children deemed to have IQ scores below 50 were regarded as ineducable and unable to learn. Their physical and emotional needs were catered for by social and health service providers who were able to give parents a respite from the burden of continuous caring.

It is in this negative context that a pedagogy for children with severe and complex learning disabilities developed. It had grown out of work done by psychologists in the back wards of long-stay hospitals who found that institutionalized adults who had been labelled as 'idiots' and assumed to be unable to learn any social skills could be trained to do tasks for themselves. These might involve such mundane actions as putting a coat on and off, eating with a knife and fork, opening a door or selecting a drink out of two alternatives. The significant attitude underlying these teaching approaches which set specific learning outcomes is that all human beings, whatever the severity of their disability, have the capacity to learn and adapt. To realize these capacities this learning has to fit their individual circumstances and their motivation. Perhaps, the concept of a pedagogy for *individual wants* rather than special needs would be a more apt description of what tends to make for success in any form of specialist pedagogy.

Two of the most long established and major areas of specialist pedagogy are those which involve communication strategies for deaf and blind children. Whilst the teaching of braille has been seen as an essential component of traditional pedagogy for blind children, helping them to communicate and to participate in the National Curriculum, it is not always appropriate for children whose visual impairments are just part of their multiple disabilities. These learners may need a flexible range of sensory stimuli to connect with their means of expression. Traditional methods of teaching deaf children to communicate have developed out of a social attitude that has denigrated any form of communication other than speech. Attempts by deaf children to use the natural language of signing used to be punished and they were forced to try to speak even though the severity of their hearing loss might have made this an almost impossible task. Part of the development of pedagogy in this specialism has been the widespread adoption of a method of 'total communication' which involves the simultaneous use of signing and speech, effectively helping to connect the child into their special deaf language at the same time as ensuring their exposure to the dominant language of speech.

The teaching of deaf children illustrates important aspects of the politics of pedagogy. Teaching or learning signing becomes a crucial element within the process of adopting a deaf cultural identity and a failure to induct a deaf child into their cultural heritage in this way is seen by many disability rights activists as a betrayal. The politics of pedagogy for deaf children comprises two learning landscapes, delineated by boundaries between mere integration on the one side and true inclusion on the other. A pedagogy which demands the exclusive use of speech is placing assimilation into the status quo as the dominant aim; a pedagogy which encourages the use of signing is validating the significance of a proud identity. These pedagogic practices must be understood as political acts if the wider significance of an inclusive ideology is to be properly understood.

Special educational needs has a strong historical association with the medical profession and the application of medical ideas to the identification and teaching of children with disabilities and difficulties. When government first made legislative provision for children with disabilities and difficulties at the end of the last century, medical officers played a central role in the identification and placement process. With the emergence of professional educational psychologists, particularly after the Second World War, this role was taken over by them. The intelligence tests introduced at the start of this century were designed to provide systematic evidence with which to identify children who were assumed to have intellectual impairments which prevented them from benefiting from mainstream school teaching. The identification process was in the medical tradition of defining areas of deficiency and applying this to teaching and learning. This focus on individual deficits in functioning has come to be associated with what is called the medical model in the field of special needs education. One of the longstanding criticisms of the medical model from an educational perspective has been that it is negative in focusing on what the child cannot do; not on what she or he can do and learn. This criticism has been fundamental to the growth of professional interest amongst teachers and psychologists in the educational needs and provision for children with disabilities and impairments.

Much of the criticism of the medical model can be understood to derive from professional rivalries between health and educational professionals. The focus on deficits does not in itself define an exclusively medical perspective and set of assumptions, especially as the deficits talked about in education are functional ones relating to performances. These are different from the deficits identified in the medical diagnostic process which searches for underlying biological and other causes of these functional deficits. Nor does a medical approach assume necessarily that all functional deficits are unalterable, even if there are underlying conditions, such as Downs Syndrome, which are lifelong conditions. Psychologists who took over the key professional responsibilities for identification by the mid-1970s continued the deficit focus of assessment, but did so in terms of psychological processes presumed to underlie school learning and attainment. This interest in underlying psychological deficits was developed in a series of tests of perceptual, memory and linguistic processes presumed to be necessary for school learning and progress, such as the Illinois Test of Psycholinguistic Abilities (Kirk and Kirk, 1971) and the Frostig Test of Visual Perception (Frostig and Horne, 1964). The focus on underlying deficits was meant to be positive in that once the profile of perceptual and memory deficits was identified, a programme of remedial teaching could be designed to restore these processes. The pedagogic implication of these approaches was that specific groups of children – those with mild and specific learning difficulties – needed to receive special teaching programmes in settings separate from mainstream classes and focused on remediating these general underlying deficits. In practice, this tradition of remedial teaching came into disrepute for several reasons. First, there was scant evidence that any gains in underlying perceptual and memory functioning transferred to improved learning of basic educational skills relevant to the curriculum (Ysseldyke, 1973: Solity 1993). Secondly, there were doubts about the validity of the psychological deficit constructs and risks of stigmatizing children through false identification of these underlying deficits. Thirdly, the specialist remedial programmes kept these children separate from their peers in mainstream classes and schools.

This tradition of special education teaching assumed that certain children have specific educational needs which require distinct pedagogies. In terms of the conceptual framework introduced in the second section, it ignored those educational needs which are common to all and those which are unique to individuals. With the growth of interest during the 1970s in the rights of children with disabilities to be in mainstream schools and the criticisms of the relevance of deficit categories to planning teaching programmes for them, there was a sharp move away from deficit focused approaches in SEN teaching. Behavioural analytic models were proposed as offering a pedagogic alternative which focused on performances in particular contexts. Underlying processes and deficits were swept away in a refocusing on the conditions and consequences of learning specific tasks. The behavioural framework did not depend on pedagogic approaches derived from general categories of difficulties. Each child's difficulties in learning were to be analysed in individual terms, with the focus on what individual teaching was needed.

The concept of special educational needs was introduced by the Warnock Committee (DES, 1978) during this period and was strongly influenced by this focus on individual learning performance. Statements of special educational needs were designed to identify a child's individual needs in terms of goals and objectives and the provision required to meet these needs. In this way behavioural objectives were introduced as a positive teaching approach which was not side-tracked into futile and stigmatizing efforts to remediate deficits (Ainscow and Tweddle, 1978).

The basic principles of using behavioural objectives in teaching have been and continue to be very influential in special needs education. They have been adopted and adapted in government guidance on provision in the form of Individual Educational Plans (IEPs) for the wider group of those with special educational needs in the SEN Code of Practice. These principles imply that the assessment of the individual learner's attainment is relative to some common curriculum goal, such as literacy or numeracy. Learning is assumed to be cumulative and progressive, so the next step is identified towards the goal and this is defined in specific performance outcome terms. Optimal teaching methods are then adopted relevant to the specific learning objective based on what is known about the individual learner and appropriate approaches. Learning progress is monitored with the collection of performance data which is used to inform and guide the teaching and learning.

It is interesting to note in passing that many of these principles have been adopted in the moves by recent governments to raise educational standards generally through systematic school development planning, in regulations over target setting for schools and in guidance for teaching literacy and numeracy. These similarities between the principles of general school improvement and objectives teaching approaches in special education reflect the adoption of a more technical approach to education. It is an approach which appears to become more or less dominant depending on changing social, economic and political circumstances. Since the 1960s its adoption came first in special education through the influence of empirically based behavioural psychology and subsequently in mainstream schools through school effectiveness research and technically based management approaches. We conjecture that these performance planning and outcome principles are adopted when social and political conditions call for greater control of educational outcomes. This would explain how they were adopted first within special education, which had been for many decades a backwater in education until the advent of the movement supporting greater rights for the disabled from the 1960s. The political need to raise standards in the general school system was subsequent to this in the 1980s, in response to what were seen to be serious skill gaps in Western societies.

Pedagogies can become punitive, destructive and ineffective, however, if they overlook individual identity to focus only on the disability rather than the person. Again, just as any good teacher tries to treat their students with respect, so the pedagogy has to be used appropriately. Any form of behaviour modification programme is potentially abusive and controlling. It involves an unequal power relation and is using methods which are designed to instil patterns of learned behaviour. Whilst it may be presented as a negotiated process entered into with the agreement of the learner, there is an implicit reliance that both sides accept responsibility for making necessary changes to the learning patterns or behaviour patterns of one of them. Behaviour contracts might be viewed as primarily concerned with the well being of the school community as a whole and with maintaining order, rather than with individual needs. There are extreme examples, however, now most often found in special residential provision, where a behaviour modification programme can be mainly concerned with preventing a child from severely injuring themselves, perhaps smashing their head onto hard surfaces or biting their skin so deeply that it bleeds. Such behaviour can become life-threatening and clearly any pedagogy which helps to prevent this is valuable. In the direct practitioner experience of one of us (Jenny Corbett), a most successful programme in a special school was seen to lessen significantly the incidents of head-injury to one adolescent girl. She used to bang her head on hard surfaces and we always responded by giving her lots of attention, so she did it more often. The visiting psychologist told us to hold her onto a soft mat on the floor when she began banging her head but not to reward this behaviour with the usual positive attention. When she was not banging her head, we were told to make a big fuss of her. Within only a few weeks the learned behaviour of thirteen years was 'faded out', as the terminology goes. It seemed like common sense on reflection but, without this intervention, we may well have persisted in what was unhelpful practice.

CURRENT RANGE OF PEDAGOGIC PRACTICES: ISSUES AND EXAMPLES

In special schools

In a recent research study, Adams (1998) examines the pedagogy of special schools which teach children with moderate or severe learning disabilities. She found that the essential element of a pedagogy for children with moderate learning disabilities was control. Much of the teaching was dull and repetitive rote learning with group tasks set and scant signs of differentiation. There was nothing special about it. The blandness of approach was such that could commonly be found in those mainstream classrooms where pedagogic practice lacked imagination. She concluded her evaluation of this pedagogy with these reflections:

> What emerged most strongly from the analysis of learning activities was the difficulty which teachers perceived in dealing with the learning needs of this group of pupils. The challenging behaviours which the class had demonstrated early

in the academic year had led to formal structures, rules and regulations for the classroom. Managing behaviour remained foremost in the minds of teachers and in many lessons this influenced the styles of teaching and learning . . . A mistrust of collaboration, which was thought to lead to pupils being off task, to chatter and to disruption, meant that pupils spent much time working individually on similar tasks, not on individualised work.

(pp. 182–183)

The latter comment is particularly revealing. It illustrates the fallacy of assuming that working individually is in any way special. Recent emphasis upon the importance of Individual Education Plans (IEPs) in all mainstream schools, including the secondary sector, suggests that individual work is particularly appropriate for children with learning disabilities. However, many secondary teachers find this extremely difficult to support and antipathetic to their commitment to group learning. If, as Adams says, each child is working individually on an identical task because teachers in a special school with fewer than ten pupils in the classroom find differentiation impractical, it is not surprising that secondary teachers often feel that they are being asked to do the impossible.

In contrast, Adams found that the pedagogy for severe learning disabilities was generally thoughtful and child-centred. It recognized individual differences and sought to connect with the specific interests and understanding of each child. She observed that teachers managed classrooms to facilitate learning and that:

This resulted in a great degree of fluidity in the environment with pupils moving around the classroom for differing activities . . . With help almost always close at hand there were few occasions when pupils were not occupied, so that the atmosphere was at once informal and calm.

(ibid., p. 208)

She noted in particular that this style of classroom management helped to avoid incidents of challenging behaviour from children whose past record had been one of emotional volatility. In adopting a pedagogy which relates to the child as an individual and then helps to include them in classroom activities, such teaching promotes personal growth and dignity through high levels of empathetic awareness.

It is clear from research like this that current pedagogic practices in special schools vary considerably in quality. This research contrasts practices between special schools providing for different degrees of learning disabilities. There have also been recent expressions of concern about the quality of provision and teaching in special schools for children with emotional and behaviour difficulties from OFSTED school inspectors (Cole *et al.*, 1998). The introduction of the National Curriculum has probably had the most impact on teaching in all special schools over the last ten years. It has connected curriculum and teaching in special schools with mainstream schools within a common framework and challenged special schools teachers to find ways of applying the national framework while adapting it to the needs of pupils in their schools.

In mainstream schools

With more than 50% of children having Statements of SEN in mainstream schools in England, any discussion of pedagogy and SEN needs to consider pedagogic practices in ordinary primary and secondary schools (Norwich, 1997). This proportion represents about 1.4% of all pupils in the English school system. But these are children with significant SENs, who represent only about one-tenth of all children considered to have a difficulty in learning at some stage in their school careers, about 1 in 5 of all children. This wider group of children who have always been in ordinary schools were the focus of the legislation in 1994 which introduced the SEN Code of Practice. All schools including special schools have since then been required to have regard to the Code in making provision for those with special educational needs. Amongst many other provisions, the Code introduced a five stage system of identification and provision for individual children with SEN. The first three stages related to children (the wider group of 1 in 5) with increasing degrees of need for additional or different provision to be provided by the ordinary school. Stage four involved the statutory assessment process in which the LEA takes multidisciplinary advice about whether to issue a Statement which represents its obligations to provide additional or different provision either in an ordinary or special school. Stage five represents special provision determined by the LEA.

Within this legislative framework, the Code of Practice has specified pedagogic approaches under what is called individual educational plans (IEPs), which are for children at stages two and three. Stage one relates to the identification of a child causing concern to the class teacher and the teacher adopting some special teaching approach. At stage two the school's special educational needs coordinator (SENCO) becomes involved in working with the teacher to identify the child's needs and plan some relevant teaching, perhaps with some extra teacher or learning support assistance. These plans are recorded in an IEP. At stage three the SENCO involves an outside support professional, an educational psychologist or external support teacher, to assist in assessing needs and planning appropriate teaching responses, also recorded in an IEP. These IEPs have become the main pedagogic requirement within ordinary schools for developing individual teaching for children with SEN. Similar individual learning plans are supposed to be formulated in special and ordinary schools for children with Statements. However, there is some uncertainty about this as Statements are themselves more generalized records of individual children's special educational needs which also include details about general teaching approaches.

We will confine our discussion to IEPs for the larger number of children at stages two and three. IEPs are short records of the child's strengths and difficulties, parental views and the views of the child where appropriate. They also include learning targets, relevant teaching strategies, staff involvement and how progress is to be monitored and assessed. IEPs are meant to set targets for a period of between one and two terms in specific terms which makes assessment of progress possible.

IEPs were partly introduced as a system of accountability and a way of ensuring that schools were providing adequate pedagogy for those with less significant SENs who did not need a Statement. The paperwork involved in formulating and regular reviewing of IEPs has been greeted by many teachers as a bureaucratic nightmare, especially in larger schools (Cooper, 1996). However, IEPs have also been seen in a more positive light as a constructive way of planning individual teaching. Initial research and inspection summaries within two years of their implementation pointed to the need for more guidance about their purpose, format and implementation. Since then the DfEE has issued further guidance about IEPs (DfEE, 1997b) and the research team which advised the DfEE has published further details (Todd *et al.*, 1998). Much could be said about the administrative aspects of IEPs as part of the operation of the SEN Code of Practice and of differences between primary and secondary schools, for example. But, for the purposes of this chapter, we will confine the discussion to the main issues we are considering.

As noted above, the influence of behavioural objectives in teaching, an approach based on performance planning and outcome principles, is evident in the form and use of IEPs. A generic kind of planning is assumed irrespective of the area or kind of learning. Planning is considered to be about setting specific single learning objectives for which specific strategies are selected. There is no place for teaching which has multiple and related objectives which call for inter-connected strategies. Neither is there a place for general teaching strategies where there are open-ended objectives. The IEP format may be relevant to the learning of certain basic educational skills, but there are difficulties when a single approach is applied to other areas, such as in personal and social development, creative and problem-solving areas of learning.

IEPs have also been criticized for their potential to separate out and stigmatize those who have them. In so doing their operation can be seen to bolster a mainstream system which is insensitive to individual needs if there is no feedback and connection with general curriculum planning and teaching. IEPs are often thought to be for planning individual teaching on a one-to-one basis. However, this is not necessarily so. The setting of individual targets does not require separate or withdrawal individual teaching strategies. It may be considered preferable to arrange teaching to be done in group settings as part of regular class learning activities.

It has also been suggested that all children, not just those on SEN stages 2 and 3, could have records of their individual educational needs. There are already examples of schools which undertake some individual targeting with all their pupils with a focus on specific pedagogies. The advantage of applying this system to all children means that those with SENs would not need to be treated differently. The risk with this kind of individual planning is that it could become excessively wasteful of precious time needed for learning activities. Also, there might still be the need for more detailed individual planning for those with greater difficulties in learning. But, whether there are individual learning plans for some or for all, individual planning cannot be separated from curriculum planning and teaching which is sensitive to individual needs. No individual planning process can cover the range and depth of planning involved in providing a broad and balanced curriculum. IEPs are not meant to be a substitute for a curriculum and pedagogy which is suitable for the diversity of learners. What is needed is a combination of appropriate curriculum differentiation which takes place at a school or department level and individual planning which supplements this by fine tuning and focusing the priority areas for teaching a children with SEN. This is a combination of top down systemic curriculum planning which builds flexibility into teaching approaches and bottom up individual assessment and planning. This point relates back to the earlier discussion in the introduction about the need to see the inter-connections between pedagogy and curriculum.

As we have said in our introduction, pedagogy cannot be isolated from its organizational and policy context. Meeting the needs of the minority with difficulties is connected to meeting needs of the majority through differentiated curriculum and pedagogic practices. It also connects with the grouping and placement of pupils both within and between schools. The move towards greater placements of those with Statements in ordinary schools over the last decade (Norwich, 1997) has been associated with two types of organizational arrangement. One has been the additional resourcing of particular schools which specialize in some area or areas of SEN. The other type of arrangement is the placement of individual children with Statements in mainstream class with the support of specialist teaching and/or learning assistant support. This might involve some withdrawal teaching for individuals or small groups during regular class time or outside class time. It will be clear that the kinds of teaching used for the range of significant SENs now met by teachers in ordinary schools depend on the particular organizational and grouping arrangements. The kind of teaching required by a child with a significant SEN will depend on whether her or his mainstream class is ability grouped or not, on whether there is withdrawal teaching or not, how such teaching relates to the mainstream class teaching programmes and whether there are other children with significant SENs in the class. Figure 6.1 shows how pedagogy cannot be isolated from the policy and organizational context. It is a summary of the relationships between school specialization, learner diversity, differentiation practices and pedagogy just discussed.

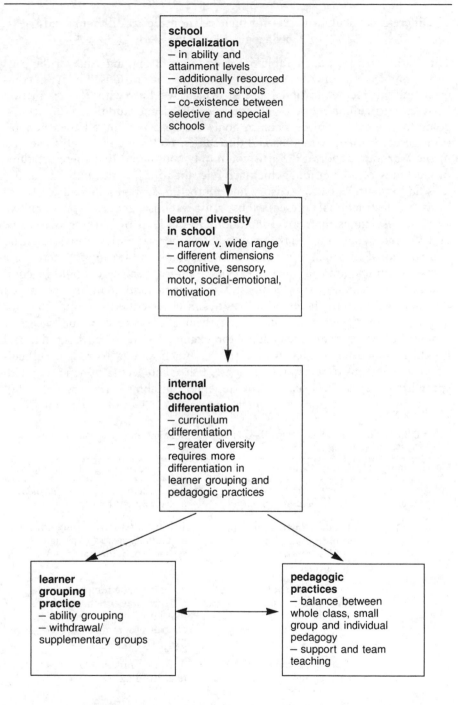

Fig. 6.1 Model of relationship between school specialization, learner diversity, school differentiation and pedagogic practices

Different curriculum goals and their relationship to different kinds of pedagogic adaptations

This framework set out in Table 6.2 is one way of making sense of the pedagogic implications of the central distinction we have proposed between common and distinct educational needs, which we link with the distinction between curriculum goals for all and specialized and additional curriculum goals for some. Where curriculum goals are common for all then adaptations accept learners' strengths and difficulties. Following the analysis set out in the Warnock Report 1978 it is commonly considered that there are three broad kinds of adaptations which are relevant to different kinds of disabilities and impairments: for sensory and motor impairments there are adaptations to instructional presentations and response modes; for cognitive learning disabilities there are adaptations to the level of learning objectives; and for emotional and behaviour difficulties there are adaptations to social and emotional climate and interactions in teaching and learning. Where there is more than one kind of impairment or disability then there would be combinations of adaptations. By contrast, where curriculum goals are specialized for some, adaptations focus on difficulties in order either to reduce them or circumvent them. When circumventing them alternative communication or mobility access systems are taught, for example, sign systems, spatial and building orientation strategies and braille. When aiming to reduce difficulties, teaching aims to reinstate functions, such as intellectual functioning with specialized programmes such as Instrumental Enrichment (Feuerstein, 1980) and self-control functioning through cognitive-behavioural programmes for

Table 6.2 Framework of relationships between different curriculum goals and pedagogic adaptations

Curriculum goals	Common to all	Specialized goals for some
Pedagogic adaptations	*which accept learner's strengths and difficulties*	*which focus on learner's difficulties to circumvent or reduce them*
	1. adapt instructional presentation and learner response modes (sensory and motor impairments)	1. learn alternative communication or mobility access (e.g. sign system, spatial/building orientation, braille)
	2. adapt level of learning objectives (cognitive learning disabilities)	2. lessen deficit/impairment (e.g. instrumental enrichment for intellectual impairments (Feuerstein); self-control programmes (for conditions like ADHD))
	3. adapt social-emotional climate and interactions of teaching-learning (emotional and behavioural adjustment difficulties)	3. restore function (e.g. Reading Recovery)

(Based on Norwich, 1990)

children with attentional and activity difficulties (sometimes identified as ADHD). There are also specialized programmes which aim to restore function not just to improve functioning in area of difficulties, such as Reading Recovery (Clay, 1985).

PEDAGOGIC PRACTICES FOR A MORE INCLUSIVE SCHOOL SYSTEM

Booth and Ainscow (1998) have recently explored the area of pedagogic practices which support inclusion by presenting field work from several different cultural settings. This international perspective is interesting as it takes the ideology of inclusion into many real-life settings to see how teachers translate ideology into practice. Their concluding reflections are particularly challenging in saying that:

> The examination of the nature of perspectives permits an understanding of the way research in this field has been constrained by a particular history of special education, dominated by a particular medical and psychological view of why students experience difficulties in schools, and how they might be resolved. We suggest that a perspective which fully utilises the fertility of the concepts of 'inclusion' and 'exclusion' allows a break from such a history and the creation of a new one. (p. 246)

A phrase which refers to 'the fertility of the concepts' can be seen to epitomize that degree of introspective theorising which Clark et al. (1998) acknowledge can be constricting in the development of pedagogic initiatives relating to inclusion.

Perhaps an appropriate analogy for the current state of pedagogic practices for inclusion is that they are sandwiched between two opposing forces, different in flavour and texture and coming from completely different origins, but complementary. The top layer (and most conspicuously high-profile) is the theory of inclusion which relates to ethics, civil rights and conceptions of social justice. It is essentially about values and sets out idealized systems and relationships unsullied by practical realities. This is where critics of inclusive ideologists condemn their ideas as utopian and unrealistic. The under-layer of this sandwich is the voice of practitioners, administrators and policy-makers, embedded in day-to-day responsiveness and coping strategies. Their lives have been made more difficult in recent years by increased demands from external evaluators and it is not surprising if they resist any potentially stressful new elements to challenge their pedagogy. Inclusive practices, such as mixed ability teaching, team teaching and collaborative learning, for example, can seem intolerable to them, when they measure these in the context of league tables and SATs. It is unrealistic to expect that teachers can give equal status to the competing demands made on them: to demonstrate successful performance against externally imposed criteria and to be responsive and flexible towards differentiation in the classroom. In between the philosophical ideals and the daily practice, it is all too easy to lose sight of what kind of pedagogy is inclusive to all learners.

In their recent analysis of special education theorizing, Clark *et al.* (1998, p. 162) suggest that in some models of special education it is assumed that there are:

> no really-existing 'special needs' which necessarily cause problems for educators and call for some carefully-worked-out response.

This seems to be a denial of the very tangible difficulties which many children do experience and a rejection of the specific pedagogies which we have discussed as having been developed as a response to their apparent disabilities and difficulties in learning. This kind of statement may be intended as a powerful challenge and can be a painful provocation to teachers working with children with disabilities and difficulties. These teachers often feel that they have devoted their careers to developing and enhancing distinct pedagogies which they have felt was beneficial to children they were deeply committed to supporting.

Teachers decide to work in the special school sector for many different reasons, some of which may be unconsciously connected to their own feelings of vulnerability. What many of them learn to develop is a caring pedagogy which is essentially founded upon their insights into the nuances of each individual child's behaviour patterns and means of communicating (Corbett, 1992; 1997). Whether this differs significantly from what might be expected of any good teacher is the critical factor to consider when addressing an inclusive pedagogy. In tracing the historical developments which led to a special needs pedagogy, a key assumption was that it was possible to help most people learn new skills and that behaviour patterns could change. This is an inclusive attitude in that it does not exclude some learners as being unable to learn and develop.

The pedagogy of itself is not the problem; adopting pedagogical practices which have been successful in the special school sector can be a valuable means of supporting inclusion, as the earlier example from the school for children with severe learning disabilities illustrates. Task analysis and the creation of manageable steps towards achieving skills in literacy and numeracy can be seen in many aspects of differentiated mainstream practice and what is termed 'precision teaching' or 'objectives teaching' (e.g. Kessissoglou and Farrell, 1995; Cornwall, 1997; Sinclair, 1997). The widespread popularity of systems like the use of Circle Time and Behaviour Contracts in primary and secondary schools also illustrates the successful transfer of pedagogy from the special to the mainstream sector (e.g. Curry, 1997; Myers, 1998).

Clark *et al.* (1998) say that both special education and concepts of special needs are products of particular social processes rather than descriptions of the reality of children's characteristics or rational responses to those characteristics. But we consider that the specific example offered above illustrates how a rational response to a child's self-destructive behaviour was useful and beneficial to that child, enabling her to regain considerable dignity as well as preventing any further physical damage. The social processes which foster a special pedagogy can be positive as well as negative: positive, in assisting a learner to acquire meaningful and transferable knowledge and relevant and self-determining actions and dispositions, and negative, in focusing on isolated facts and skills and short term behaviours to suit others' needs. In the example described above, there were instances of children on programmes which appeared to make minimal difference to their quality of life and which did inhibit and constrain them in a way which could be seen as punitive. The deciding factor is whether there is meaningful and rewarding learning or whether there is a predominance of disconnected and controlled learning unsuited to the genuine needs of the learner.

For a pedagogy to enhance the quality of inclusive practices in the mainstream, there has to be an accurate evaluation of just what an inclusive pedagogy means in practice. There is a major dilemma in trying to promote inclusive values and maintaining a commitment to genuine individual learning and development in practical contexts. One way of dealing with the mismatching is to assess the process by which the teacher relates to the learner and then the learner is brought into a wider social inclusion. This could be seen as having two key aspects: the first, to connect with the individuals; the second, to connect them with the wider community of the classroom, school, recreation or housing. These two aspects are not one-off processes but ongoing expressions of responsiveness, which require imaginative, lateral thinking and high levels of flexibility.

'Connection' is an apt way of describing a pedagogy relevant to inclusion for it captures the central role of the teacher in the process, what we wish to call a connective pedagogy. Connecting in an inclusive learning environment presents challenges to the teacher. It is much easier to connect in selective settings of homogeneous, academically able and motivated learners. The level of empathy required to understand diverse learning styles is considerable. In their range of examples, Booth and Ainscow (1998) show how useful subjects like drama can be in opening up attitudes and helping disabled students to feel more included, deliberately introducing topics which include the outsider.

Assuming that inclusion refers to all learners, it is interesting to consider what connective pedagogy means for a wide range of individual differences. Beginning with a child who is deaf and blind, connection here cannot mean speaking to the child from any distance. It has to involve touch. To connect with this learner, the teacher needs to help the child feel safe and secure in the familiarity of daily rituals. This may be done through massage, stroking and feeling familiar textures. To gain some sense of time and space, the routine may include feeling a different texture at the beginning of each school day. In this way, the teacher can first connect on a one-to-one level and then connect the child into their surroundings through using all the senses as appropriate and allowing the child to use them as a communication or enabling tool in making contact with objects in their daily lives (Park, 1997; 1998). Children who have profound and multiple disabilities may respond to the connection of mother-infant interaction, leading them into a wider exploration of their environment, through play and reflecting back to them their own sounds and gestures (Watson and Fisher, 1997).

In contrast, making connection with a child who shows emotional and behavioural difficulties involves recognizing her or his experience of the world. The teacher has to act as a link for them into social behaviours that are acceptable in a school setting, whilst validating their identity and way of perceiving themselves and others. It should be clear that inclusion and connection relate to many varied differences among school students, not just those traditionally seen as 'special needs'. It has especial relevance to that level of connection which can help children from different ethnic minorities feel included and validated. It also includes that connection which helps young people discovering their sexuality is outside the norm to feel that their identity is valued and their experience of difference is given equal respect as is their desire to be part of the school community.

These two aspects of connection, if operating successfully, will promote respect for individual identity and participation in group activities in differing ways which are comfortable for those involved. But, for connection to be enduring, what is individually comfortable needs to be respected. Forced social participation, even if subtle, threatens respect for the individual and runs counter to valuing individuality. Similarly, some forms of individual connection can isolate the child from the wider social context which runs counter to inclusive values. So, if these two aspects of connection are taken into account, then casualties are less likely in mainstream practices. Where disabled young people are placed in classrooms and playgrounds without this degree of connection, they are more likely to suffer from isolation, bullying and an inappropriate curriculum with inadequate pedagogic responses. This is an example of locational integration (DES, 1978) with all its inherent weaknesses. A connective pedagogy is costly in time, effort, concentration, consistency, continuity and funding. However, it becomes easier with familiarity and practice. Connective pedagogy will incorporate some of the best of 'special needs' teaching. But it does not ignore differences; it celebrates rather than pathologizes the disabled child. And in connecting the specific learner to the group, it is an anti-discriminatory pedagogy which seeks to educate all of the learners in how to be more responsive and understanding of the individual differences in any of them.

CONCLUDING COMMENTS

In this chapter we have examined ways of moving forward in dealing with the dilemma of trying to promote inclusive values and a commitment to supporting genuine individual learning and development in practical contexts. We present the idea of a connective pedagogy as a way of conceptualizing how teaching has two interrelated aspects, that of connecting with the individuals and connecting individuals with the wider social context and community. In recognizing this duality we, as authors, see ourselves, despite any other differences of view, as unlike some theorists about inclusive education. This is because we are unable to discount the very real difficulties which some learners experience in trying to access the practical demands of an operational curriculum. The politics of pedagogy is concerned with issues of cultural identity and we believe that the concept of bicultural identity is useful in moving forward with developing new ways of combining teaching which is relevant to common and distinct educational needs. The concept of bicultural identity aptly illustrates the experience of simultaneously requiring a recognition of individual difference and an acknowledgement of addressing active inclusion. There needs to be a balance between common cultural needs and specific needs which may justify some use of a distinct pedagogy. Distinctness also applies to learners whose difference relates to different religions, in which cultural identity is presented as an integral element of educational growth. Distinctness does not deny commonality. Rather than fostering a false invisibility which can be destructive to those whose fragility requires positive affirmation, it recognizes difference positively. For these reasons we support the notion of connective pedagogy.

REFERENCES

Adams, J. (1998) *A Special Environment? Learning in the MLD and SLD Classroom*, PhD thesis, University of Northumbria at Newcastle.

Ainscow, M. (1995) Education for all: making it happen, *Support for Learning*, 10(4): 147–157

Ainscow, M. and Tweddle, D. (1978) *Preventing Classroom Failure: An Objectives Approach*, London: Wiley.

Booth, T. and Ainscow, M. (eds.) (1998) *From Them To Us: An International Study of Inclusion in Education*, London, Routledge.

Clark, C., Dyson, A. and Millward, A. (1998) *Theorising Special Education*, London: Routledge.

Clay, M. (1985) *The Early Detection of Reading Difficulties*, London: Heinemann.

Cole, T., Visser, J. and Upton, G. (1998) *Effective Schooling for Pupils with Emotional and Behavioural Difficulties*, London: David Fulton.

Cooper, P. (1996) Are individual educational plans a waste of paper?, *British Journal of Special Education*, 23(3): 115–119.

Corbett, J. (1992) Careful teaching: researching a special career, *British Educational Research Journal*, 18(2): 235–243.

Corbett, J. (1997) Teaching special needs: 'tell me where it hurts', *Disability & Society*, 12(3): 417–425.

Corno, L. and Snow, R.E. (1986) Adapting teaching to individual differences among learners, in M. Wittrock (ed.) *Handbook of Research in Teaching*, New York: Macmillan.

Cornwall, J. (1997) *Access to Learning for Pupils with Disabilities*, London: David Fulton.

Curry, M. (1997) Providing emotional support through circle-time: a case study, *Support for Learning*, 12(3): 126–129.

DES (1978) *Special Educational Needs: Report of the Committee of Enquiry into the Education of Handicapped Children and Young People (The Warnock Report)*, London: HMSO.

DfEE (1997a) *Special Educational Needs: Excellence for All* (Green Paper).

DfEE (1997b) *The SENCO Guide*.

DfEE (1998) *The National Literacy Strategy: Framework For Teaching*.

Feuerstein, R. (1980) *Instrumental enrichment: an intervention program for cognitive modifiability*, Philadelphia: University Park Press.

Frostig, M. and Horne, D. (1964) *The Frostig Programme for the Development of Visual Perception*, Chicago: Follett.

Kessissoglou, S. and Farrell, P. (1995) Whatever happened to precision teaching?, *British Journal of Special Education*, 22(2): 60–63.

Kirk, S.A. and Kirk, W.D. (1971) *Psycholinguistic Learning Disabilities*, Chicago: University of Illinois Press.

Myers, J. (1998) Inside the circle, *Special*, Spring: 34–35.

Norwich, B. (1997) *A trend towards inclusion : statistics on special school placements and pupils with statements in ordinary schools 1992–1996*. Bristol: CSIE.

Park, K. (1997) How do objects become objects of reference?, *British Journal of Special Education*, 24(3): 108–113.

Park, K. (1998) Form and function in early communication, *The SLD Experience*, 21: 2–5.

Sinclair, L. (1997) Researching classroom practice in order to accommodate more able children, *Support for Learning*, 12(2): 81–82.

Skilbeck, M. (1984) *School-Based Curriculum Development*, London: Harper Education Series.

Solity, J. and Bull, S. (1987) *Special Needs: Bridging the Gap*, Buckingham: Open University Press.

Solity, J. (1993) Assessing through teaching: a case of mistaken identity, *Division of Educational and Child Psychology*, 10(4): 27–47

Todd, J., Castle, F. and Blamires, M. (1998) *Implementing Effective Practice*, London: David Fulton.

Watson, J. and Fisher, A. (1997) Evaluating the effectiveness of intensive interaction teaching with pupils with profound and complex learning difficulties, *British Journal of Special Education*, 24(2): 80–87.

Ysseldyke, J.E. (1973) Diagnostic-prescriptive teaching: the search for aptitude treatment interactions, in L. Mann and D.A. Sabatino (eds.) *The First Review of Special Education*, Philadelphia: JES Press.

7

Teaching for Supercomplexity: A Pedagogy for Higher Education

Ronald Barnett and Susan Hallam

In 1997, in the UK, the report of the National Committee of Inquiry into Higher Education was published (NCIHE, 1997). That Report, over 400 pages in length together with several volumes of appendices, has helped to stimulate a national debate about higher education. Among the major issues that have held general public attention in the wake of that Report have been the funding of higher education, especially the research base but also the responsibility of students towards the costs of their education; access to higher education; standards; the professional development of lecturers and the nature of the curriculum. Largely overlooked in that debate, however, have been issues of pedagogy. For example, given any educational aims that might be determined, how might they be translated into pedagogic practices? What forms of learning and teaching are appropriate to 'a learning society' and 'globalization'? Both of these latter features help to form the context in which the Report is situated but neither are discussed there in relation to pedagogical issues.

In this chapter, we aim to address this silence and we shall attempt to do so precisely at the level missing from the Dearing Report. That is to say, we shall develop our analysis of contemporary approaches to and understandings of pedagogical matters by placing it in the wider context of a higher education for the twenty-first century. In doing so, we shall implicitly work with two levels of meaning of 'pedagogy'. Firstly, we shall identify different teaching approaches and conceptions, and their associated learning processes, as they are developing in higher education (call this Pedagogy I). However, the identification of emerging teaching approaches and learning processes in itself will be inadequate for developing a pedagogy for the twenty-first century, even if we critically interrogate – as we intend – the research on such practices. To achieve our aim, pedagogical practices will have to be evaluated against a sense of the aims of a higher education set in the context of globalization and a general will to bring about a learning society. Secondly, therefore, the task requires – and we shall seek to offer – a normative theory or view as to the kinds of pedagogical processes appropriate to the twenty-first century (call this Pedagogy II).

Our argument is quite simple. The world is one of – as we term it – *super-complexity*. A genuinely higher education is faced with the challenges of preparing graduates not just to cope with this world but to prosper in it and to go on adding to its supercomplex character. This will require considerable thought and collective effort, if our pedagogical processes are to be adequate to that task. There are, however, signs of movement in just that direction.

A SUPERCOMPLEX WORLD

We are faced not just with a world of complexity but with a world of supercomplexity. Complexity is that state of affairs in which entities, data, or even theories *within a particular domain or framework* exceed one's resources for handling them. Doctors have too many patients to see in the time available, managers have too many considerations to entertain in making decisions, and lecturers have too many students to supervise and support. Characteristically, these are examples simply of complexity. In each case, the task is largely given: it is just that the immediate demands go beyond the available resources for solving the presenting problems.

Such cases, however, when examined further, often turn out to be examples of *supercomplexity*. Supercomplexity is that state of affairs where one is faced with alternative frameworks of interpretation through which to make sense of one's world and to act purposively in it. Increasingly, doctors, managers and teachers are faced with just such a situation. Is a doctor to understand herself as a manager of the resources of the nation's health service or as a physician attending to health? Is a company manager to understand himself as a 'steward' of the world's scarce material resources or as an executive of a particular company? Is a lecturer to understand herself as a purveyor of a valued form of intellectual life represented by a particular discipline, or as a producer of skills required by the labour market or as a facilitator of each student's 'emancipation'? Situations such as these present their subjects with alternative and possibly incommensurable frameworks to understanding not just those situations but themselves. The dilemmas that supercomplexity presents us all with are dilemmas of understanding (the world), of action (in the world) and of identity and self-understanding (in that world).

Supercomplexity, it is clear, acts upon pedagogy in higher education in two ways. Indirectly, it is represented in the calls of employers for higher education to develop in students not just 'core skills' but 'self-reliance' (AGR, 1995). If we are faced with an inchoate, unpredictable and continually challenging world, then graduates will have to have powers of 'self-reliance' in order to cope with and to act purposively in that world. Responsibility is placed on the self for surviving in an uncertain world. In turn, if this call is to be heeded, pedagogies in higher education will presumably need to be those that foster such human qualities.

Directly, supercomplexity finds its way into the pedagogies of higher education since, as we have already seen, lecturers in higher education are now being faced – for the first time – with multiple and contesting invitations to interpret, and to act out, their professional selves. Does the lecturer fall in with managerial imperatives to abandon the closed curricula that emerged out of *The Academic Tribes and (their) Territories* (Becher, 1989), designed around the discrete callings of the disciplines, and to substitute instead a modular programme, the units of which are intended to do duty for a range of student programmes? Do teaching staff in higher education fall in with the so-called 'McDonaldization' of higher education (Hartley, 1995) in which the students become customers, to be managed in predictable ways? Is the suggestion of the recent National Inquiry into Higher Education that teaching become a matter of 'skill' development helpful, even if there are multiple forms of skills that come into view (NCIHE, 1997)? These are arguably contesting views as to the pedagogical relationship that, in turn, call for alternative pedagogies.

How, then, might we appraise contemporary pedagogical practices in higher education? To what extent do conventional pedagogies develop the kinds of human quality appropriate for a supercomplex world? Are the changes that might be detected in pedagogies likely to enhance higher education towards that end or, even, to place it further away? In what follows, we shall investigate a number of actual or possible trends that might shed light on the matter.

FROM RESEARCH TO TEACHING?

If the world in which graduates are having to make their way is a world of supercomplexity, the relationship between research and teaching at least has to be rethought. Since the birth of the Humboldtian tradition – with Humboldt's founding of the University of Berlin in 1810 – the Western university has had a self-understanding built upon a tight relationship between research and teaching. In that self-understanding, indeed, research has come to be prior – logically and chronologically – to teaching. 'Gladly would he lerne and gladly would he teche': Chaucer's Clerk of Oxenforde has his institutional legacy in the 'modern' university. Teaching is the fruit of the labour of research. The university is, in the first place, a site of free, organized inquiry. Teaching, accordingly, has come to be the transmission of the understandings – especially the form of life in the different disciplines – that have developed and accrued through that research. In this tradition, research and teaching are, therefore, inseparable components of a dual belief in the possibility and the value of (i) free inquiry; and (ii) disinterested knowledge emerging from that process of free inquiry.

This is a self-understanding of the modern university. For the post-modern university, in contrast, both of these two axioms are in doubt. Inquiry is necessarily saturated with tacit and unexaminable understandings. At the same time, the university has become subject to a state agenda in which the key criterion of knowledge is less its truth and more its usefulness (Lyotard, 1984). As a result, the university can no longer contain a naive sense of objective knowledge at the centre of its self-understanding. Indeed, for some commentators, the university has to understand that it is faced, in several senses, with 'the end of knowledge' (Delanty, 1998).

Supercomplexity, accordingly, doubly requires that the relationship between research and teaching be reconsidered. On the one hand, no longer can the academic community fall back on naive preconceptions as to its being in possession of objective knowledge. On the other hand, the conditions of supercomplexity that face graduates as they make their way through life call for a fundamental reappraisal as to the extent to which an educational project framed solely within the context of the research enterprise could any longer be adequate.

As it happens, the relationship between research and teaching has begun to attract the attention of researchers. The question has been: 'what is the relationship between teaching and research?' Notably, in this 'debate', the two terms are invariably placed in this order: the focus is on teaching and the underlying critique is that, within a university, research is not so central in informing effective teaching as has been assumed. A separate question, but springing from a similar agenda, focuses directly on the ways in which academics frame their research: do they see their teaching activities as compatible or incompatible with their research? Clearly, if incompatibility can be demonstrated to any extent, this might suggest that teaching in universities can and even does take place separately from research. In other words, this particular focus on the teaching/research relationship springs from a technocratic and bureaucratic agenda, intended to drive down the unit of resource by separating teaching and research. If the evidence supported this it would then assist in legitimizing possible moves towards a differentiated system of higher education, in which some universities were effectively denied the resources to conduct research and became 'teaching universities'.

Unsurprisingly, the research has been inconclusive. Drawing on a cross-national study, Clark (1997) suggests that the incompatibility thesis is over-simple, in that it overlooks 'critical linkages' between research, teaching and learning. But, as Clark admits, his paper does not seriously tackle the relationship between research and teaching in relation to undergraduate education. In focusing on advanced study, Clark notes the moves across the world to restructure teaching and research units, for example, through the creation of graduate schools, in which cross-institutional centres are developed for advanced teaching purposes. In other words, we may note that the continuing reorganization of *even research-led universities*, beset with the challenges of maximizing their research effort within limited resources, is having the effect of reducing the linkages between research and teaching at the local level within university departments.

Clark (1997, p. 252) suggests that 'we need to move conceptually beyond the dichotomy of research *and* teaching' and, instead, look towards the organizational development of 'a culture of inquiry'. Unfortunately, it is unclear to what extent, if at all, a culture of inquiry requires the immediate presence of large-scale research. As with other papers addressing the same issue, we are told that academics 'view research as necessary for effective undergraduate teaching' but we are offered no independent evidence to support that view. Where the relationship has been examined in such a way that goes beyond the views and values of academics, it emerges that 'research production or scholarly accomplishment "is only slightly associated with teaching proficiency" ' (Feldman, quoted in Martin, 1997, p. 156). In general, academics value research more than teaching although this is true to a much lesser extent with women members of staff (Gottlieb and Keith, 1997). Where academics 'perceive their role to be primarily concerned with teaching', it is hardly surprising if academics experience 'frustration' in the pattern of their working lives, especially as 'they perceive judgements on research productivity to be more highly rated than teaching' (Martin, 1997, p. 157).

How, then, in the context of our concerns to sketch a pedagogy for supercomplexity, might we interpret these findings? Faculty value research more than teaching but assert that there is a positive relationship between the two. We have already said that the research on this issue is inconclusive: some talk of an indirect but weak relationship (Smeby, 1998); others talk simply of 'coexistence' between teaching and research (Gottlieb and Keith, 1997). However, the main difficulty lies in the way in which the teaching-research relationship is in general conceptualized. Even if it was established that research was reflected in teaching, we would still be left with the need to identify the form of that relationship and, more importantly, the value that might be attributed to it. As some have come to argue, it may be that much of the research into the supposed teaching-research relationship is itself founded on an impoverished notion of research.

In other words, we are faced – in the first place – with a conceptual matter rather than an empirical matter. Helpful here is the view of Brew and Boud (1995) who argue that the key link between research and teaching is that of learning: both sets of practices are concerned with learning, albeit in different contexts. Teaching may lead to learning. Learning may occur through the process of undertaking research. Teaching will gain most from research where these relationships are understood and are reflected in the nature of the teaching. What is key so far as research is concerned in this context is *not* the knowledge and new understandings that research has spawned but, rather, the process of inquiry, that is to say 'the ways in which knowledge is generated and communicated' (Brew and Boud, 1995, p. 261). In turn, just as researchers' own understandings and offerings are crucial if research based inquiry is to develop so, if we are to introduce the key elements of research into the pedagogical situation, 'students' understandings should be taken seriously' (Rowland, 1996, p. 7).

This line of inquiry is helpful but it does not go far enough. If we are to develop a pedagogy for supercomplexity, then the aims of teaching in higher education have to be redefined to acknowledge this. Intellectual inquiry and communication have themselves to be interpreted widely to embrace the human qualities of coping with uncertainty, the projection of self amidst that uncertainty and the determination and resilience to take matters forward, to engage in the messiness of human dialogue and to act with some delibera-tion. All this is required in the activities of research and scholarship. Increasingly, too, these activities require scholars and researchers to com-municate their findings and understandings to wider audiences, to voice themselves in different registers and to attempt to take disparate and con-tending audiences with them.

It is, therefore, possible to develop a pedagogy for higher education which is research based but only if – for this purpose – research is understood as a process rather than the quest for objective knowledge.

FROM STUDENT OUTCOMES TO LEARNING PROCESS?

A pedagogy for supercomplexity – Pedagogy II – has to be based on a view of learning construed as, at least in part, the acquisition of those human capabilities appropriate for adaptation to conditions of radical and enduring uncertainty, unpredictability, challengeability and contestability (Barnett, 1999). In turn, teaching would itself have to become a set of practices likely to bring about such complex learning outcomes. Teaching considered as a set of competent performances on the part of academics would be inade-quate. Much research into pedagogy in higher education undertaken thus far is therefore of limited applicability: it addresses the ways in which teaching assists students in the acquisition or construction of a body of knowledge rather than their adaptation for conditions of supercomplexity.

One line of study has focused on identifying 'award winning' or 'excel-lent' teachers (Dunkin and Precians, 1992; Johnston, 1996). We are told that they possess complex and flexible concepts of teaching effectiveness and use a wide range of criteria for evaluating its effectiveness, placing greater empha-sis on their own feelings than the evaluative judgements of others. They have a clear sense of purpose related to their students' learning and mastery of the subject matter *in the long term*, a willingness to manipulate the learning environment to satisfy teaching aims, and a lack of perceived constraints to change their teaching and experiment with new ideas. This is relatively uncontroversial as it stands but fails to consider the aims against which the teaching is being evaluated. If these ultimately focus on the acquisition of domain specific knowledge they may be inappropriate in relation to the devel-opment of adaptability to conditions of supercomplexity.

Another strand of research has attempted to explore and define criteria for judging 'effective' teaching (Saunders and Saunders, 1993). The characteristics which have emerged include effective and enthusiastic communication of subject matter; the stimulation of thinking, understanding and intellectual development; the provision of regular and informative feedback and appropriate means of assessment; and taking a personal interest in the students, being willing to help and support them and enhancing their confidence and self-esteem (Ingleton, 1995). Is this line of inquiry helpful in working towards a pedagogy for the twenty-first century? Certainly an exclusive stress on subject domain knowledge would be inappropriate for adaptation to conditions of supercomplexity. But combined with an emphasis on students' intellectual and personal development, there may be the basis for a theory of teaching – one that embraces learning in its broadest sense, with a genuine view of learners as social and personal selves (Francis, 1994) – that can satisfy the conditions of adaptability for supercomplexity.

So what can the research tell us about learning in this sense? Dominant for twenty years as *the* paradigm of research in this domain has been that which has developed from 'phenomenography'. Phenomenography explores the qualitatively different ways in which phenomena are experienced and perceived (Marton, 1981). Fundamental is the idea that 'how' we go about experiencing and understanding the world cannot be separated from 'what' we experience and understand (Marton, 1988). Learning occurs when we come to see and understand something in a qualitatively different way to our previous understanding.

Over time, phenomenography has itself undergone considerable development, from initial research focusing on learning (Marton and Saljo, 1976a, b), through the study of understanding of basic concepts in economics and physics (Dahlgren and Marton, 1978; Johansson *et al.*, 1985) to studies which focus 'on the "pure" phenomenographic interest in describing how people conceive of various aspects of their reality' (Marton, 1986, p. 38).

Early work identified the so-called 'deep' and 'surface' learning distinctions. 'Deep' learning is that in which the student invests her learning with her own meanings; 'surface' learning is not necessarily – as some believe – devoid of meaning but is learning whose meaning is alien to the learner (for example, where it is undertaken for instrumental reasons with which the learner does not identify). From the initial identification of deep and surface approaches, an extensive research programme developed, which varied in its degree of identification with phenomenography. Some research relied on quantitative rather than qualitative techniques and linked motivation to deep (intrinsic – interest) and surface (extrinsic – concern with demands) intentions to learn (Entwistle *et al.*, 1979). Later, a range of other characteristics, for example, learning processes (Entwistle and Waterston, 1988); environmental study preferences (Murray-Harvey, 1994); fear of failure and anxiety (Entwistle, 1987); personality variables, locus of control and academic self-concept (Drew and Watkins, 1998); and self-esteem (Abouserie, 1995) were explored in terms of their relationships with learning approaches. Pure phenomenographic research, describing students' conceptions of their reality, has identified six conceptions of learning: a quantitative increase in knowledge;

memorizing; the acquisition for subsequent utilization of facts, or methods; the abstraction of meaning; an interpretative process aimed at understanding reality (Saljo, 1979) and later developing as a person (Marton *et al.*, 1993). It has also led to the exploration of lecturers' conceptions of teaching and learning.

What is the contribution of this research? Essentially it is to remind us that there is a world of the learner and that learners bring to bear on learning their often quite separate and disparate perceptions, intentions, motivations, conceptions and understandings of the context in which they find themselves (Marton, 1981). Although phenomenography does not prescribe methods of teaching, by focusing on the world of the learner it has offered principles to guide the practice of teaching and learning which may additionally provide a helpful aid in developing a pedagogy appropriate to the conditions of supercomplexity. That students variously adopt 'surface' and 'deep' learning approaches, often dependent on their own judgement of the learning that tacitly is being called for in different learning environments (Svensson, 1977), suggests that pedagogies can all too easily produce inappropriate learning approaches. 'Inappropriate' is, of course, a value judgement; but it is also here a logical category. If we intend that students should have a first-hand appropriation of the texts and experiences put their way, if we intend that students should be able to construct knowledge themselves, if we intend that students should attempt to form understandings that begin to develop linkages between their disparate learning experiences, then certain kinds of learning are going to be 'appropriate' while others will be 'inappropriate'.

Has this research effort achieved any more than to give some empirical warrant for what now appears to be a self-evident set of conceptual truths? It has shown that students separately hold conceptions of learning on the one hand and approaches to learning on the other, which are often related (van Rossum and Schenk, 1984); that their approaches to learning are relatively plastic (a student may adopt a deep learning approach in one learning environment and a surface learning approach in another) (Laurillard, 1979); that their learning approaches can change over time (and that higher education in general actually acts to transform deep learning approaches on the part of students into surface learning approaches) (Gow and Kember, 1990); that learning approaches characteristically vary across subject domains (some subjects being apparently more likely to predispose students to adopt surface learning approaches) (Smeby, 1996); and that the learning perceived by students as tacitly embedded in assessments acts to frame their general learning approaches (Biggs, 1996).

This research is significant in that it demonstrates – through its international and cumulative character sustained over twenty years – that educational responsibilities fall upon lecturers, faculty and the institutions within which they function. Evidence is now *there* to the effect that the quality and character of the way that students are taught and the learning environment they experience has profound impacts on the quality of their learning (Entwistle *et al.*, 1992). Where the desire is to engage students in learning in ways which sustain their motivation and interest, to allow them to develop deep and critical understandings of the issues and relate them to their everyday concerns, to develop as individuals, in other words to adopt a deep approach, the learning environment should avoid an overloaded and narrow syllabus, a heavy workload and timetable, time pressure, the creation of anxiety, and the adoption of assessment procedures which require the memorization of factual information. A deep approach is encouraged by being given choice in what and how to learn, a broadly based syllabus and a supportive and lively relationship with staff (Sheppard and Gilbert, 1991).

This research has demonstrated that lecturers now cannot evade their responsibilities to act as educators. As well as being authorities in their epistemic fields, teaching professionalism now requires that they give some attention to the ways in which they construct the learning environment and orchestrate students' learning. In doing so, the research also issues health warnings: it shows that improving pedagogy in higher education cannot be a matter of a technological fix, of simply inserting new modes of learning (such as problem-based learning or computer-based learning). Any change, to be effective, has both to take account of the students' experiences and perceptions of the new learning environments and to be monitored so as to ensure that appropriate learning approaches are likely to be adopted.

Yet, for all that, the gains secured from much of this research effort – across time, across the world – may be limited from the point of view of the practical task of constructing a pedagogy adequate to preparing students for adapting to the conditions of supercomplexity. There are three considerations. Firstly, a supercomplex world is a world without stable meanings; it is a world in which the handling of uncertainty, ambiguity and contestability come to the fore. Developing a truly 'deep' understanding may subsume issues of doubt and uncertainty but, in practice, the development of deep understanding has often been interpreted within disciplinary confines and accepted research paradigms – the development of understanding of a specific and accepted body of knowledge. Secondly, the world, despite its supercomplexity, calls upon students to act purposefully. Much of the research focusing on students' approaches and conceptions has overlooked their being, their engagement with others and their preparedness and capacity to place that learning in practical situations. This has continued to endorse the academics' perception of higher education and learning in higher education as being largely concerned with cognitive processes.

Third, some strands of the research in focusing upon students' conceptions of, approaches to and strategies for learning, have tacitly driven a wedge between students and the objects of their learning. Although Marton and Booth (1997, p. 139) argue that 'person and world, inner and outer are not separated' in phenomenography, the overwhelming body of research has implied that learning is in some ways outside the student: it is the vehicle, the means, by which a portion of the external world is appropriated. As a result much of the research overlooks the most important point in the learning process, the learner herself. Similarly, although encouraging a deep approach implicitly suggests the promotion of the key ideas within the modern Western university of critical thinking, reflection and critical self-reflection, most are given short shrift, especially in the sense of the development of the self that these concepts embody. In her paper, Abouserie (1995) showed that the quality of a student's learning could be improved through an enhancement in his or her self-esteem. It may well be that, before concerning themselves with students' meanings, lecturers intent on bringing about a lifelong love of learning and a resilient self in their students should pay attention to the students' sense of themselves, their self-confidence and the sense of their own worth (as was indicated earlier).

The phenomenographic research tradition, since its inception in Goteborg in the 1970s, has been influential in spawning a vast research programme, much of which is not within the phenomenographic tradition. Some aspects of this research venture are now exhausted seams. Others, which may prove to be richer seams, now need to be mined so as to complement the ore already brought out.

FROM TEACHING TO LEARNING?

Both in parallel to phenomenographical research and within it, there has rightly been interest in the conceptions of teaching held by lecturers in higher education (Fox, 1983). Hardly surprisingly, it turns out that lecturers' conceptions of teaching may be placed upon a continuum between knowledge-centred and student-centred conceptions (Kember and Gow, 1994). More sophisticated relational conceptions, which provide both disciplinary frameworks and students' understandings, exploring the relationships between them are hinted at, but have hardly been studied systematically.

The conceptions of teaching embedded in lecturers' pedagogical practice often diverge from their espoused views of teaching (Murray and Macdonald, 1997). Lecturers claim frequently to value critical thinking among their students, or students' independence of mind, or their autonomy, but often adopt strategies that severely limit students' pedagogical space, deny their own voice, or place students in hock to their lecturers' own frames of thinking. Placed in such a position, students are likely to fall in with the dependent role in which they are cast. For example, both lecturers and students have misgivings about the worth of lectures (Willcoxson, 1998) and yet this pedagogical device – which made good sense in mediaeval universities in an era before the printing press and before the existence of libraries – continues to dominate pedagogical transactions in higher education. A conspiracy has grown up between both teacher and taught to ensure that pedagogical processes are as free as possible of unpredictability, stress, openness and multiple contending voices. But just these conditions are characteristic of supercomplexity and await graduates in the wider world.

In general, we can observe, current pedagogical practices in higher education run the risk of selling students short, a situation we can hypothesize is likely to deepen in the absence of countervailing measures. As students come literally to finance more heavily their own higher education, having to meet increasing proportions of the teaching costs, they are hardly likely actively to seek out pedagogical processes that place more responsibility upon them for their own learning and have, as they might see it, more uncertain outcomes. Accordingly, the ground is laid whereby the conspiracy between teacher and taught for a risk-free, non-challenging learning environment is likely to become more prominent. It is an environment that is inadequate to meet the challenges of supercomplexity.

FROM KNOWING TO DOING?

A pedagogy for supercomplexity has to concern itself with individuals' capacity to act purposively in the world. In the UK, the state, it might seem, has picked up this challenge and, over the last ten years or so, has gone further than any other advanced nation in attempting to reposition higher education by encouraging the explicit inculcation of *skills* in the curriculum. Skills come in various guises. Firstly, they are embedded in the practices of disciplines: not only overt skills, such as laboratory skills, but more inward skills, such as those demanded by the practices of the historian, have received explicit attention. Secondly, skills are integral to particular areas of professional life to which courses may be directed: nursing, social work, teacher education, engineering join the other one hundred or so professional fields represented in higher education, the skills of which lecturers feel they have some responsibility for developing. Thirdly, so-called transferable, core or generic skills are skills that purportedly carry across discrete domains. It is the last of these that the state in the UK has especially sought to enhance in the higher education curriculum, firstly through the Enterprise in Higher Education initiative – in which individual institutions were given substantial grants for whole-institutional programmes of action – and subsequently through particular projects.

The matter of skills in higher education is largely a curriculum matter. It invites the question: to what degree is a focus on skills appropriate in the higher education curriculum? An answer to that question presupposes that we are clear as to what is meant by 'skills' – almost any human activity can be viewed as a skill – the term has become over-saturated with ambiguity. The existence of 'transferable skills' is by no means generally accepted although some universities have put in hand a cross-institutional programme for their implementation. Historically, acquiring a university degree was viewed as providing the essential grounding in critical thinking and analysis which was deemed to provide the necessary skills – which were presumably considered as transferable – for a range of careers. The increasing demands of the post-modern industrial and commercial world for more undergraduates, who also possess a wider range of skills, has led to the questioning of the adequacy of current curricula. This is, as yet, a relatively unexplored area. For example, we do not know whether 'communication skills' are transferable until we have identified what we mean by communication skills, attempted to facilitate their development in students across a range of domains and contexts and evaluated these efforts. However, if transferable skills are to be taught and taken seriously as outcomes of learning they will need to be assessed (Biggs, 1996). If students are not to be increasingly pressured, with the detrimental effects that this can have on their learning and self-development, other assessment demands will need to be reduced.

FROM SKILLS TO SELF?

In addition to transferable skills and discipline-specific skills, research has also taken a particular interest in wider domains of skill application such as work experience and undergraduate projects. Following practice in the United States, the stratagem of enabling students to work on projects that are linked directly to lecturers' research activities has several benefits (McGill, 1990). However, insofar as that research focuses on the presence or otherwise in undergraduate projects of such elements as the criteria for their assessment, the adequacy of their supervision, and the facilities for undertaking them (Henry, 1994) – important though these matters may be – research will and does miss the likely significance of such experiences.

What is possible, and is deserving of more empirical research, is that projects are valuable to the students for multiple reasons, key among them being that they provide students with pedagogical space to develop their own ideas, to inject something of themselves into their learning and to make and to substantiate – even in the form of technological projects – their own truth claims in and on the world. In short, through their projects, students construct themselves as selves, as pedagogical subjects. This set of possibilities, at least, is worthy of inquiry but, for that, empirical research is going to have become more theoretically and, indeed, philosophically adept than it has proved itself hitherto, exploring learning outcomes in relation to a wide range of criteria which might reflect adaptability to the conditions of supercomplexity.

Supercomplexity requires that a pedagogy be operative in three domains – of knowledge, action and self. *In each domain*, pedagogy has the challenge of encouraging the formation of 'authoritative uncertainty' (Goodlad, 1995, p. 30). That is, students have in some way to fashion some kind of stability where no stability is available. A higher education for supercomplexity is faced with this pedagogical challenge in a particularly acute sense because higher education is faced – in the Western tradition – with making problematical that which may be unproblematical. At least, the domain of knowledge and the domain of action are recognized as pedagogical domains in higher education; explicitly much less recognized is the domain of self. But without attention to the domain of self, a pedagogy that attends just to the other two domains of knowledge and action will be unstable: the self will be liable not to be a subject of its destiny but an object, prey to the ideologies and power complexes present in the situations encountered in the wider world.

Although seldom, if ever, construed in these terms, pedagogical practices that have the power to develop the student's self have been increasing in recent years. The keeping of reflective 'logs' or 'diaries', the requirement that students – in certain professional fields – should be able systematically to reflect on and to appraise their own practices, the use of small group learning, and of peer tutoring (in which students are placed in a situation of pedagogical responsibility for others) are all pedagogical practices that can strengthen the student as a subject, capable of effecting purposive change in their environments. However, the widespread adoption within higher education of practices such as these is likely to prove problematic given that their serious usage calls for a diminution within the curriculum of the presence of the interests of subject based communities or those of the professional or industrial sectors.

TEACHING FOR SUPERCOMPLEXITY: TOWARDS A STRATEGY

The instantiation, nationwide, of a higher education pedagogy for the twenty-first century is a long way off, but it is a feasible aspiration. Strategies will have to be developed at national, institutional and departmental levels but the strategies will be ineffective unless put into the service of large, overarching, theoretically sound policies. We have sketched out the outlines of such a pedagogical theory built upon the idea of supercomplexity. The world of the twenty-first century into which graduates will have to make their way is likely to be one of ever-widening uncertainty, challenge and conflict, bearing on the three domains of knowledge, action and self. Criteria of truth, the will to act and the sense of one's identity will be relentlessly tested and will be subject to continuing change. In addition, graduates from universities will have placed upon them particular expectations to exercise leadership in public knowledge, collective action and self-development. Graduates will be expected continually to reinvent themselves as well as their environment. Amidst contending frameworks in the three domains of knowledge, action and self, they will be expected to be triply creative.

Such a conception of pedagogy requires *not* a paradigm change for that would imply that approaches to pedagogy are entirely awry. That, as we have seen, is not the case. There are many examples of pedagogy moving in appropriate directions. There are, however, three system-wide issues that need to be addressed. Firstly, pedagogy has to recognize that it is faced with educational challenges; that is to say, the academic community has to become interested in education as such. Secondly, fora have to be developed that enable the different interests that are bearing on pedagogy in higher education to come together, including academics in their separate academic groupings, employers, professional bodies and students. Lastly, means have to be found in which new models of pedagogy can be tried, developed and evaluated that have a serious chance of addressing and developing the student subjectivities demanded by a supercomplex world.

It just may be that, in the UK, the new national Institute for Learning and Teaching in Higher Education can address all three of these challenges; but no one body can by itself bring off such an ambitious and far-ranging agenda. For anything approaching success, all the parties have to work together, including the universities separately and collectively, the government, academic epistemic communities and the students' representative bodies. There are, in fact, signs of just such a conjunction of interests now developing.

The desirable strategy that emerges, therefore, is a kind of matrix structure in which the various ingredients of faculty development, dialogue and experimentation (the horizontal axis, as it were) have to be implemented at the different levels of national system, institution and department (the vertical axis). It may well be that subject networks and regional groupings of institutions might have to be inserted as additional vertical layers. It is also clear that the establishment of widespread pedagogical development, experiment and evaluation (constituting yet a third axis) would open up pedagogic innovation. Accordingly, any tendency to develop a favoured pedagogical approach for the whole of higher education has to be ruled off-side.

The critical level of strategy implementation is that of the lecturers and their self-definitions. It depends on the extent to which academics frame themselves as 'physicists', 'engineers', 'historians' and so on and the extent to which they are receptive to considering pedagogical matters. That consideration suggests, in turn, that pedagogical innovation has to be driven forward departmentally (Willcoxson and Walker, 1995) but, to be effective, it will have to be aimed at raising awareness of and probably transforming the students' learning environment (Entwistle et al., 1992; Biggs, 1993). It is easy enough to urge that pedagogic innovation depends on lecturers feeling that they have some ownership of any such changes (van Driel et al., 1997). But the issue remains: what might be meant by 'ownership'? Surely, it must in part incorporate an acknowledgement that faculty have themselves to believe in any such innovation which, in turn, means that such innovations have to be bound into the self-identity of members of faculty but that self-identity may have little, if any, space for a concern with pedagogical issues.

There is a conundrum here: faculty in higher education may be resistant to pedagogic change and yet pedagogic change is dependent on their assimilating it to their self-understanding if it is to get successfully off the ground. Clearly, the resolution of this conundrum calls for institutional leadership which is able to form the communicative conditions in which externally perceived possibilities may be internalized in such a way that they are worked through and bring about sustained changes in professional practices which ensure that the students' experience of learning facilitates them for adaptation to conditions of supercomplexity.

Initiatives such as the training and systematic professional development of lecturers and the inclusion of pedagogical matters within staff appraisal will be counterproductive unless set within an open-ended professional environment. If higher education institutions reward staff for demonstrable interest, and involvement in pedagogical innovation, this will assist in the development of receptivity to new ideas. However, this may also be ineffective unless supported by the injection of ongoing opportunities enabling faculty to discuss and explore the theoretical and practical challenges such innovations present.

Institutions will need to adopt the same principles in reshaping the ways that faculty approach teaching as faculty need to adopt in relation to the reshaping of student learning. The process must be authentic, the learning environment open, there must be an alignment of the learning process with educational goals and assessment criteria must encourage the highest levels of intellectual functioning. The characteristics that are called for *within* the pedagogic situation have to become characteristic of the institutional hinterland that bears *on* that pedagogic situation.

CONCLUSION

Worldwide, higher education has been undergoing rapid and considerable change. The degree of change experienced in the UK has probably been more severe than almost any other advanced country in the world, as the system has – within a decade or so – been transformed from an elite system to a mass system of higher education (albeit one that continues to incorporate 'important elite elements' (Trowler, 1998, p. 18). Unit costs, evaluation systems, managerial disciplines, curricula, professional space, stakeholder claims, and accountability practices: all have changed in ways that have brought about an intensity of academic work and an openness. Many of the academy's fundamental practices have changed. But, so far, pedagogical practices have exhibited a resistance to change.

However, change is now evident in the innermost 'intimacy' of higher education (Scott, 1995), in precisely those pedagogic practices. Less evident are signs that the changes in pedagogy are attributable to thought-through understandings of the scale of the pedagogical challenges facing higher education. To return to our starting point, the globalization of which the Dearing Report spoke is but a symptom of the much larger complex of features of the world that we have termed *supercomplexity*. A genuinely higher education, as the highest form of education, has a responsibility to prepare students fully for that world of uncertainty, challenge and turbulence. Appropriate pedagogies for such a world are not to be caught by talk of the production of competences and skills, however 'generic' or 'transferable'. Instead, they will be pedagogies that enable graduates purposively to effect change in that world, and to have the enduring will to do so, even though those graduates realize – through their higher education – that there can in such a world be no final warrant for their actions and claims, and their own sense of self.

It follows that a higher education for the twenty-first century not only calls for a pedagogy for supercomplexity; it calls for new thinking about higher education itself.

REFERENCES

Abouserie, R. (1995) Self-esteem and achievement motivation, *Studies in Higher Education*, 20(1): 19-26.

AGR (Association of Graduate Recruiters) (1995) *Skills for Graduates in the 21st Century*, Cambridge: AGR.

Barnett, R. (1999) *Realizing the University*, Buckingham: Open University Press (in press).

Becher, T. (1989) *Academic Tribes and Territories*, Buckingham: Open University Press.

Biggs, J. (1993) From theory to practice: a cognitive systems approach, *Higher Education Research and Development*, 12(1): 78–86.

Biggs, J. (1996) Enhancing teaching through constructive alignment, *Higher Education*, 32(3): 347–64.

Brew, A. and Boud, D. (1995) Teaching and research: establishing the vital link with learning, *Higher Education*, 29(3): 261–273.

Clark, B.R. (1997) The modern integration of research activities with teaching and learning, *Journal of Higher Education*, 21(1): 31–42.

Dahlgren, L.O. and Marton, F. (1978) Students' conceptions of subject matter: an aspect of learning and teaching in higher education, *Studies in Higher Education*, 3(1): 25–35.

Delanty, G. (1998) The idea of the university in the global era: from knowledge as an end to the end of knowledge?, *Social Epistemology*, 12(1): 3–26.

Drew, P.Y. and Watkins, D. (1998) Affective variables, learning approaches and academic achievement: a causal modelling investigation with Hong Kong tertiary students, *British Journal of Educational Psychology*, 68(2): 173–188.

Dunkin, M. and Precians, R. (1992) Award-winning university teachers' concepts of teaching, *Higher Education*, 24(4): 483–502.

Entwistle, N. (1987) Motivation to learn: conceptualisations and practicalities, *British Journal of Educational Studies*, XXXV(2): 129–48.

Entwistle, N., Hanley, M. and Hounsell, D. (1979) Identifying distinctive approaches to studying, *Higher Education*, 8(4): 365–80.

Entwistle, N., Thompson, S. and Tait, H. (1992) *Guidelines for Promoting Effective Learning in Higher Education*, Edinburgh: Centre for Research on Learning and Instruction, University of Edinburgh.

Entwistle, N. and Waterston, S. (1988) Approaches to studying and levels of processing in university students, *British Journal of Educational Psychology*, 58(3): 258–65.

Fox, D. (1983) Personal theories of teaching, *Studies in Higher Education*, 8(2):

151–63.

Francis, H. (1994) *Teachers Listening to Learners' Voices*, the thirteenth Vernon-Wall Lecture. Leicester: British Psychological Society, Education Section.

Goodlad, S. (1995) *The Quest for Quality: Sixteen Forms of Heresy in Higher Education*, Milton Keynes: Open University Press.

Gottlieb, E.E. and Keith, B. (1997) The academic research-teaching nexus in eight industrialized countries, *Higher Education*, 34(3): 397–420.

Gow, L. and Kember, D. (1990) Does higher education promote independent learning?, *Higher Education*, 19(3): 307–322.

Hartley, D. (1995) The 'McDonaldization' of higher education: food for thought?, *Oxford Review of Education*, 21(4): 409–23.

Henry, J. (1994) *Teaching through Projects*, London: Kogan Page.

Ingleton, C. (1995) Gender and learning: does emotion make a difference?, *Higher Education*, 30(3): 323–55.

Johansson, B., Marton, F. and Svensson, L. (1985) An approach to describing learning as a change between qualitatively different conceptions, in A.L. Pines and T.H. West (eds.) *Cognitive Structure and Conceptual Change*, New York: Academic Press.

Johnston, S. (1996) What can we learn about teaching from our best university teachers?, *Teaching in Higher Education*, 1(2): 213–25.

Kember, D. and Gow, L. (1994) Orientations to teaching and their effect on the quality of student learning, *Journal of Higher Education*, 65(1): 59–74.

Laurillard, D.M. (1979) The processes of student learning, *Higher Education*, 8(4): 395–409.

Lyotard, J-F. (1984) *The Postmodern Condition: A Report on Knowledge*, Manchester: Manchester University Press.

Martin, G. (1997) Teachers or researchers? The perception of professional role among university lecturers, *Innovations in Education and Training International*, 34(2): 154–59.

Marton, F. (1981) Phenomenography: Describing conceptions of the world around us, *Instructional Science*, 10(2), 177–200.

Marton, F. (1986) Phenomenography: A research approach to investigating different understandings of reality, *Journal of Thought*, 21: 28–49.

Marton, F. (1988) Phenomenography: a research approach to investigating different understandings of reality, in R. Sherman and R.B. Webb (eds.) *Qualitative Research in Education: Focus and Methods*, London: Falmer Press.

Marton, F. and Booth, S. (1997) *Learning and Awareness*, Mahwah, New Jersey: LEA.

Marton, F. and Saljo, R. (1976a) On qualitative differences in learning I: Outcome and process, *British Journal of Educational Psychology*, 46: 4–11.

Marton, F. and Saljo, R. (1976b) On qualitative differences in learning II: Outcome as a function of the learner's conception of the task, *British Journal of Educational Psychology*, 46: 115–27.

Marton, F., Dall'Alba, G. and Beaty, E. (1993) Conceptions of learning, *International Journal of Educational Research*, 19(3): 277–300.

McGill, T.E. (1990) Special projects laboratory in experimental psychology, in J. Hartley and W. McKeachie (eds.) *Teaching Psychology: A Handbook*, Hillsdale: Erlbaum.

Murray, K. and MacDonald, R. (1997) The disjunction between lecturers' conceptions of teaching and their claimed educational practices, *Higher Education*, 33 (3): 331–49.

Murray-Harvey, R. (1994) Learning styles and approaches to learning: distinguishing between concepts and instruments, *British Journal of Educational Psychology*, 64(3): 373–88.

NCIHE (1997) *Higher Education in the Learning Society*, Report of the National Committee of Inquiry into Higher Education, London: HMSO.

Rowland, S. (1996) Relationships between teaching and research, *Teaching in Higher Education*, 1(1): 7–20.

Saljo, R. (1979) *Learning in the Learner's Perspective. I. Some Commonsense Conceptions*, Reports from the Department of Education, No 76, Goteborg: Goteborg University.

Saunders, C. and Saunders, E. (1993) *The Identification of Teaching Skills: Expert Teachers' Perceptions of University Teaching*, Research Report. Coleraine: Education Department, University of Ulster.

Scott, P. (1995) *The Meanings of Mass Higher Education*, Buckingham: Open University Press.

Sheppard, C. and Gilbert, J. (1991) Course design, teaching method and student epistemology, *Higher Education*, 22(3): 229–51.

Smeby, J. (1996) Disciplinary differences in university teaching, *Studies in Higher Education*, 21(1): 69–79.

Smeby, J-C. (1998) Knowledge production and knowledge transition: the interaction between research and teaching at universities, *Teaching in Higher Education*, 3(1): 5–20.

Svensson, L. (1977) On qualitative differences in learning: III. Study skill and learning, *British Journal of Educational Psychology*, 47: 233–43.

Trowler, P. (1998) *Academics Responding to Change: New Higher Education Frameworks and Academic Cultures*, Buckingham: Open University Press.

van Driel, J.H., Verloop, N., van Werven, H. I. and Dekkers, H. (1997) Teachers' craft knowledge and curriculum innovation in higher education engineering, *Higher Education*, 34(1): 105–22.

van Rossum, E.J. and Schenk, S.M. (1984) The relationship between learning conception, study strategy and learning outcome, *British Journal of Educational Psychology*, 54(1): 73–83.

Willcoxson, L. (1998) The impacts of academics' learning and teaching preferences on their teaching practice: a pilot study, *Studies in Higher Education*, 23(1): 59–70.

Willcoxson, L. and Walker, P. (1995) Valuing teaching: a strategy for changing the organizational culture of an academic department, *Higher Education Research and Development*, 14 (2): 269–78.

8

Pedagogy in Work-based Contexts

Toni Griffiths and David Guile

This chapter aims to analyse learning and pedagogy in work-based contexts, a term derived from two strands of the research and policy literature which are often assumed to be distinct. One strand encompasses the literature on apprenticeship, a concept which in the UK has historically been associated with craft and technician occupations. It is now more associated with a much wider range of occupations and describes a structure within which young people in transition from school or from higher education to work can learn and, most importantly, demonstrate their workplace abilities and potential whilst at the same time developing their civic and social identity (Heikkinen, 1995; Fuller and Unwin, 1998). Apprenticeship encompasses in the UK such disparate schemes as the Modern Apprenticeship, launched in 1994, but also company initiatives aimed at postgraduates, for example, the Teaching Company scheme (Senker et al., 1993) and is now being broadened to include the idea of a Graduate Apprenticeship.

From its outset, the Modern Apprenticeship was seen to serve many purposes (Fuller, 1996). Following the failure of the Youth Training scheme and the collapse of traditional apprenticeships in a relatively narrow range of occupations, it represented an attempt by the then Conservative Government to strengthen the UK's historically weak vocational education and training provision by trying to involve industry more closely with the design and development of the programme (Fennell, 1994). However, the Modern Apprenticeship principally represented a work-based programme which provided young people with an opportunity to gain a National Vocational Qualification (NVQ) at Level 3.

The second strand of the literature on which our term, 'work-based contexts', rests consists of the 'family' of work-based activities, such as work experience, work shadowing, work visits, work simulations. These are commonly offered to students in full-time 14–19 education in the UK and are viewed as part of a larger spectrum of activities and programmes of work under the umbrella of the 'work-related curriculum' (Wellington, 1993; Harris, 1997). The chief of these, work experience, is a characteristic feature of UK education and is also a significant component of several major education business partnerships initiated by big companies (Miller et al., 1995) as well as being a feature of the Labour Government's New Deal. This strand of work-based activities represents relatively recent developments within the UK and other European education and training systems (Griffiths *et al.*, 1992; Jamieson *et al.*, 1988). These have now become invested with assumptions, traditionally associated with apprenticeship, about rites of passage, initiation and completion rituals and learning how to become an independent adult.

Although these different approaches to learning in work-based contexts have always been seen as distinct in the UK and elsewhere in Europe, they appear increasingly to have more in common than has traditionally been recognized, something borne out by the UK and EU education and training policy literature (EC, 1997). Further, there is evidence that research on apprenticeship and the 'family' of work-based activities has turned to similar theoretical traditions to formulate ideas about what pedagogies may best support learning in work-based contexts (Enkenburg, 1995; Rainbird and Ainley, 1999).

This chapter will refer first to the UK and EU policy and research literature to establish the basis of pedagogic comparison between work experience, work shadowing, work visits and work simulations and the Modern Apprenticeship programme. We will also note trends to convergence between UK and EU education and training policies and agendas for learning in work-based contexts – and the growth of company-initiated programmes for various forms of education business partnership.

Having clarified the context, we will address three questions concerning (a) the dominant assumptions about human development and models of learning which have underpinned approaches to learning in work-based contexts, (b) the extent to which reconceptualization of learning as a social process points to the need for new pedagogic models for supporting learning in work-based contexts and (c) the challenges which this poses. We will explore the implications of these issues and go on to identify approaches to or models of work-based learning which avoid narrow definitions of learning as a form of training or simulated experience or mechanistic outcome. These ideas will be further explored through a model embodying the concept of connectivity and the extent to which new pedagogical and curriculum frameworks may develop from a social theory of learning across formal and informal contexts.

LEARNING IN WORK-BASED CONTEXTS: UK AND EU CONSIDERATIONS

There is widespread acceptance throughout the UK and the European Union more generally that current and predicted changes in the organization of work are generating new skill requirements and occupational profiles (Brown, 1997). These changes are related amongst other things to new product and process technologies, changing production concepts (for example, 'just-in-time', 'diversified quality production') and business improvement strategies (for example, Total Quality Management, Business Process Re-engineering). One consequence has been an increasing focus upon the role of post-16 education and training policies in enhancing the overall 'human capital' within the EU (Lasonen and Young, 1998). Alongside a desire to reform post-16 curricula so as to promote opportunities for progression into higher education, there has also been a renewed interest in the contribution of work-based learning to strategies for enhancing productivity and economic growth (Rubenson and Schuetze, 1993). In particular, there has been a marked interest in the different forms of learning which are possible in work-based contexts as a strategy for assisting young people in making a more effective transition to and progress through the world of work (EC, 1995).

Recent policy documentation provides clear evidence of the similarities between the UK and the European Union with respect to policies to promote learning in work-based contexts. The White Paper, *Success for All* (DfEE, 1997a), which articulated the Labour Government's commitment to providing all students with access to high quality education and training, emphasized the contribution of 'partnership activities' and the provision of opportunities to learn in work-based contexts as ways of enhancing motivation, raising standards and preparing young people for the challenges of working in the twenty-first century. It also reaffirmed the Government's intention to ensure that the Modern Apprenticeship programme provided a high quality alternative to full-time study. Research on school effectiveness and improvement has complemented many of these themes. For instance, it has shown that an openness to partnership in learning is a characteristic feature of effective schooling. Sammons *et al.* (1995) offer a summary of the most common factors found to be associated with effective and improving schools and partnerships, often involving businesses and work-based learning, have a significant role to play.

In relation to the EU, several key texts – for example, *Teaching and Learning: Towards the Learning Society* (EC, 1995) and *Learning in the Information Society: Action Plan for a European Initiative* (EC, 1997) – have acknowledged that learning in work-based contexts is a significant concern of EU education and training policy. Nevertheless, as Green *et al.* observe (1997), on the basis of the evidence available there is significant variation in the quality and standard of learning in work-based contexts across Europe. The European Commission's EUROPROF project represents one initiative in addressing this variation through the professional development of Vocational Education and Training (VET) professionals and through fostering an innovative research and development culture (Brown, 1997). Whereas quality may vary, common assumptions may nevertheless be detected about the nature and significance of learning in work-based contexts. For example:

(a) a human capital perspective of the value of learning in work-based contexts for EU human resource development which has emphasized

investment in education and training whilst neglecting the study of pedagogic processes (some kind of human capital perspective is, of course,
an inescapable element of policy for public education);

(b) an emphasis both on the differences between formal and informal education and the superiority of the technical-rational model (discussed later)
of education and training;

(c) that learning in work-related contexts is multi-functional. In other words,
it can provide students with an opportunity (i) to enhance the links
between their programmes of formal education and training – either in
vocational education and training or in general education – and real work
contexts, (ii) to acquire occupationally-specific skills, economic and industrial awareness or accreditation for the development of generic competences and key skill development and (iii) to become lifelong learners
through broadening the basis of their experience;

(d) the centrality of a functional model for the delivery of apprenticeships
and work experience, the most widely accepted form of learning in work-
related contexts. (Policy models cannot, of course, avoid being functional, designed to meet particular ends or goals; however, the dominant
functional focus emphasizes management arrangements rather than pedagogic processes.)

Apart from these broad and interrelated assumptions, there are other and
more specific assumptions about different forms of learning in work-based
contexts. For example, there is an unquestioning assumption that the different forms can equally provide opportunities for young people to develop their
key skills or generic competences. Not only is the development of key skills
an explicit requirement of the UK's Modern Apprenticeship programme
(Fuller, 1996), it is also being promoted as a desirable outcome of more general programmes of work experience (DfEE, 1997b). Similarly, there is an
assumption that both learning contexts are expressions of the wider educational interest in developing more learner-centred forms of education and
training. We explore the implications of these assumptions below.

FORMAL AND INFORMAL LEARNING AND WORK-BASED CONTEXTS

Over the years, most educationists have accepted that formal and informal
contexts involve different types of learning and result in different learning outcomes. Resnick has provided a succinct exposition of this traditional view,
arguing that educationists have assumed that the characteristics of mental
activity outside formal education contrast with the learning processes typical
of formal education. She suggests that learning in formal educational contexts
(i) is an individual process, (ii) involves a purely mental activity based on the
manipulation of symbols and (iii) results in the production of generalized concepts. Learning in work-related contexts is, by contrast, a collaborative process

leading to highly context-specific forms of reasoning and skills (Resnick, 1987).
Resnick summarizes the ways in which learning in educational institutions
may differ from learning outside institutions as shown in Table 8.1.

Table 8.1   Differences between learning in and outside institutions

Learning in institutions	Learning outside institutions
decontextualized	has 'real' content
second-hand	first-hand
needs motivating	comes easily
tends to be individualistic	is co-operative/shared
assessed by others	self-assessed
formal structure	few structures

The acceptance of such differences between formal learning and learning
in work-based contexts has been associated with certain policy priorities in
most EU countries. First, formal learning is heavily privileged in relation to
other types of learning on the understanding that it provides the basis or
foundation of scientific knowledge about human activities and practices.
Second, curricula in schools, colleges and universities have been organized
through the classification and framing of discipline-based knowledge on the
understanding that the purpose of education is to build the student's sense
of mastery of a discipline (Barnett, 1997). Third, the acceptance that formal
learning is superior to informal learning has led to much greater value being
placed upon decontextualized knowledge and skills than 'situated' or contextual knowledge (Dall'Alba and Sandberg, 1996) and therefore the consideration of the relationship between the two and the implications for
pedagogy have been neglected. Fourth, it has produced a view of the process
of education and training in which bodies of knowledge and types of skill
are separate and bounded entities which can be taught independently of their
actual, practical application (Lasonen, 1997; Lasonen and Young, 1998).

The legacy of decontextualized pedagogy for learning in work-based contexts is considerable. Assumptions about the superiority of formal learning
underlie divisions within education and training systems and between academic and vocational curricula in the UK and across Europe – as the EC
Leonardo da Vinci project at the Institute of Education on parity of esteem
has demonstrated (Lasonen and Young, 1998). These divisions have meant
that work experience, work shadowing and work visits have, at the very best,
been seen as a marginal activity within academic curricula. In so far as work-
related activities have been associated with the academic curriculum, this
remains the case chiefly in the UK and to a degree in such Northern European
countries as Sweden. In such cases, work-related activities have tended to be
part of broad-based programmes of general education or closely aligned with
courses in Business and Economics.

There are also quite differing views about the relationship between formal
and informal learning within apprenticeship across the EU. The UK's Modern

Apprenticeship is characterized by quite different approaches to this issue. Some schemes try to reconcile the relationship between formal and informal learning to support apprentices in developing their Key Skills, while other schemes only choose to use the NVQ framework to accredit workplace learning and minimize the key skill component (Fuller, 1996). The UK's Teaching Company scheme, however, (Senker et al., 1993) is an example of how companies and higher education institutions have jointly negotiated the formal education component of postgraduate schemes. By contrast, Siemens AG in Berlin has established its own on-site integrated training school, enabling it to provide both the work-based and the education-based components of the dual system's apprenticeship scheme and the trainers and teachers to plan modules of work together, producing a more flexible pattern of training (Griffiths and Miller, 1996). Overall, greater thought has been given in 'dual' systems like Germany's to the relationship of the work experience component with formal study (Bremer and Heidegger, 1997). Where research has explicitly addressed the transition to work from school and from higher education, it has tended to adopt a functional and normative view, concentrating upon models of delivery and institutional arrangements.

Another neglected aspect is an exploration of how work-based activities can provide the context for 'deep' learning, as opposed to 'surface' learning (see, for example, Ramsden, 1992) and to what extent pedagogy in relation to work-based contexts may or may not support such a form of learning (Engestrom, 1995). Contrasting these approaches to learning points to the potential of work-based learning contexts for the active engagement of the learner (see Table 8.2).

Recognition of the different approaches to learning is necessary in developing appropriate pedagogies. In work-based as in other contexts this implies engaging students in ways that are appropriate to the deployment of deep approaches and involves a pedagogy that is challenging and hard work. Later in this chapter we describe a model aimed at facilitating this deep approach.

THE LEGACY OF HUMAN CAPITAL THEORY FOR LEARNING IN WORK-BASED CONTEXTS

The broad acceptance in the UK and EU education and training policy literature of the premises of human capital theory (Becker, 1964) has had a considerable effect upon recent thinking about learning in a variety of work-based contexts (Griffiths, 1999).

In human capital theory, the rationale for and the level of investment in education and training is related primarily to perceived economic return. It has therefore proved particularly attractive to policy makers in their attempts to justify investment in education and training to employers and within EU member states more generally (EC, 1995; Lasonen, 1997; DfEE, 1997a). In

Table 8.2 'Deep' and 'surface' approaches to learning

Deep approach

Focusing, for example on concepts applicable to solving the problem.
Relating previous knowledge to new knowledge.
Relating knowledge from different courses.
Relating theoretical ideas to everyday experience.
Relating and distinguishing evidence and argument.
Organizing and structuring content into a coherent whole.

Surface approach

Focusing on 'signs'.
Focusing on unrelated parts of the task.
Memorizing information for assessments.
Associating facts and concepts unreflectingly.
Failing to distinguish principles from examples.
Treating the task as an external imposition.

(Summarized from Entwistle and Marton, 1984)

the UK, this has also involved an attempt to address social exclusion through the introduction of the New Deal which aims to provide access to training for unemployed people. Further, it has fuelled the growth of education business partnerships initiated by companies such as Rover, BT, BP, The Post Office, BA and many others (Miller *et al.*, 1995). These developments, including the New Deal approach, while interesting and stimulating from several perspectives, do not necessarily have a great deal to say about the development of pedagogy in relation to work-based learning. The schemes have attempted several approaches to lifelong learning and to the world of work. For example, in the case of Rover, work experience placements aimed to be based upon learning agreements linked with teacher placements (Simpson, 1991). In the case of the Ford programme, however, the well-known Employee Development and Assistance Programme encourages employees voluntarily to undertake learning activities without necessarily any reference to the workplace (DfEE, 1995). From a different perspective, and possibly getting closer to pedagogical concerns, The Post Office's partnership programme with the University of Warwick included a three-day residential course for students following the University's Postgraduate Certificate in Education course. The aims of the residential course were to explore the potential of education business links for developing teaching and learning and to lay the foundations for further professional development through links with business (Abbott *et al.*, 1996).

Many of the developments in recent years are consistent with one of the main tenets of human capital theory which sees the whole question of innovation and continuous improvement as primarily the result of exogenous, technological processes. Innovation within human capital theory is not, in general, perceived as being particularly affected by the introduction of new learning processes (Ellstrom, 1997) nor by the development of the types of 'learning environment' within workplaces which support learning (Gherherdi *et al.*, 1998; Guile and Young, 1999b). Human capital theory tends not to be concerned with the contribution which different models of education and training, and their different assumptions about the process of human development, might make to future competitiveness and 'employability' (Ellstrom, 1997). However, it is increasingly accepted in the industrial management literature (Lundvall and Johnson, 1994) that these issues are at least as significant to the process of innovation. Whatever else education business partnership programmes have accomplished, companies have generally neglected the need for a broader definition of human capital theory which could take a more strategic view of the role of learning processes. The consequence has been a failure at policy level to press for new theoretical and conceptual frameworks for relating learning in work-based contexts to formal education and training.

THE TECHNICAL-RATIONAL MODEL OF EDUCATION AND TRAINING AND LEARNING IN WORK-BASED CONTEXTS

Traditionally, in both formal education and work-based contexts, competence has been viewed in terms of the attributes of the individuals and the tasks to be performed. By and large, these attributes have typically been described in terms of the knowledge, skills and attitudes required for programmes of study or the areas of work in which students intended to engage or the tasks they were expected to perform. This technical-rational model of education and training involves a functional perspective of the role of education and training, with an emphasis on adaption, that is to the attitudes and tasks referred to above (Ellstrom, 1997). Further, conventional views of developing competence make an additional assumption: that it is possible to decontextualize competence not only from practice but also from its underlying knowledge and its context (cultural, social, technological and organizational). In fact, the technical-rational model of education and training treats practice and context quite separately and, whereas at a policy level, it is recognized that there will always be a tendency to decontextualize, it is important to remember that learning always takes place in contexts. A challenge for policy makers lies, therefore, in incorporating into strategy both the importance of 'context' in learning and the broader learning goals which transcend specific contexts.

A prime aim of workplace learning has been to mould and adapt skills and this has influenced ideas about pedagogy. Students engaged in different forms of work-based practice have been viewed as 'containers' (Lave, 1993), while knowledge and skills have been viewed as 'entities' which can be taught quite separately from the context of their use (Gherherdi *et al.*, 1998) – and these assumptions have influenced pedagogy. Moreover, it is assumed that, once work-based learning has contributed to 'filling people up' with new knowledge, skills and attitudes, they will be able to master the new skills required of them and conduct themselves in accordance with new workplace expectations (Guile and Fonda, 1999). Because individuals are assumed unconsciously to assimilate relevant workplace knowledge, skills and attitudes and to internalize the implications of occupational changes occurring in the workplace, the pedagogic practices involved have been little questioned. Once the relation between any form of work-related learning and formal education and training has been conceptualized in accordance with prevailing technical-rational assumptions, there then appears to be little reason to question the process of learning or the form of competence development, as the research literature makes clear (cf. Dall'Alba and Sandberg, 1996).

A philosophical basis of the curriculum critique of the traditional model of education and training lies in the work of Dewey (1966). As Prawat has noted (Prawat, 1993), many educationists have interpreted Dewey as the key proponent of the ideas that all stages and phases of education should be made 'relevant' to students and that pedagogy should involve a more problem-based approach to education and greater use of inquiry-based models. Dewey's influence can be seen quite clearly in much of the literature that addresses learning in work-based contexts and many of its academic and professional advocates turned to him to provide its rationale (see in Jamieson *et al.*, 1988, Miller *et al.*, 1991). Dewey has frequently been cited in justification of the long tradition of 'learning by doing' central to many models of apprenticeship (Guile and Young, 1999a). It is questionable, however, as to how far Dewey's influence informed thinking at a political and policy level in the UK where developments have been pragmatic and not noted for their philosophical or theoretical justification, owing more to broad political feeling than to theory – as, for example, in the famous 'Ruskin' speech of Prime Minister James Callaghan (TES, 1976).

One consequence of this critique of the technical-rational model of education and training is that the experiential learning paradigm, specifically Kolb's idea of the experiential learning cycle derived from the work of Dewey (Kolb, 1984), has been perceived as providing a more sophisticated, theoretical framework for understanding the challenge of learning in work-based contexts. It appeared to offer apprentices a more relevant framework within which to analyse their work-based learning than the 'assimilation' (Coy, 1989) or 'intuition' (Dreyfuss and Dreyfuss, 1986) theories of learning which were previously associated with the 'institution of apprenticeship' (Guile and Young, 1999a). In the case of activities like work experience, this appeared to complement the Deweyan inquiry-based methodology of teaching and learning (Watts, 1991).

Building the theoretical case for learning in work-based contexts and defining the pedagogic approach to such forms of learning around the idea of experiential learning has in effect, however, maintained the distinctions and status differences between formal and informal learning identified by Resnick. Those who advocated a distinct pedagogy for work-related activity in schools and colleges did so on the basis that the framework of experiential learning implied a separate and different pedagogy and model of learning from that of the mainstream academic curriculum (Miller *et al.*, 1991).

By and large, this left the mainstream curriculum broadly unaffected and the 'work-related curriculum' effectively separate from it – despite the Employment Department's Technical and Vocational Education Initiative (TVEI) which attempted a better integration of the two. An alternative course would have been to formulate a more unified approach to the curriculum involving new curriculum concepts and a pedagogy which might produce better articulation between formal and informal learning and a reconsideration of the process of teaching and learning (Young, 1998). In the case of apprenticeship, it has been acknowledged that the emphasis on experiential learning has rarely led to any fundamental rethinking of pedagogy but has served only to reinforce the tradition of 'learning by doing' (Heikkinen, 1995; Rainbird and Ainley, 1999). Neither has it led to the development of new theoretical and conceptual frameworks with the purpose of relating apprentices' learning in work-based contexts to programmes of formal education and training (Gherherdi *et al.*, 1998).

Another development which also led to a critique of the technical-rational model of education and training was the emergence of the 'outcomes' model (Jessup, 1990). Although initially geared towards achieving the reform of vocational awards and qualifications in the UK – and hence its association with the Modern Apprenticeship – specific aspects of the 'outcomes' ideology have slowly become assimilated into mainstream educational thinking and practice (Hodgson and Spours, 1997). The vision of education and training articulated by Jessup tried to address two objectives. First, it tried to reform the traditional conception of education and training by emphasizing the outcome rather than the process. Second, it in effect adopted a deliberately agnostic position on any particular pedagogic practice within education and training. The 'outcomes' model of education and training suggested that it was more liberalizing and egalitarian to adopt a system which attached prime importance to the 'outcome', the result, and did not prescribe the form of teaching and learning necessary to gain a qualification (Jessup, 1990). Initially, these ideas were received with a certain hostility by the educational community (Hyland, 1992; Whitty and Wilmott, 1992) and they informed the design and delivery only of vocational qualifications such as National Vocational Qualifications (NVQs) or general vocational awards such as the General National Vocational Qualification (GNVQ). Over the last few years, however, the idea of 'learning outcomes' has increasingly become associated with the 'work-related curriculum' (Harris *et al.*, 1995). Learning outcomes have been perceived as providing a concrete focus for students in relating the learning and knowledge gained from their work-based experiences and presenting it for accreditation. They have also been used more generally and academic syllabi and even degree courses are sometimes expressed in these terms. We shall return to the implications of these issues.

PEDAGOGY IN WORK-BASED CONTEXTS

Three underlying features of learning in work-based contexts have been identified: the reaction to the differences between formal and informal learning; the limitations of human capital theory which has emphasized investment in education and training whilst neglecting the study of pedagogic processes; and the limitations of the technical-rational model of education and training which has marginalized the study of work-related practice. In this section we address the influence of these factors on ideas about pedagogy in work-based contexts.

Both in the UK and more generally across the EU, the different traditions of learning in work-based contexts have all tended to see experience as the key source of learning. Further, experience has also been seen as the central means by which students acquire worthwhile knowledge and skill about the world of work. As noted above, the philosophy of experiential learning has been widely endorsed in the literature on learning in work-based contexts. It has generally led to teaching strategies – in schools, colleges and the best company programmes – designed to help students/apprentices 'capture' the essence of their work-based experiences either through a debriefing process or through the use of a diary to record experience. (Fuller, 1996; DfEE, 1996).

A parallel development in the relevant UK literature, however, has been to view the idea of 'learning outcomes' as complementary to the objectives of experiential learning. They have been seen as possessing several strengths. First, it has been argued that they provide a way of supporting the development of learner autonomy and learner self-discipline, which is a key objective of UK and EU policy makers (Green et al., 1997). Second, it has been asserted that learning outcomes are central to improving the quality of teaching and learning in work-based contexts and that they should be specified as rigorously as possible if students are successfully to use their experience as the basis of learning (Harris et al. 1995). Third, it has been suggested that they provide a more concrete focus for helping students develop their key skills (Miller, 1996; Oates and Fettes, 1997). Thus, the idea that experience provides incontestable evidence of learning and that learning outcomes provide stronger guarantees of learning has become axiomatic from the evidence of the literature. The key challenge has therefore been seen as how to define a series of work-based learning outcomes which students or apprentices may acquire, for example during their work experience or on-the-job learning, and which they may present for formal or informal accreditation. The situation is, however, rather more complex than this.

As the debates on adult education have noted (Usher and Edwards, 1994; Usher et al., 1997), there is a danger that, once experience is taken to be 'foundational' and 'authoritative', educationists tend not to challenge its value, intelligibility and meaning. Further, as Boud et al. have noted (1993), the conception of experience that lies at the heart of pedagogies of experiential learning, including learning in work-based contexts, is rooted in a rational/positivist epistemology in which experience is constructed as being transparent and giving students unmediated access to the world. From this perspective, knowledge of the world of work is deemed possible because it is assumed that there is a direct correspondence between the world and the way it is represented in the student's experience. As we noted above, there is a consensus in the literature as to how effectively to link experience and understanding.

There are several problems with these assumptions about the process of learning in which experiential learning tends either to be presented as a natural characteristic of all learners or as a substitute for a pedagogic technique. In the case of the former, it is assumed that the 'raw material' of work experience, work shadowing, work visits or apprenticeships can be 'worked up' into some form of meaningful knowledge through the controlled use of the senses (observation) and the through the application of reason (teacher-facilitated reflection). The pedagogic process can, however, easily become little more than checking whether particular information has been 'processed', a very narrow view of learning (Prawat, 1993). It overle ks the extent to which learning is a 'situated' process (Lave and Wenger, 1991), influenced by the social and cultural context in which it occurs and therefore not resulting in context-free information. As Guile and Young (1999b) point out, the limitation of most of the theories of information processing is that (i) they fail to acknowledge the extent to which learning involves a mediated pedagogic process involving discussion, negotiation and the resolution of conflicting views and (ii) that they focus upon the assimilatory aspect of learning existing knowledge at the expense of the production of new knowledge.

The idea of teacher-facilitated reflection is not itself unproblematic. Most worthwhile reflection involves teachers' exploring with learners the extent to which experience is influenced by the constraints of its context. As Young and Lucas in this volume (Chapter 5) have argued, this is likely to involve the use of concepts to provide a theoretical framework in which learners can reflect critically upon their experience. Such concepts and theories have to be introduced to the learner by the teacher in order to facilitate the process of reflection – a practice which would appear to contradict the idea that the authenticity of the learner's experience is in some sense sacrosanct and that critical questioning of that experience could damage the nature of the learner's recollection of the experience (Usher et al., 1997). Thus, the literature on learning in work-based contexts repeatedly demonstrates pedagogic considerations being reduced to the application of a specific set of methodological procedures designed to facilitate the recollection of experience. The procedures themselves have generally been derived from the Kolb learning cycle and involve pre-set learning outcomes. They are assumed to be constant across all contexts and capable of guaranteeing the authenticity and validity of the experience.

There are serious problems involved in denying the integral role of theory in the process of learning. 'Experiential learning' is not a 'natural' category and is itself endowed with assumptions about how learners can be helped to make sense of their experience. As Bray and Hoy (1989) point out, the meaning and significance of experience depends not only on the experience as such but also on how and by whom it is interpreted. A process of mediation therefore underpins the process of learning and this involves learners being immersed in ideas as well as in the world of experience (Guile and Young, 1999b). This provides learners with a basis for connecting their context-specific learning with ideas or practices which may have originated outside those contexts – and has significant implications for pedagogy.

The literature isolates a further problem which emanates from the positivist assumptions influencing much of the research on learning at work: an insensitivity to the opaque nature of many modern workplaces. The literature tends to assume that workplaces, work practices and work cultures are transparent and susceptible to observation, although there are some notable exceptions (Heikkinen, 1995; Fuller, 1996; Brown, 1997; Fuller and Unwin, 1998). This weakness in much of the literature can be illustrated in two ways. First, as a study of work-based science amongst A Level students revealed (Guile, 1995), even when the specific objectives of work experience have been agreed between workplaces and schools, it is not always easy to identify 'science in the workplace'. Given that science in the workplace is encoded in various forms of technology, it does not easily present itself to student inquiry. Students therefore have to be supported to 'find' the science and identify the relevant principles and concepts which underpin it. Second, much work in modern workplaces is not transparent. As the classic Zuboff and Hirschorn studies of industrial and nuclear plants illuminate (Hirschorn, 1986; Zuboff, 1988), even full-time workers struggled to understand and interpret the data they were looking at on screen. This suggests that sole reliance on the idea of experiential learning is unlikely to assist students in comprehending the reality of modern workplaces.

Another weakness stems from the idea that learning outcomes are unproblematic and inevitably provide a device through which learners' experience and the knowledge which arises from it can be assessed. Part of the problem is that this conception of learning presupposes a set of objectives which all learners can reach. Unless handled carefully, learning outcomes can become routinized and, instead of supporting the process of learning in its most emancipatory sense, can lead to learners accessing very narrow competences or forms of knowledge. As Usher et al. (1997) have argued about similar developments in adult education, learners' experience is significant to the extent to which it contributes to the learning of predetermined knowledge or skills. Experience which does not lead to predetermined knowledge tends to be discounted rather than seen as a source for future learning. Finally, the assumption that learners can easily gain access to and operate in work contexts neglects the extent to which learning ultimately involves participating in a 'community of practice' (Lave and Wenger, 1991). As Gherherdi *et al.* (1998) have observed, this requires 'host' organizations to give due consideration to providing opportunities for learners to observe, discuss and try out different practices with members of the 'community' they have temporarily joined.

A TYPOLOGY OF LEARNING IN WORK-BASED CONTEXTS: IMPLICATIONS FOR PEDAGOGY

In this final section, we address the implications of our analysis by offering a typology of approaches to work-based learning in which different models embody changing responses to policy, to the learner, to skills needed and ultimately to pedagogy. The final model which we present – the connective model – offers the possibility of an integrated response to changes in all these areas in a way which avoids the limitations described in the previous section. We developed the typology – and it is being developed further – within the European research forum established by the EU Targeted Socio-Economic Research project in which we are partners (Griffiths, 1999).

The five models naturally reflect the influence of different economic, technological and social factors prevailing within European countries – although they can be viewed as part of an ever-evolving continuum of learning in work-based contexts. Thus, although the models may be specific to periods of economic and technological development and reflect changing educational ideas about the process of learning, the models can and do co-exist in different countries.

The models are analytical rather than descriptive; no specific work-based programme fits neatly into any of the models and some programmes may contain elements of more than one model. The typology is not prescriptive but, as with any analytical framework, it is not without its own values and priorities. It is a fifth model – the connective model – which we will describe in some detail since its innovatory features are relevant to future approaches to pedagogy and effective learning in work-based contexts. The models are as follows:

- **Model 1. Traditional model: the 'bridge into work'** – typically in most EU Member States providing a technical-rational perspective of work-based learning. The role of formal learning is to acquire knowledge and skills; the role of work-based learning is directed towards learning tasks.

- **Model 2. Experiential model** – representing an attempt to reform the traditional model in response to the need for students to acquire less occupationally specific knowledge and skills and more generic knowledge and understanding about the content of work. The role of formal learning is to familiarize students with occupational changes and to develop their economic and industrial awareness. The role of work-based learning is to undertake activities to acquire an awareness of economic and occupational change.

- **Model 3. Generic model: Key skill/Competence development** – an explicit attempt to develop an alternative to the traditional model, based on slightly different principles which emphasize using work-based experience to acquire learning outcomes (accreditation of knowledge, skills). The role of formal learning is very limited: competent work-based activity is all that is required and workplace learning is the major source of evidence for accreditation.

- **Model 4. Work process model: facilitated learning** – an attempt to address the omissions of Models 2 and 3 and to reassert the key role of the teacher/trainer/HRD personnel. Thus, the role of pedagogy is to facilitate the process of reflection-in-action but not necessarily reflection-on-context. Model 4 seeks to combine the emphasis in the traditional model on the role of the teacher with the commitment to self-management and self-development of models 2 and 3. The role of work based learning is to provide an opportunity to develop work process knowledge and the role of formal learning is to support that.

- **Model 5. A connective model of pedagogy and learning in work-based contexts** – our fifth model, the 'connective' model, is innovative in several senses. First, it integrates and goes beyond the principles of the reformist, alternative and dualist models (2–4) and makes a fundamentally different assumption about learning and development. Instead of adhering to the technical-rational perspective about learning (a matter of adapting to new contexts, acquiring new skills and manifesting the desired attributes) the model is based on a 'reflexive' theory of learning (Guile and Young, 1999b). In other words, although it accepts that any form of learning is 'situated' (Lave and Wenger, 1991), it also assumes that learning involves the use of concepts which may or may not be external to the context (Guile and Young, 1999b). The pedagogic task is to allow learners to conceptualize their experiences in different ways and for this conceptualization to serve different curriculum purposes.

Second, the connective model differs fundamentally from the technical-rational model of education and training. It requires a pedagogy which helps learners to experience different combinations of theoretical and practical learning, enabling them to relate their formal programmes of study to trends in labour and work organization. For example, a work experience placement may provide an opportunity to understand new principles of business organization and their implications for work roles as well as an opportunity to develop personal and social skills. Understanding either dimension of the work experience requires learners to use ideas and concepts external to the work context – and external to their personal experience – and this is a pedagogic challenge, albeit a rewarding one, for their teachers. Diana Laurillard's reflections on teaching and learning in higher education (Laurillard, 1993, p. 93) are pertinent to our present considerations, particularly in the light of our earlier observations on 'deep learning': 'Students will not suddenly switch to being the model of holistic, deep and epistemologically sophisticated learners . . . Teaching must create a learning environment . . . at every level of description of the learning situation; i.e. conceptual structure, actions, feedback and goal must relate to each other so that integration can work.' Furthermore, as Beach's work indicates, teachers must recognise the extent to which students have to 'learn to negotiate how they learn' in workplaces (Beach and Vyas, 1998). Learning in work-based contexts involves students having to come to terms with a dual agenda. They not only have to learn how to draw upon their formal learning and use it to interrogate workplace practices; they also have to learn how to participate within workplace activities and cultures. Without the type of assistance described above, both types of learning are highly troubling activities, since they involve students in having to reconcile the relationship between formal learning and workplace practices. As Beach has further argued, this form of learning is best characterized as a form of 'horizontal development' and not the transfer of learning (Beach and Vyas, 1998).

Third, the connective model explicitly reflects our argument that 'host' organizations for work-related activities must consider how they can provide 'environments for learning' (or opportunities to participate in 'communities of practice') if they are to maximize the learning potential of these activities and this very much requires a rethinking of pedagogy by workplace managers, trainers and teachers. In this sense, the model goes beyond previous applications of human capital theory since it acknowledges the need for investment in education and training as well as paying attention to the process of learning in the workplace.

Fourth, the model replaces the notion of 'transferability' with the concept of 'boundary crossing' to be developed by students through their work-based experience (Engestrom et al., 1995). This concept reflects the gradual recognition that learning is not simply a matter of acquiring knowledge and skill in one context (a workplace) and reapplying it in another (another workplace) and offers the possibility of reconciling Resnick's (1987) distinctions between forms of learning described earlier. Teaching and learning in the connective model is more a process and product of interaction within contexts and between contexts – and the successful mediation of these relationships is a pedagogic priority which includes recognizing that learning involves negotiation of learning as part of workplace experience.

A pedagogic aim in the connective model is to introduce theories and concepts which learners can use to interrogate and assess critically workplace practice and contexts. Work-based learning should involve the identification of problems for analysis and for applying theory and also concepts for exploring the implications of different solutions to problems – thus enabling the learner to develop broader forms of expertise than could be acquired within formal education and training alone. The pedagogic goal of the model is to encourage students to develop critiques of and alternatives to existing practice and to apply them in the process of developing their capabilities.

The pedagogy of the connective model requires an approach to workplaces wherein they actively become environments for learning. Its development and application will demand the active involvement of teachers, researchers, policy makers and employers alike for it is not a model of learning which can be superficially or spasmodically engaged. It has the potential to avoid the limitations of past practice and to engage creatively with the challenges of the future. The connective model could come to offer a living, continually developing illustration of what theory can offer practice and how learning can be an active product of their informed connection.

REFERENCES

Abbott, I., Coldicott, C., Foley, M., Huddleston, P. and Stagg, P. (1996) *Developing Education Business Links: Initial Teacher Education Getting Down to Business*, paper presented at the Symposium on European Education Business Partnership, 'Learning for the Future', Frederiksborg County, Denmark.

Barnett, R. (1997) *Higher Education: A Critical Business*, Buckingham: Open University Press.

Beach, K. and Vyas, S. (1998) *Light Pickles and Heavy Mustard: Horizontal Development Among Students Negotiating How to Learn in a Production Activity*, paper presented at the Fourth Congress of the International Society for Cultural Research and Activity Theory, University of Aarhus, Denmark.

Becker, G. (1964) *Human Capital. A Theoretical and Empirical Analysis with Special Reference to Education*, New York: Columbia University Press.

Boud, D., Cohen, R. and Walker, D. (1993) Introduction, in D. Boud, R. Cohen and D. Walker, (eds.) *Understanding Learning from Experience*, Buckingham: SRHE/Open University Press.

Bray, A. and Hoy, J. (1989) Experiential learning: a new orthodoxy? in S.W. Weil and I. McGill, (eds.), *Making Sense of Experiential Learning*, Buckingham: SRHE/Open University Press.

Bremer, R. and Heidegger, G. (1997) Combining the apprenticeship system and the German dual system with access to polytechnics, in J. Lasonen, (1997) *Reforming Upper Secondary Education*, University of Jyvaskyla: Institute for Educational Research.

Brown, A. (ed.) (1997) *Promoting Vocational Education and Training: European Perspectives*, Hameenlinna: Finland.

Coy, M. (1989) *Anthropological Perspectives on Apprenticeship*, New York: SUNY Press.

Dall'Alba, G. and Sandberg, J. (1996) Educating for competence in professional practice, in *Instructional Science*, 24(3): 411–437.

Dewey, J. (1966) *Democracy and Education*, New York: The Free Press (Macmillan).

DfEE (1997a) *Success for All*, London: The Stationery Office.

DfEE (1997b) *Improving Work Experience*, Sudbury: Suffolk.

DfEE (1995) *Employee Development Schemes: Developing a learning workforce*, Sheffield.

Dreyfuss, H.L. and Dreyfuss, S.E. (1986) *Mind Over Machine*, Oxford: Blackwell.

Ellstrom, P-E. (1997) The many meanings of occupational competence, in Brown, A. (ed.) *Promoting Vocational Education and Training: European Perspectives*, Hameenlinna: Finland.

Engestrom, Y. (1995) *Training for Change*, London: International Labour Office.

Engestrom, Y. Engestrom, R., and Karkkainen, M (1995) Polycontextuality and boundary crossing, *Expert Cognition, Learning and Instruction*, 5: 319–337.

Enkenburg, J. (1995) Situated cognition and cognitive apprenticeship. A new framework for professional skills, in A. Heikkinen, (ed.) *Vocational Education and Culture. European Prospects from Theory and Practice*, Hameenlinna: Finland.

EC (1995) *Teaching and Learning: Towards the Learning Society*, Brussels: EC.

EC (1997) *Learning in the Information Society: Action Plan for a European Initiative*, Brussels: EC.

Entwistle, N.J and Marton, F. (1984) Changing conceptions of learning and research, in F. Marton *et al.* (eds.) *The Experience of Learning*, Edinburgh: Scottish Academic Press.

Fennell, E. (1994) Comment, in *Insight*, Winter, Sheffield: Employment Department Information Branch.

Fuller, A. (1996) Modern apprenticeships process and learning: some emerging issues, in *Journal of Vocational Education and Training*, 48(3): 229–248.

Fuller, A. and Unwin, L. (1998) Reconceptualizing apprenticeship; exploring the relationship between work and learning, in *Journal of Vocational Education and Training*, 50(2): 12–20.

Gherherdi, S., Nicolini, D. and Odella, F. (1998) Towards a social understanding of how people learn in organisations: the notion of a situated curriculum, in *Management Learning*, 20(3): 273–297.

Green, A., Leney, T. and Wolf, A. (1997) *Convergence and Divergence in European Education and Training Systems*, Institute of Education: University of London.

Griffiths, T. (1999) *Work Experience as an Education and Training Strategy: New Approaches for the 21st Century*, interim report of an EC Fourth Framework (TSER) research project.

Griffiths, T. and Miller, A. (1996) *European Education Business Partnership and Germany*, paper presented at the Symposium on European Education Business Partnership, 'Learning for the Future', Frederiksborg County, Denmark.

Griffiths, T., Miller, A. and Peffers, J. (eds.) (1992) *European Work Experience: Principles and Practice*, Centre for Education and Industry: University of Warwick.

Guile, D. (1995) *Work-Related Learning in A Level Science*, Post-16 Education Centre, Institute of Education: University of London.

Guile, D. and Fonda, N. (1999) *Managing Value Added Learning*, London: IPD.

Guile, D. and Young, M. (1999a) Beyond the institution of apprenticeship: towards a social theory of learning as the production of knowledge, in H. Rainbird and P. Ainley, (eds.) *Apprenticeship: Towards a New Paradigm of Learning*, London: Kogan Page.

Guile, D. and Young, M. (1999b) *The question of learning and learning organisations,* paper from Past 16 Education Centre, Institution of Education, University of London.

Harris, A. (1997) Equipping young people for working life: the workplace versus the school, *Economic Awareness*, January: 3–5.

Harris, A., Jamieson, I., Pearce, D. and Russ, J. (1995) *Equipping Young People for Working Life: Effective Teaching and Learning in Work-Related Contexts*, Research Studies RS46, London: The Stationery Office.

Heikkinen, A. (ed.) (1995) *Vocational Education and Culture. European Prospects from Theory and Practice*, Hameenlinna: Finland.

Hirschorn, L. (1986) *Beyond Mechanization*, Cambridge, Mass: MIT Press.

Hodgson, A. and Spours, K. (eds.) (1997) *Dearing and Beyond – 14–19 Qualifications, Frameworks and Systems*, London: Kogan Page.

Hyland, T. (1992) Expertise and competence in further and adult education, in *British Journal of In-Service Education*, 18(2): 23–28.

Jamieson, I., Miller, A. and Watts, A.G. (1988) *Mirrors of Work*, Brighton: Falmer Press.

Jessup, G. (1990) *Outcomes: NVQs and the Emerging Model of Education and Training*, Brighton: Falmer Press.

Kolb, D. (1984) *Experiential Learning: Experience as the Source of Learning and Development*, New York: Prentice Hall.

Lasonen, J. (ed.) (1997) *Reforming Upper Secondary Education*, University of Jyvaskyla: Institute for Educational Research.

Lasonen, J. and Young, M. (eds.) (1998) *Strategies for Achieving Parity of Esteem in European Upper Secondary Education*, University of Jyvaskyla: Institute for Educational Research.

Laurillard, D. (1993) *Rethinking University Teaching*, London: Routledge.

Lave, J. (1993) The practice of learning, in S. Chaiklen and J. Lave, (eds.) *Understanding Practice: Perspectives on Activity and Context*, Cambridge: Cambridge University Press.

Lave, J. and Wenger, E. (1991) *Situated Learning*, Cambridge: Cambridge University Press.

Lundvall, B. and Johnson, B. (1994) The learning economy, *Journal of Industrial Studies*, 1(1): 1–12.

Miller, A. (1996) To boldly go . . . work experience but not as we know it? in A. Miller and G. Forrest, (eds.) *Work Experience for the 21st Century*, CEI: University of Warwick.

Miller, A., Cramphorn, J., Huddleston, P. and Woolhouse, J.G. (1995) *Making Education Our Business*, CEI: University of Warwick.

Miller, A., Watts, A.G. and Jamieson, I. (eds.) (1991) *Rethinking Work Experience*, Brighton: Falmer Press.

Oates, T. and Fettes, T. (1997) Work experience and key skills, in G. Forrest, (ed.) *Work Experience for the 21st Century: Changing Priorities, Changing Practice*, CEI: University of Warwick.

Prawat, R. (1993) The value of ideas, *Educational Researcher*, 23(7).

Rainbird, H. and Ainley, P. (1999) *Apprenticeship: Towards a New Paradigm of Learning*, London: Kogan Page.

Ramsden, P. (1992) *Learning to Teach in Higher Education*, London: Routledge.

Resnick, L.B. (1987) Learning in school and out, *Educational Researcher*, 16(9): 13–40.

Rubenson, K. and Schuetze, H. (1993) Learning at and through the workplace. A review of participation and adult learning theory, in N.J. Cresskill, *What Makes Learners Learn?*, New York, OECD: Hampton Press.

Sammons, P., Hillman, J. and Mortimore, P. (1995) *Key Characteristics of Effective Schools: A Review of School Effectiveness*, Research Report commissioned by the Office for Standards in Education. London: Institute of Education and Ofsted.

Senker, J., Senker, P. and Hall, A. (1993) *Teaching Company Performance and Features of Successful Schemes*, Brighton: Science Policy Research Unit, University of Sussex.

Simpson, G. (1991) The key to lifelong learning, TEC Director, February/March.

Times Educational Supplement (22 October 1976) J. Callaghan, speech at Ruskin College, Oxford.

Usher, R., Bryant, I. and Johnston, R. (1997) *Adult Education and the Post-Modern Challenge*, London: Routledge.

Usher, R. and Edwards, R. (1994) *Postmodernism and Education*, London: Routledge.

Watts, A.G. (1991) The concept of work experience, in A. Miller, A.G. Watts and I. Jamieson, (eds.) *Rethinking Work Experience*, Brighton: Falmer Press.

Wellington, J. (1993) *The Work-Related Curriculum*, London: Kogan Page.

Whitty, G. and Wilmott, E. (1992) Competency-based teacher education: an approach and issues, *Cambridge Journal of Education*, 21(3): 27–32.

Young, M.F.D. (1998) *The Curriculum of the Future*, London: Falmer Press.

Zubboff, S. (1988) *In the Age of the Smart Machine*, London: Heinemann.

9

Adults as Lifelong Learners: The Role of Pedagogy in the New Policy Context

Ann Hodgson and Maria Kambouri

There has been a growing interest in adults as learners because of the emerging national and international policy focus on lifelong learning (OECD, 1996). Lifelong education, in itself, is not a new concept and has been the subject of debates in this country and beyond since it was adopted as a 'master concept' by UNESCO in 1970 (Tight, 1996). What is new is the fact that lifelong learning has increasingly been seen by policy makers and national governments as one of the major strategies for addressing the effects of national and international economic, demographic, social and organizational change. The education of adults, therefore, which has traditionally taken a clear second place to the education of children in most countries, has crept up the political agenda in this country, as in many others. This is mainly for economic reasons, but also increasingly for broader social and cultural reasons, because of the role education is seen to play in relation to the promotion of social cohesion and democracy.

It is commonly recognized that the pace of economic change, largely resulting from globalization and the rapid spread of information and communications technologies, has, and will continue to have, a powerful effect on the way that societies organize production and employment (Green, 1997). In consequence, it is suggested that the knowledge and skills acquired through compulsory education, although an important foundation for life and work beyond school, will not equip adults to cope adequately with the new context in which they find themselves at the end of the twentieth and beginning of the twenty-first century. The major policy response to the demands of this new context and, in particular, to the requirements of the labour market, is the development of strategies for promoting lifelong learning. In the United Kingdom, lifelong learning, although seen by the current administration as a 'cradle to grave' framework (DfEE, 1998), is largely focused on the education and training of adults.

This chapter focuses generally on adults as lifelong learners at all stages of their life and in different types of learning environments. We feel it is important here also to define what we mean by lifelong learning in relation to adults, since there is no one concept of it. Definitions range from a very narrow deficit model, where the focus is on compensation for previously incomplete or inadequate foundation education, to a much broader model, which encompasses all types and levels of learning. This latter model is premised on the need for all adults, whatever their previous level of educational attainment, to undertake the kind of education, training and self-development activities which will equip them to cope with the challenges of economic, social, demographic and technological changes. It is this broader model which frames what we discuss in this chapter, although we do highlight the issues of compensatory education and training within this model, because of their significance in current policy debates on adults and lifelong learning.

We will argue that there are three major factors which underpin the way in which adults learn – their personal characteristics, their reasons for participation and the context in which they learn. These factors underline the major differences between the education of children up until the end of compulsory schooling and the education of adults which takes place beyond compulsory education. Adults have a variety of needs and demands of education at different points in their lives, depending on their previous education, the roles that they currently perform and the goals that they wish to achieve. They are also limited as to where, when and how they can study and often there is no specific curriculum which they are expected to follow or a body of knowledge which they are expected to assimilate. Clearly, all of these factors have a determining effect on the type of pedagogy that will be perceived as practicable, useful or relevant to different groups of adult learners; and certainly there is an issue over whether any one type of pedagogy might be effective with all adult learners.

For these reasons, the major theories of adult learning have focused largely on the learner and her/his requirements of the learning process, rather than on pedagogy *per se* (e.g. Freire, 1972; Knowles, 1980, 1996; Jarvis, 1983; Kolb, 1984; Boud *et al.*, 1985; Brookfield, 1986; Rogers, 1989). Indeed, the usefulness of the term pedagogy itself, when applied to the teaching of adults, has been questioned by a number of academics and practitioners involved in the education of adults (e.g. Knowles, 1980; Mezirow, 1981) and an alternative term – andragogy – has often been used to refer to the teaching and learning of adults.

The first of our five sections will look at adults as learners and will provide a brief overview of the existing literature on theories of adult learning, with particular reference to the pedagogy/andragogy debate. The second section will highlight some important links between adult learning and teaching and will attempt to draw out some principles for effective teaching which result from this review. Section three will discuss the context for adults as lifelong learners and will raise some issues about how far the current national policies on lifelong learning address the needs and wants of adult learners.

This will be followed by a section on the potential role of the adult educator in the current policy context. The final section will argue for the need for research which connects the debates on adult teaching and learning to the debates on policies for promoting lifelong learning, in order to ensure that adults are genuinely given the opportunity to become effective lifelong learners.

ADULTS AS LIFELONG LEARNERS

What is it that is so different about adults as learners and why have the debates about the teaching and learning of adults often been carried out in isolation from the debates about the teaching and learning of children? If, as Rogers claims 'Learning means making changes – in our knowing, thinking, feeling and doing' (Rogers, 1992, p. 9), then it is clear that this is an activity which involves both children and adults. However, it is also equally clear that the starting points for change in relation to children and adults will be significantly different. What adults know, think, feel and do is related both to their own personal characteristics and to the context in which they find themselves, but also to the extent to which they are prepared to change or learn at any particular time.

These three factors – personal characteristics, context and motives for learning – therefore underpin what, how and why adults learn and, ultimately, whether they choose to participate in any organized form of learning. Since these factors are all, to a greater or lesser extent, determined by life experiences, there is a strong argument for treating adult learners, with their greater life experience and formative personal histories, as different from children. In addition, adults, unlike children, have a degree of choice about whether they participate in education and training; they are not necessarily educated in the same type of institutions as children (or, indeed, in any institution at all); and there is no set curriculum which they are required to follow, unless they are working towards national qualifications.

It is not surprising, therefore, that those who write about education, learning and teaching have seen adults as different from children and that a separate literature, debates and theories have emerged in relation to adult teaching and learning. We would contend that this separateness has its strengths, in that it takes into account the psychological and social difference between adults and children, but that there is still much that those who write about pedagogy could learn from those who write about andragogy and vice versa.

ADULTS AS LIFELONG LEARNERS: THE PEDAGOGY/ANDRAGOGY DEBATE

What is so unique about learning in adulthood? Several adult educators have attempted to answer this question proposing models, sets of principles or adult learning theories. Malcolm Knowles has been one of the stronger voices in trying to separate the field of adult education from other areas of education. He argued that pedagogy, the art and science of teaching, is clearly directed at children and suggested another term which would more specifically address adults as learners as distinct from children. Andragogy, 'the art and science of helping adults learn', was then adopted (Knowles, 1980, 1996).

The assumptions that differentiate andragogy from pedagogy are that:

> as a person matures:
> (1) her or his self-concept moves from one of being a dependent personality toward one of being a self-directed human being, (2) he accumulates a growing reservoir of experience that becomes an increasing resource for learning; (3) his readiness to learn becomes oriented increasingly to the developmental tasks of his social roles; and (4) his time perspective changes from one of postponed application of knowledge to immediacy of application, and accordingly his orientation toward learning shifts from one of subject-centeredness to one of problem-centeredness.
>
> (Knowles, 1996, p. 84)

For Knowles, as for us, the basic differences between adults and children are related to prior experience:

> Adults have more to contribute to the learning of others; for most kinds of learning, they are themselves a rich source for learning; adults have a richer foundation of experience to which to relate new experiences (and new learnings tend to take on meaning as we are able to relate them to our past experience); adults have acquired a larger number of fixed habits and patterns of thought, and therefore tend to be less open-minded.
>
> (ibid., pp. 89, 90)

However, this last point can be seen as a rather negative aspect in a person's learning effort, and Knowles suggests planning an initial 'unfreezing' exercise to free learners' minds from preconceptions. We will return to this important point later in the chapter when we talk about the role of the adult educator.

Andragogy was therefore premised on humanistic assumptions about the adult learner as a self-directed human being who possesses rich prior experiences, has a readiness and orientation to learn related to the roles and responsibilities of adult life, and is internally motivated. As Pratt (1993, p. 17) suggests:

> andragogy appears to rest on two implicit principles of learning: first, knowledge is assumed to be actively constructed by the learner, not passively received from the environment; and second, learning is an interactive process of interpretation, integration and transformation of one's experiential world.

Mezirow's theory of 'perspective transformation' follows a similar direction towards a process of becoming critically aware of how and why we are constrained by our own assumptions about the world we live in and begin to transform these assumptions (Mezirow, 1981). More recently, criticism and close scrutiny of the assumptions underlying Knowles' work and their implications for practice have led Knowles to soften his position and to speak of a continuum from pedagogy to andragogy. This continuum ranges from teacher-directed to student-directed learning that is suited to both adults and children depending on the situation in which learning takes place. In the case of adults, for instance, who know little about a topic, a teacher-directed approach may precede the self-directed learning that is assumed to take place. Looking at andragogy as a theory for instruction rather than a theory for learning may well be a way of settling this debate which is ultimately rather artificial (Hanson, 1996). We therefore agree with Merriam's comment:

> while andragogy does not define the uniqueness of adult learning, it does provide a set of guidelines for designing instruction with learners who are more self-directed than teacher-directed

> (1993, p. 9)

Certain lessons can be drawn from these theories which could help improve a learner's and a teacher's own practices. We will now discuss several key concepts related to learning in adulthood that have influenced practice.

ADULTS AND THEORIES OF LEARNING

The question of how adults learn has been at the centre of the debate on adult education since the beginning of the century when it became a distinct discipline. Some educators believe that adult 'learners', because of their longer histories and therefore experiences, require a different treatment than younger learners. They propose that differences in background, educational or not, some more extensive than other, will influence the way adults experience learning. The issue of whether ability to learn declines with age has preoccupied research from the beginning of the existence of adult education as a separate field of practice.

Initially, exploring differences in the ways adults and children learn was driven by psychological theories of learning: research paradigms concentrated mostly on behavioural and cognitive learning processes examining the obvious difference between children and adults and the effects of age on learning. In one of the first systematic investigations of adult learning, Thorndike *et al.* (1928) and his colleagues tested people between the age of fourteen and fifty on various memory and learning tasks. They concluded that teachers should expect twenty-five to forty-five year olds to learn at nearly the same rate and in the same manner as they would have learned the same topic at the age of twenty. They estimated only one per cent decline in this period of learning. Other researchers in the 1930s found a similar decline in learning curves over time, but with later onset and not as sharp (e.g. Miles and Miles, 1932). However, when the time pressure was removed from the testing conditions, older adults performed as well as younger ones. And when instead of focusing on rate of learning and age *per se*, research studies turned to issues such as power and ability to learn, results showed that adult test scores were related to previous education and skills.

Later studies deriving from psychometric theory and methodology – a branch of psychology which focuses on measures and tests of intellectual abilities – confirmed these findings (e.g. Wechsler, 1958) and noted that decline occurred on some types of tests, suggesting that only some aspects of intelligence may decline but not others. An influential theory based on two types of intelligence; 'fluid' and 'crystallized' intelligence has been developed by Horn and Cattell (1968). Fluid intelligence, which is linked to biological, universal development and is 'culture' fair, decreases with age, while crystallized intelligence, which is linked to abilities which are normally associated with experience and social processes, increases, leaving intellectual functioning balanced overall. Long (1971, 1972) studied physiological changes, asking the question of whether anyone may be too old to learn. In general, most of the studies resulted in a positive, optimistic outlook for the learning ability of ageing adults (Lumsden and Sherron, 1975; Birren and Schaie, 1990). Other research focused on the development of expertise and practical intelligence or even wisdom. Sternberg (1990) examined differences between everyday and academic problem solving, noting that everyday problem solving can be more complex since it requires not only the solution of problems but also the ability to recognize and define them based on incomplete, ambiguous and even conflicting information. Comparisons between novices and experts on the other hand, (e.g. Chi *et al.*, 1988) reveal that experts perform better than novices, mainly within the domain of their expertise, and that experience is key to this superiority.

However, the process by which experts arrive at an acquired expertise – or sages to their wisdom – is yet unclear. Piaget's work on cognitive growth and different stages of development which represent qualitatively different ways of making sense, understanding and constructing a knowledge of the world is pertinent for adult learning. Although his research did not extend into adulthood, it has nevertheless provided us with valuable information about the development of thinking from childhood to adulthood (formal operations) as well as the development of the kind of knowledge which arises from acting in the world and reflecting on our actions and experiences (Piaget, 1978). Piaget's theory has found applications such as Kohlberg's (1981) work on moral judgement that is also assumed to develop in different stages with age. Other perspectives including those proposed by Gagne and Bruner will be discussed in the next section when we examine the link between learning and instruction.

So, depending on how learning is defined, measured and assessed, people can learn in adulthood as well as in childhood. The importance of additional non-cognitive factors underpinning learning which involve personal histories such as level of education, training, and health or indeed, factors related to social and cultural contexts (Jarvis, 1987; Merriam and Caffarella, 1991; Tennant, 1997) and theories which stress reflecting upon experience (Freire, 1972; Mezirow, 1981) have gained increasing support in the discussions on how adults learn. Feminist theory is another important perspective which suggests that women may have different learning needs from men (such as learning best in environments where knowledge that comes from life experience is valued) and identifies power issues that affect the learning process (Tisdell, 1993). There is evidence that feminist theory and feminist pedagogy literature are beginning to have an impact on adult learning theory (e.g. Hart, 1992).

Yet no single perspective or general theory of adult learning has prevailed. This is not only due to the characteristics of adult learners – a point Brookfield makes:

> Learning activities and learning styles vary so much with physiology, culture, and personality that generalised statements about the nature of adult learning have very low predictive power.

> (1986, p. 25)

but also, due to differences of context, culture and power. This point is clearly captured in the quotation from Hanson below:

> All-embracing theories only get in the way of developing an understanding of the differing strategies necessary to enable diverse adults to learn different things in different settings in different ways

> (1996, p. 107)

To date, theories of adult learning have largely been untested by specific research into their efficacy. Any research in this area has often been focused on small-scale studies in specific learning contexts (e.g. the workplace, HE, FE) or with specific groups of learners (e.g. those acquiring basic skills or access learners). We would suggest that this is partly because of the complexity of the area of adults as learners and the education of adults, which results in fragmented studies of a fragmented field, but also partly because of a traditional lack of focus in national government policy in this country and elsewhere on adult learners, in comparison with the focus on schools and younger learners.

Recently however, as we have noted earlier, there has been a significant change in policy focus, which has resulted in a greater interest in the role of adult education and training in promoting economic competitiveness, as well as supporting social inclusion and democracy. However, there is little evidence that theories of adult learning have had a major impact on the way that national governments decide on policies for lifelong learning. We see the new policy context opening up the potential for a new line of research into the impact of major theories of adult learning on adult teaching, which could result in the advancement of teaching theory and practice in this area. We would argue strongly not only that there is a need for such research, but that this research should also be used to inform national policies on lifelong learning.

CONNECTIONS BETWEEN ADULT LEARNING AND THE TEACHING OF ADULTS

Several thinkers have influenced, through their work, the way we see the link between learning and teaching. Among the many who have contributed to the development of adult education, Dewey could be seen as the most significant. His ideas also provide a strong basis for the more recent concept of lifelong learning as he firmly believed that education should be reconceived to include all stages in life because all human beings are born with an enormous potential for growth and development (Dewey, 1938). Among other things, he stressed that teachers should be made intelligently aware of this learning capacity, the needs and the past experiences of those under instruction, and also to be receptive to learners' suggestions. In this way teachers should facilitate or guide learning but should not interfere or control the learning process as with didactic teaching. We would suggest that these ideas are as fresh and relevant for today's adult educators as they were for teachers of children in the 1930s.

Another influential thinker, Bruner (1990), also bases his learning and teaching theories on the belief that the human being is a natural learner. His theory of instruction (1966, pp. 40–1) is based on certain principles which are also relevant to adult teaching particularly when this is viewed as teacher-directed. These are that instruction should specify:

- the experiences which most effectively implant in an individual a predisposition towards learning;
- the ways in which the body of knowledge should be structured so that it can be readily grasped by the learner;
- the most effective sequences in which to present the materials to be learned;
- the nature and pacing of rewards and punishments in the process of learning and teaching.

Bruner also recognizes the need to distinguish between different ages, styles of learning and subject matter in teaching adults.

Another significant contributor to the understanding of a relationship between learning and instruction is Gagné (1977; Gagné et al., 1992). His work on the concept of problem solving is particularly significant since problem solving is a teaching method frequently used by educators of adults. He proposed a problem-solving cycle which begins by regarding experience as a problem, formulating possible solutions through observations and reflections, testing each hypothesis by action and assimilating solution. A flexible learner is thought to have mastered more sets of rules than a rigid learner and this degree of flexibility is crucial for learning to solve a problem effectively. It is significant to note here that theories of learning and teaching of adults have focused largely on the learner, his or her characteristics and previous experiences because it is believed that through these the ground for further learning will be prepared.

Personal characteristics of adults may therefore influence the ways they learn, where they learn and ultimately, whether we can do anything to encourage, support or facilitate their learning endeavours throughout life. We will now look at some characteristics of the adult learner which have been at the centre of the debate on learning and teaching.

LEARNER CHARACTERISTICS

A foundation concept in adult education is 'self-directed learning', which is defined as a process in which individuals take the initiative in designing learning experiences, diagnosing needs, locating resources and evaluating learning (Knowles, 1980).

As discussed above, for some educators this concept is considered the main distinction between the prescribed ways children learn in the conventional schooling system and the voluntary ways in which adults engage in education. However, as a characteristic of the adult as learner, self-initiated learning varies and this must be taken into consideration when teaching adults. We would suggest that the different ways in which learners direct their own learning should be examined through careful research in order to inform practice.

A similar idea, that of deliberate learning, was exemplified through work on 'learning projects' carried out by Tough (1979, 1996). In pursuing his interest in major personal change Tough concentrated on individual needs and how major personal change leads to personal growth. Implications drawn from this research suggest putting the focus on educators, not merely as people who help others learn, but as learners themselves. We will come to this important point in a later section on the role of the educator of adults.

Brookfield, who has written extensively on the topic, states:

> At the heart of self-directedness is the adult's assumption of control over setting goals and generating personally meaningful evaluative criteria. One cannot be a fully self-directed learner if one is applying techniques of independent study within a context of goals determined by an external authority . . . it is rather a matter of learning how to change our perspectives, shift our paradigms, and replace one way of interpreting the world by another.
>
> (1986, p. 19)

Such individual differences in interpreting the world have led to another important concept underpinning learning that is based on learners' characteristics as well as context, that of different 'cognitive' or 'learning styles'. These refer to an individual's characteristic ways of organizing and processing information and originated in work based on individual differences in making simple perceptual judgements led by Witkin (1950; Witkin et al.,

1977). He found that context influenced some people's perceptual judgements consistently and spoke of this mode of perception as 'field dependent' and the other extreme of perceiving an item independently of context as 'field independent'. Based on several years' work on cognitive styles, Witkin also provided a comprehensive analysis of their educational implications for teacher training, educational guidance and vocational preparation. For example, it was found that the relative superiority of field dependent people in remembering material with a social context is due mostly to their preference for such material and that if field independent people focused on this material they performed as well. This is a useful result for adult education because it shows that learning styles are modifiable through education or training. A useful overview of styles and strategies can be found in Riding *et al.* (1991).

A further approach to learning styles has been developed by Kolb and Fry (1975) following Kolb's experiential learning model which is based on the following propositions:

- learning is best achieved as a process, not in terms of outcomes;
- learning is a continuous process grounded in experience; and
- the process of learning requires the resolution of conflicts between dialectically opposed modes of adaptation to the world.

Although it is not clear how and whether this model can be generalized to all environments, it provides a good framework to plan teaching and learning activities and can be employed as a guide to vocational counselling, understanding learning difficulties and so on. Caution about handling learning styles in practice is emphasized by Tennant (1997, p. 88):

> Ideally learning styles should be on the agenda of any adult learning group, not as an instrument of the adult educator, but as an item for discussion and mutual scrutiny.

These two important concepts underlying adults' learning processes, namely self-directed learning and diverse learning styles, should therefore lie at the heart of any formal or informal teaching setting.

Turning the focus away now from the individual learner on to learning in the group, we would like to mention briefly the study of group dynamics, a field of enquiry within social psychology, which documents the powerful influence of the group on individual actions, perceptions, judgements and beliefs. The individualistic focus on group studies has been compared with the collective and shows that groups promote self-understanding, sharing support and exchanging feedback. Learning in groups has been suggested as the ultimate way of learning how to learn (Olmested and Hare, 1978).

SOME UNDERLYING PRINCIPLES FOR THE TEACHING OF ADULTS

Effectively teaching adults may then mean taking more time to find out the conditions under which each person can learn best. Brookfield (1986, pp.

9–11) for instance, discusses six principles of effective practice in facilitating learning which are not far from Knowles' idea of 'superior conditions' of learning and principles of teaching:

- participation in learning is voluntary;
- effective practice is characterized by a respect among participants for each other's self-worth;
- facilitation is collaborative;
- action and reflection are placed at the heart of effective facilitation (action in a sense of exploring a wholly new way of interpreting one's own work, personal relationships or political allegiances);
- facilitation aims to foster in adults a spirit of critical reflection;
- the aim of facilitation is the nurturing of self-directed, empowered adults.

These principles are well-respected and endorsed by many educators, as are those of other scholars who have formulated their perspectives on teaching by relying on their intuition, experience and beliefs on how adults learn best (Joyce and Weil, 1986; Rogers, 1989, among others). Unfortunately, few empirically derived perspectives on teaching adults are available and, as we discussed earlier, this reflects the need for more research in the area.

There is a recent publication of an empirical study of teaching perspectives, however, that describes such evidence, collected over several years, which concludes that 'there is no single, universal, best perspective on teaching adults' (Pratt *et al.* 1998; p. 11). Pratt studied 253 teachers of adults in several countries asking them what they meant by 'teaching'. The investigation involved questions about learning, motivation, the goals of education, the nature of their students, the influence of context on their teaching. Each perspective is presented in contexts of the actual practice of several educators who were invited to choose the perspective closest to them and to describe it in their own words.

It is the diversity of learners, content, context and ideals in the field that led Pratt to address types of commitment in teaching rather than a series of techniques. This commitment is expressed in terms of:

> actions, intentions, and beliefs regarding: (a) knowledge and learning, (b) the purposes of adult education or training, and (c) appropriate roles, responsibilities, and relationships for instructors of adults.
>
> (1993, p. 17)

Pratt is suggesting that teaching can be improved through reflection not only of the teacher's actions (e.g. improving technique) but also of the underlying intentions (e.g. clarifying goals) and beliefs (e.g. 'articulating what is taken for granted about learning') (1998, p. 11). The five adult teaching perspectives that emerged from this work are:

- transmission, as the effective delivery of content;
- apprenticeship, as modelling ways of being;

- developmental, cultivating ways of thinking;
- nurturing, facilitating self-efficacy; and
- social reform, seeking a better society.

Most teachers were reported to hold two or three perspectives although one tended to be more dominant, and no one was found to hold all five. Because these perspectives are based on actions, they are often mistaken as techniques. Pratt stresses the 'invisible' part, the core of each perspective; that is the teacher's beliefs and intentions. Pratt's work is influenced by a form of learning named 'perspective transformation' (Mezirow, 1981) which is based on fundamental structures of thinking and perceiving the world and the ways in which we see ourselves and our relationships. This study provides valuable evidence and an important contribution to the literature on teaching adults both as a theoretical analysis and as empirical research.

In conclusion, there is no single best perspective on how to teach adults just as there is no single theory of learning that can describe the diversity of the adult learner. Instead, what emerges as a central message from the literature in this field is that plurality is encouraged in both processes. The richness provided by the coming together of diverse disciplines such as philosophy, psychology, sociology and even economics and history cannot be underestimated when researching the field of adult education and lifelong learning, which is practice-based and has no single underlying discipline. Further research evidence of the impact different teaching perspectives have on the learning processes of adults, an example of which we discussed above, should therefore draw on all these other disciplines. Moreover, it is evident from this review of the literature that systematic research of practical knowledge in this area has been much more frequent and extensive in America than in the United Kingdom and we would therefore recommend that there should be more replication of such studies in order to investigate whether some apparent similarities in findings hold for this country as well. It is equally clear that the need for areas such as educational gerontology, vocational training and continuing professional education will continue to grow in the future as these areas increase in importance.

THE CONTEXT FOR LIFELONG LEARNING

Thus far we have discussed principles for effective adult learning and teaching in a somewhat context-free way and we have focused almost exclusively on the effects of learners' personal characteristics on their learning. However, as we argued earlier in the chapter there are two other major factors which influence the way adults learn – their reasons for participation and the context in which they learn. Moreover, there is an important link, we would argue, between these two latter factors. The reasons for adults participating in formal and informal education and training are intimately related to the wider sociopolitical and economic context within which education and learning takes place, as well as the physical and social environment within which adults learn (Pratt *et al.*, 1998). This section of the chapter explores this broader context and comments on the role that current and proposed policies for lifelong learning might have in relation to it.

Recent studies of adult participation in education and training in the United Kingdom (Sargant, 1991; RSA, 1996; Uden, 1996; Sargant *et al.*, 1997; McGivney, 1997; Coffield and Vignoles, 1997; FEFC, 1997; Robertson and Hillman, 1997) report the low percentage of adults who are currently involved in learning or who wish to participate in some form of education or training in the near future. These studies also highlight the current inequitable distribution of learning opportunities and the significant barriers which exist for adults who wish to become lifelong learners. These include structural and systemic obstacles, such as hostile institutional environments and delivery modes, the traditional inequitable distribution of learning opportunities in the workplace and inappropriate forms of accreditation, as well as the more obvious financial barriers, such as lack of study grants and loans, the uncertain rates of return to certain types of education and training and the high costs of child care, transport and fees.

The majority of adults study part-time, which means that they have to juggle a number of roles in addition to that of learner, and are often faced with education institutions which are organized and run for the benefit of full-time rather than part-time learners. Those who may well have the greatest need to undertake further learning, because of deficits in their earlier education or lack of marketable qualifications and skills, are often those who feel most disempowered by their past negative experience of education (Munn and MacDonald, 1988). These learners often also find themselves the subject of isolation and discrimination in formal education institutions (Coffield and Vignoles, 1997) and may face problems of cultural alienation in relation to the curriculum and qualifications on offer (Robertson and Hillman, 1997). As Coffield (1997a and 1997b) points out, it is important, therefore, to consider policies for education and training alongside more fundamental questions about social and structural change, in order to create a context within which lifelong learning can flourish. Otherwise, aspirations for creating a nation of lifelong learners will founder for the same reasons that the movements for recurrent education and lifelong education foundered in the 1960s and 1970s. An over-reliance on the ability of individual learners even to be able or willing to take charge of their own learning in a hostile context, let alone to change the society in which they find themselves, is doomed to failure, because it ignores the social character of learning and the power of context. It also ignores some of the fundamentally important characteristics of adults as learners highlighted earlier in this chapter, particularly the need for adults to have clear reasons for learning and relevant goals and rewards to pursue.

There is little evidence yet, however, that national policy makers concerned with lifelong learning are fully aware either of what theories of adult learning tell us about adults as learners, or of how important the context for learning is for adult learners. The government's recent Green Paper, *The Learning Age* (DfEE, 1998), for example, begins with a vision of lifelong learning which is both broad in its conception and inspirational in its tone. The document asserts the importance of lifelong learning, recognizes that learning can take many different forms with equally diverse purposes and outcomes and understands that it can take place in a wide range of formal and informal settings. However, the policy proposals in *The Learning Age* are based on two assumptions which, we would argue, do not adequately take cognizance of the characteristics of adult learning as discussed earlier in this chapter nor of the research to date on effective adult learning and teaching.

First, there is an emphasis on the responsibility of the individual learner to make lifelong learning a reality within the current context, rather than on changing the context itself. Second, insofar as teaching and learning is discussed at all in the document, there is an assumption that information and communication technologies (ICT) are the most appropriate way of facilitating lifelong learning. The first assumption ignores the evidence from studies of adult participation in education and training (e.g. Sargant, 1991; RSA, 1996; Uden, 1996; Sargant *et al.*, 1997; McGivney, 1997; Coffield and Vignoles, 1997; FEFC, 1997; Robertson and Hillman, 1997) on the power of structural barriers to lifelong learning. The second fails to recognize the importance of human interaction and collaborative peer relationships for effective adult learning and teaching. Cooper (1996) and Kirkup and Jones (1996), among others, spell out the dangers of an over-reliance on the pedagogic uses of ICT because of their potentially isolating effects, their inflexibility of content and study method, their inaccessibility to large groups of learners and the current lack of teacher expertise in this area. We will not explore these ideas more fully here since they are pursued in more detail in the following chapter.

Here, however, we would simply like to suggest that satisfying the needs and wants of adult learners, in order to ensure that they participate in and learn effectively within a system of lifelong learning, will require policy makers to take note of the research literature on adult teaching and learning alongside the policy literature on post-compulsory education and training.

THE ROLE OF THE ADULT EDUCATOR

How then should the adult educator see her/his role in supporting adults as lifelong learners within the present policy context? We propose that a useful starting point might be the three factors which we identified above as making adult learners to some degree different from children as learners – i.e. the personal characteristics of the adult learner, the context in which s/he is learning and her/his motives for learning. This suggests to us three interrelated major roles for the adult educator in supporting adults as lifelong learners: facilitator of learning; curriculum developer and critical evaluator of the learning process. In each of these roles the adult educator is being asked to address all three of the factors which define adults as learners.

Facilitator of learning

The role of facilitator has been extensively and eloquently described elsewhere (see, for example, Hirst and Peters, 1970; Brookfield, 1986; Rogers, 1992) and will not, therefore, be discussed in any depth here. There are, however, a number of key points which emerge from this literature which we feel are worth highlighting because they are of significance to the role of the adult educator in the current context. These include the need for the facilitator of learning to promote autonomous learning by:

- encouraging learners to define their own goals and purposes and, where appropriate, to explore these with other learners;
- helping learners to understand how they learn best and to use this knowledge to make their learning as effective as possible;
- creating an environment in which the views of all learners are valued and explored and which promotes the development of self-esteem;
- challenging both the learner's own views and, more broadly, promoting the concept of critical reflection within a supportive environment.

This role might be succinctly summed up in the words of Boud *et al.* (1996, p. 52):

> We believe that if teachers and others assisting learners are to have an effective role in promoting learning that role is essentially to provide a stimulus for learning, to support the learner in the process and to assist the learner in extracting the maximum benefits from what occurs.

In supporting the role of teacher as facilitator we would like to underline that this does not necessarily suggest that we believe there is one particular non-directive teaching style which should be adopted. Rather, in common with Pratt *et al.* (1998), we stress the importance of using a range of teaching styles or strategies which, in discussion with the learner, appear to be most appropriate for addressing the specific needs and wants of the learner in a particular context.

Curriculum developer

Earlier in this chapter we stated that there is no one set of curriculum objectives for adult learners, unless they are following programmes which are defined by the requirements of national qualifications. The curriculum for adults is often therefore seen by practitioners as comprising mainly that which the adult learners themselves identify that they wish or need to learn.

This, as Rogers (1992) points out, will usually revolve around three areas – occupation, social roles and interests – and is a useful starting point for curriculum development. However, there is arguably a role for the adult educator as curriculum developer to introduce problems, ideas and themes which go beyond the individual experiences of the learners and which encourage them to see their learning in a broader social, cultural and political context so that they can challenge that context and the assumptions which underlie it. This is allied to what Freire (1972) describes as 'conscientization', Mezirow (1981) terms 'perspective transformation' and Schon (1996) sees as 'problem framing'. It also encompasses the type of activities which Jansen and van der Veen (1996) discuss in relation to a methodology for adult education in the risk society, for example, community education for critical debate and social action, the envisaging of future scenarios and a thematic approach to social problems, rather than a focus on individual problems.

As Brookfield (1986, p. 284) says:

> The task for the educator, then, becomes that of encouraging adults to perceive the relative, contextual nature of previously unquestioned givens. Additionally, the educator should assist the adult to reflect on the manner in which values. beliefs, and behaviours previously deemed unchallengeable can be critically analyzed.

Critical evaluator

As stated earlier in this chapter, the importance of the adult educator learning, and being seen to learn, alongside her/his students cannot be underestimated as a way of demonstrating the universality of the concept and application of lifelong learning A further major role for the adult educator, as for all educators, is therefore, we would argue, the role of critical evaluator. By this we mean that the adult educator has the responsibility constantly to reflect on the impact of her/his practice and role, on the curriculum experience s/he is providing for her/his learners and on the learning that is taking place. Boud et al. (1996) model of reflection in learning, although intended by the authors to be used with adult learners, might, in addition, provide a useful paradigm for the adult educator as critical evaluator. In this three-stage model, the learner is asked first to return to an experience and to describe it in as dispassionate a way as possible. Second, she/he is encouraged to attend to the feelings that were present during the initial experience. Finally, the learner proceeds to re-evaluating her/his experience. It is not difficult to imagine how this cycle of learning might prove useful for the adult educator when s/he is reflecting on her/his own practice.

Finally, there is, we would argue, a potential fourth, but rather different role the adult educator can play through her/his research and writing – that of policy commentator. We feel that the adult educator, as a policy commentator, has a responsibility not only to participate in her/his own personal development as a learner and teacher but also to become an active contributor to the policy debates on improving the context for adults as lifelong learners. It is this role which we explore briefly below in the final section of this chapter.

THE NEED FOR RESEARCH IN THE NEW POLICY CONTEXT

In conclusion, what emerges from a review of the literature on adult teaching and learning is that there is no one dominant adult learning theory and little empirical evidence of one model of instruction being any more effective than another with adult learners. In fact, the effectiveness of different models of teaching adults has not been fully explored. As we have argued earlier, there is therefore a need for more research into this area to inform policy on lifelong learning.

From what we have highlighted earlier in this chapter, what stands out as the major principle of adult learning and teaching is that adults' previous life and learning experiences and the social context in which they currently find themselves are both significant in how successful they are as lifelong learners. Depending on how learning is defined, measured and assessed, people can learn as effectively in adulthood as in childhood. The difference therefore between adults and children as learners lies in the way adults approach learning. Educators of adults may well need to differ from educators of children because they have to invite adults to become and remain active learners by supporting and encouraging them to participate or to continue to participate in some form of lifelong education.

We would therefore argue that there is a need for the education of adults to have a separate place and weight in the field of education and to draw on a range of disciplines such as philosophy, psychology, sociology as well as economics and history to inform research and practice in this area. Given this viewpoint, we would argue that one of the major skills which the educator of adults needs to develop is an awareness of the importance of adults' previous life and learning experiences and the social context in which they find themselves. The adult educator also needs to develop the ability to use this awareness positively in the teaching context. What we do know is that adults learn well when they are self-directed, particularly when they receive feedback from a supportive peer group. They also need clear goals which relate to their life experiences and aspirations. Beyond this, how effective different teaching perspectives are likely to be is as yet unclear. It is on this area that research needs to be focused and as indicated earlier the replication of some of the American studies might prove a useful starting point.

In the broader policy context, where lifelong learning is currently seen as an important objective at national government level, we see adult educators playing four significant roles. First, as learners, they need to use their own experience of learning to develop a deeper awareness of how adults learn. Second, as practitioners, they should take account of the needs of adults for feedback, a supportive environment and relevant learning goals. Third, as researchers, they need to play a part in building up a research base about the impact of pedagogy/andragogy on the way adults learn. Fourth, as citizens, they have a role in using their experiences as practitioners and their research to contribute actively to the current policy debates related to lifelong learning. This might ensure that policies for lifelong learning in the twenty-first century are more grounded in research and practice and are therefore more likely to succeed.

REFERENCES

Birren, J. E. and Schaie, K. W. (1990) *Handbook of the Psychology of Aging* (3rd edn) San Diego, Calif.: Academic Press.

Boud, D, Keogh, R. and Walker, D. (eds.) (1985) *Reflection: Turning Experience into Learning*, London: Kogan Page.

Boud, D., Keogh, R. and Walker, D. (1996) Promoting reflection in learning: a model, in R. Edwards, A. Hanson, and P. Raggatt (1996) (eds.) *Boundaries of Adult Learning*, London: Routledge/Open University.

Brookfield, S. (1986) *Understanding and Facilitating Adult Learning*, Milton Keynes: Open University Press.

Bruner, J. (1966) *The Process of Education*, Cambridge, MA: Harvard University Press.

Bruner, J. (1990) *Acts of Meaning*, Cambridge, MA: Harvard University Press.

Chi, M., Glaser, R. and Farr, M. (1988) *The Nature of Expertise*, New Jersey: Lawrence Erlbaum.

Coffield, F. (1997a) Can the UK become a learning society?, 4th Annual Education Lecture, London: RSA.

Coffield, F. (1997b) Nine learning fallacies and their replacement by a national strategy for lifelong learning', in F. Coffield, (ed.) *A National Strategy for Lifelong Learning*, University of Newcastle Department of Education.

Coffield, F. and Vignoles, A. (1997) Widening participation in higher education by ethnic minorities, women and alternative students, in *Higher Education in the Learning Society*, London: NCIHE.

Cooper, C. (1996) Guidance and coherence in flexible learning, in P. Raggatt, R. Edwards, and N. Small (eds.) *The Learning Society: Challenges and Trends*, London: Routledge.

Dewey, J. (1938) *Experience and Education*, London: Collier Macmillan.

DfEE (1998) *The Learning Age: A Renaissance for a New Britain*, London: DfEE Cm 3790.

FEFC (1997) *Learning Works: Widening Participation in Further Education* (The Kennedy Report), Coventry: FEFC.

Freire, P. (1972) *Pedagogy of the Oppressed*, Harmondsworth: Penguin.

Gagné, R. M. (1977) *The Conditions of Learning and Theory of Instruction*, Florida: Holt, Rinehart and Winston.

Gagné, R. M., Briggs, L. J. and Wager, W. W. (1992) *Principles of Instructional Design* (4th edn) Fort Worth: Harcourt Brace Jovanovich College Publishers.

Green, A. (1997) *Globalization and the Nation State*, Basingstoke: Macmillan.

Hanson, A. (1996) A separate theory of adult learning, in P. Edwards, A. Hanson and P. Raggatt (eds) *Boundaries of Adult Learning*, Routledge and Open University.

Hart, M. (1992) *Working and Educating for Life: Feminist and International Perspectives on Adult Education*, New York: Routledge & Kegan Paul.

Hirst, P. and Peters. R. (1970) *The Logic of Education*, London: Routledge.

Horn, J. and Cattell, R. (1968) Refinement and test of the theory of fluid and crystallized intelligence, *Journal of Educational Psychology*, 57: 253–70.

Jansen, T. and van der Veen, R. (1996) Adult education in the light of the risk society, in P. Raggatt, R. Edwards and N. Small (eds.) *The Learning Society: Challenges and Trends*, London: Routledge.

Jarvis, P. (1983) *Adult and Continuing Education: Theory and Practice*, London: Routledge.

Jarvis, P. (1987) *Adult Learning in the Social Context*, London: Croom Helm.

Joyce, B. and Weil, M. (1986) *Models of teaching* (3rd edn.) Englewood Cliffs, N.J.: Prentice Hall.

Kirkup, G. and Jones, A. (1996) New technologies for open learning: the superhighway to the learning society? in P. Raggatt, R. Edwards, and N. Small (eds.) *The Learning Society: Challenges and Trends*, London: Routledge.

Knowles, M. (1980) *The Modern Practice of Adult Education: From Pedagogy to Andragogy*, Cambridge: Cambridge Book Company.

Knowles, M. (1996) Andragogy: an emerging technology for adult learning, in R. Edwards, A. Hanson and P. Raggatt (1996) (eds.) *Boundaries of Adult Learning*, London: Routledge/Open University.

Kohlberg, L. (1981) *The Philosophy of Moral Development Vol. 1 – Essays in Moral Development*, San Francisco: Harper.

Kolb, D. and Fry, R. (1975) Towards an applied theory of experiential learning, in C. Cooper (ed.) *Theories of Group Processes*, London: Wiley.

Kolb, D. (1984) *Experiential Learning: Experience as the Source of Learning and Development*, Englewood Cliffs: Prentice Hall.

Long, H. B. (1971) *Are They Ever Too Old to Learn?*, Englewood Cliffs, N.J.: Prentice Hall.

Long, H. B. (1972) *The Physiology of Aging: How it Affects Learning*, Englewood Cliffs, N.J.: Prentice Hall.

Lumsden, D. B. and Sherron, R. H. (1975) *Experimental Studies in Adult Learning and Memory*, New York: Wiley.

McGivney, V. (1997) Adult participation in learning: can we change the pattern?, in F. Coffield (ed.) *A National Strategy for Lifelong Learning*, Newcastle: Department of Education, University of Newcastle.

Merriam, S. B. and Caffarella, R. S. (1991) *Learning in Adulthood: A Comprehensive Guide*, San Francisco: Jossey-Bass.

Merriam, S. B. (ed.) (1993) *An Update on Adult Learning Theory. New Directions for Adult and Continuing Education*, San Francisco: Jossey-Bass.

Mezirow, J. (1981) A critical theory of adult learning and education, *Adult Education* (USA), 32(1): 24.

Miles, C., Miles, W. (1932) The correlation of intelligence scores and chronological age from early to late maturity, in *American Journal of Psychology*, 44: 44–78.

Munn, P. and MacDonald, C. (1988) *Adult Participation in Education and Training*, Edinburgh: The Scottish Council for Research in Education.

Olmested, M. and Hare, P. (1978) *The Small Group*, New York: Random House.

OECD (1996) *Lifelong Learning for All*, Paris: OECD.

Piaget, J. (1978) *The Development of Thought: Equilibration of Cognitive Structures*, Oxford: Blackwell.

Pratt, D. D. (1993) Andragogy after twenty-five years, in S. Merriam (ed.) *An Update on Adult Learning Theory. New Directions for Adult and Continuing Education*, San Francisco: Jossey-Bass.

Pratt, D. *et al.* (1998) *Five Perspectives on Teaching in Adult and Higher Education*, Florida: Krieger Publishing Company.

Riding, R. and Cheema, I. (1991) Cognitive styles – an overview and integration, *Educational Psychology*, 11(3, 4).

Robertson, D. and Hillman, J. (1997) Widening participation in higher education for students from lower socio-economic groups and students with disabilities, (Report 6) in *Higher Education Higher Education in the Learning Society*, London: NCIHE.

Rogers, A. (1989) *Teaching Adults*, Milton Keynes: Open University Press.

Rogers, A. (1992) *Adults Learning for Development*, London: Cassell.

RSA (1996) *Attitudes to Learning – MORI State of the Nation Poll: Summary Report*, London: RSA Campaign for Learning.

Sargant, N. (1991) *Learning and Leisure*, Leicester: NIACE.

Sargant, N., Field, J., Francis, H., Schuller, T. and Tuckett, A. (1997) *The Learning Divide: A Study of Participation in Adult Learning in the UK*, Leicester: NIACE.

Schon, D. (1996) From technical rationality to reflection in action, in R. Edwards, A. Hanson and P. Raggatt (eds.) *Boundaries of Adult Learning*, London: Routledge.

Sternberg, R. (1990) *Wisdom: its Nature, Origins, and Development*, Cambridge: Cambridge University Press.

Tennant, M. (1997) *Psychology and Adult Learning* (2nd edn), London: Routledge.

Thorndike, E., Bergman, E., Tilton, J. and Woodyard, E. (1928) *Adult Learning*, New York: Macmillan.

Tight, M. (1996) *Key Concepts in Adult Education and Training*, London: Routledge.

Tisdell E. J.(1993) Feminism and adult learning: power, pedagogy and praxis, in S. Merriam (ed.) *An Update on Adult Learning Theory*, San Francisco: Jossey-Bass.

Tough, A. (1979) *The Adult's Learning Projects: A Fresh Approach to Theory and Practice in Adult Learning* (2nd edn.) Toronto, Ontario, Canada: Ontario Institute for Studies in Education.

Tough, A. (1996) Self planned learning and major personal change, in R. Edwards, S. Sieminski and D. Zeldin (eds.) *Adult Learners, Education and Training* Routledge in association with Open University.

Uden, T. (1996) *Widening Participation: Routes to a Learning Society*, Leicester: NIACE.

Weschsler, D. (1958) *The Measure and Appraisal of Adult Intelligence*, Baltimore: Williams and Wilkins Company.

Witkin, H. (1950) Perception of the upright when the direction of the force acting on the body is changed, *Experimental Psychology*, 40: 93–106.

Witkin, H., Moore, C., Goodenough, D. and Cox, P. (1977) Field-dependent and field-independent cognitive styles and their educational implications, *Review of Educational Research*, 47(1): 1–64.

10

The Challenge of New Technologies: Doing Old Things in a New Way, or Doing New Things?

Richard Noss and Norbert Pachler

In this chapter we will try to illustrate that the potential of new technologies has considerable implications for our current notion of knowledge, as well as for the relationships and roles of teachers and learners. We conclude that while discussion of ICT is restricted to the domain of *how* to teach and learn, its real potential will remain limited. Similarly, viewing new technologies as merely an opportunity for faster or easier access to information will severely restrict the opportunities for positive educational change, and may even bring about change in the wrong direction. For genuine (and cost-effective) change to take place, we need to address – as an urgent policy issue – what kinds of new *knowledge* is made accessible by the technology, and how these fit with the needs of the citizens of the twenty-first century.

It is, perhaps, inevitable that the emergence of a new technology is accompanied by a confusion as to what might be done with it. It took many years for the printing press to be used for anything other than reprinting the Bible or for the car to be thought of as more than a horseless carriage. The latter example is instructive as the transition from horseless carriage to a new kind of transportation was dependent upon and shaped by the emergence of an infrastructure on which horseless carriages could actually be driven at a greater speed than a carriage. Technologies and infrastructures to make those technologies work emerged together, although not in an unproblematic or necessarily harmonious way (Noss, 1992).

For educationalists the challenge of new technologies poses interesting and not always soluble problems. As each technological innovation (radio, television, video etc.) has come and gone, it has left education with a feeling that something good has happened but that nothing fundamental has changed. Only a couple of years ago, hypertext and multimedia were thought to be the panacea of educational change. Yet all that has happened so far has been the translation into hypermedia of the pedagogic approaches which characterize technologies of a previous era.[1] And now the Internet has arrived. Or rather, educationalists have noticed its arrival. Many of the questions raised by its arrival are, of course, the same as those raised by other technologies before it. What kinds of pedagogy are appropriate to using this technology and, more fundamentally, how does this technology change the epistemologies of what may or may not be taught in schools. Indeed will schools, as we know them, continue to have the educational (as opposed to social) function that they currently have?

The introduction of a new variable into the teaching and learning process has considerable implications for the role of the teacher and her relationship with the learner. One of the fundamental challenges of ICT, for educational purposes, is to ensure that it actually enhances the quality of the learning experience. In order to understand how ICT might contribute, teachers need to possess not only the requisite technical skills but also to understand the relationship between the system and the learner as well as the implicit and explicit values and assumptions of ICT applications about the way learning happens. The inclusion of ICT, in the context of formal education, impacts on the dynamic interplay between teachers and learners and can – with careful design – enhance what has previously been taught and done in schools. It can also make new things possible in new ways (Bonnett, 1997, pp. 145, 151).

In this chapter we argue from the premise that the learner, as an active meaning-maker and problem-solver, is central to the learning process and that learning takes place in the context of social interaction between the teacher, the learner and others.[2] In such a model, ICT[3] can represent a valuable attribute but, in itself, is no viable substitute for pupil-teacher and pupil-pupil interaction. On the contrary, we will show that effective use of ICT makes more complex the relationship between teacher and learner, and more urgent the need to reconsider effective pedagogies, and the knowledge they are designed to teach.

NATIONAL CONTEXT AND BACKGROUND

The history of Information Technology (IT) and more recently ICT in education in the UK is characterized by a focus on the installation of hardware on the one hand and by the concept of technology as a 'thing' – often a panacea – on the other. Whereas at one time technology might have appeared as *the* solution, particularly to educational administrators, experience has shown that it is neither a replacement for the teacher, nor a particularly cheap option. Educational computing can be seen to have evolved through three stages: topicality (the computer is seen as the focus), surrogacy (characterized by the development of 'educational software' and a view of the computer as a surrogate teacher) and progression (the use of sophisticated generic software tools for problem solving activities) (Heppell, 1993, pp. 230–2). Significant pedagogic evolution, which 'requires us to be aware that computers not only bring something new to the learning environment but that they change it and they change learners too' (Heppell, 1993, p. 233), has, however, yet to emerge as a serious facet of ICT use.

The second half of the 1990s has seen technology gain prominence in UK educational policy making; the number of documents and reports that have been published by a range of governmental, quasi-governmental and non-governmental bodies arguing the case for ICT is extensive.[4] One such report argued that if no steps are taken to intensify the use of ICT in schools 'a generation of children – and a generation of adults as teachers – will have been put at enormous disadvantage with consequences for the UK that will be difficult to reverse' (Stevenson 1997, p. 4).

The claims made for the educational purposes of ICT are not new. There is, however, one fundamental contextual difference of late: education is moving beyond the school. According to McKinsey & Company, there were already just over five million home computers in 1997 representing 22 per cent of UK households; and they predict this number to grow to 45 per cent or even 50–55 per cent by 2000-1 (McKinsey & Company, 1997, p. 18). These figures are in stark contrast to the availability of suitable hardware in schools. For example, according to a report by the quango advising on ICT (then the National Council for Educational Technology (NCET)),[5] it is doubtful whether the government's target of getting all schools wired up by the year 2002 can be met due to outdated equipment (Pyke, 1998).

HARNESSING NEW TECHNOLOGIES FOR EDUCATION

The National Grid for Learning (NGfL)

We see the question of pedagogy as intrinsically connected to the question of epistemology. In our view, in the area of new technologies and indeed more broadly, they are not separable. We begin by examining what vision current policy makers have for harnessing the Internet as the most recent and highly acclaimed new technology in the service of education. That vision has been clearly spelled out in the recent government document Connecting the Learning Society, and can be summed up quite simply as 'the delivery of subjects' (DfEE, 1997, p. 5). The National Grid for Learning, it explains, is 'a way of finding and using on-line learning and teaching materials' and 'a mosaic of interconnecting networks and education services based on the Internet, which will support teaching, learning, training and administration in schools, colleges, universities, libraries, the workplace and homes' (DfEE, 1997, p. 3).

Although these two summaries of what the 'grid' actually is are merely synoptic, the vision that is produced throughout the document is rather clear: teachers will be linked to the centres of power; the DfEE will be able to communicate directly with schools and issue its latest instructions; schools will be able to send performance data directly to each other and to the DfEE; and, an aspect with increasingly high profile in the media recently, teachers will be able to download worksheets directly into their classroom.

> Mr Blunkett said multimedia computers would lift the bureaucratic burden on teachers by allowing them to download work schemes and integrated learning systems from the Internet and grid, and to share good practice with colleagues at other schools
>
> (Thornton, 1998, p. 10)

The state of thinking about the kinds of knowledge that might be introduced into schools, or the ways in which existing knowledge might be genuinely transformed by new technologies, have clearly not advanced beyond that of the Bible or the horseless carriage.

The Initial Teacher Training National Curriculum for the use of ICT

On the pedagogical front, we can get some idea of the current state of policy thinking by examining the Initial Teacher Training National Curriculum for the use of Information and Communications Technology in subject teaching[6] (DfEE, 1998). We do not mean to suggest that the last word on pedagogical issues for ICT is to be found in this DfEE circular. Nevertheless, it serves to focus our thinking on the issues as they are seen by policy makers and allows a platform from which to offer a critique. The document is nothing if not exhaustive; indeed, it is hard to see how a student teacher might attain the exhaustive list of skills in the nine months of their course even if they were to do nothing else. But we do not mean to carp at its exhaustive nature. After all, it is reasonable for any curriculum for teacher education – if it is reasonable for a government to impose such a curriculum at all – to attempt at least to be exhaustive. And there are some aspects of the document which are laudable. For example, on p. 17 we read that 'it is the responsibility of the ITT provider to ensure that the ways trainees are taught to use ICT are firmly rooted within the relevant subject and phase, rather than teaching how to use ICT generically, or as an end in itself.' (DfEE, 1998; bold in original). This seems to represent a welcome change of heart on the part of policy makers and replaces what had previously become the fetishization of ICT for its own sake and an endless succession of injunctions to teachers about the need to introduce children to technology for the good of the nation's economic well-being.

Nevertheless, we had better state that we believe that the understanding in policy circles of the consequences for education of ICT is rather short-sighted. And at the risk of pre-empting the remainder of this chapter, we believe that government would do better to support and encourage the mapping out of the kinds of deep changes that are inevitable even within the next ten years and to try to equip teachers not only with knowledge about what they might do with technologies as they currently stand, but how they may contribute to shaping those technologies in the service of the educational system.

We begin our own analysis by considering the National Grid for Learning,[7] perhaps the most obvious manifestation of governmental commitment to the new technologies. How significant is it? Our answer is that it must be an interesting and perhaps necessary first step and it is certainly something which we would applaud. The explosive growth of Internet connectivity in homes has to some extent pre-empted the modest suggestion that schools should be connected. But given that home use is heavily contingent upon social class, we cannot but support the attempt of government to open access to all through the schools.

It is, as we have already said, significant that the vision of connectivity is one of delivery and this has technological implications as well as pedagogical ones. One might believe that even with limited financial outlay, it would be better to aim for schools to equip each child with a computer than to ensure that each school and each teacher can download pre-existing work schemes for the delivery of schemes of work conceived in ways which take little if any account of the technology. There is no mention of the computer as a potential source of empowerment either for the student or for the teacher, or as a way for the student to come to grips with knowledge of any kind. Indeed 'knowledge', *what* rather than *how*, is absent from current policy. Rather than the general but vague aims of 'improving the quality and standards of pupils' education' and 'supporting teachers, both in their everyday classroom role . . . and in their continuing training and development' (DfEE, 1998, p. 17), it might be better to have as a short term goal the serious engagement of teachers with the substantive ways in which the computer might afford students the exploration of deep and hitherto inaccessible conceptual knowledge.

To its credit, there are some signs that policy is turning in this direction. If the new (lottery-funded) programme of teacher education is successful in encouraging teachers to do more than simply acquire 'skills' related to ICT – there is, for example, a clear focus in preliminary documents on subject knowledge – then there may be a real opportunity for teachers to control the complexities of the new technologies, and harness it to their and their students' advantage.[8]

But, unfortunately, there are also countervailing tendencies. It is, for example, difficult to see how this process can proceed very far in relation to 'literacy', when the government has decreed the narrowest of definitions for the knowledge involved, and determined – to the nearest ten minutes – how it should be taught.[9] Neither can the current obsession with 'numeracy'[10] sit easily with imaginative or even cost-effective uses of new technologies which, in mathematical and scientific realms, are now beginning to offer genuinely novel and exciting potential (see, for example, the reconceptualization of geometric ideas (Laborde and Laborde, 1995), the ideas of calculus (Kaput, 1994) or the important topic of probability (Wilensky, 1997). Instead, numeracy is restricted to basic number, pedagogy to 'whole class teaching', and new technologies – at least in the case of the calculator – are all but banned.

We can, of course, continue in the old way. Perhaps it will be possible to download schemes of work from the Internet so that teachers may more effectively teach long division, or laboriously construct programmed learning systems to drill learners in calculational skills: there must be a certain irony in harnessing such a powerful technological engine to drive such a rusty – and anachronistic – vehicle. Yet, the DfEE seems to view the technology in just this anachronistic way.[11] Specifically, the functions (sic) of ICT are:

- its speed and alternaticity;
- its capacity and range;
- its provisional nature, how the provisional nature of information stored allows work to be changed easily; and
- the interactive way in which information is stored

(DfEE, 1998, p. 19)

Here then are the DfEE's assumptions about the role of ICT: it is a fast, wide-ranging, editable and interactive system for the storage and location of vast amounts of information. From this epistemological standpoint, there flows an inevitable pedagogy. It is a pedagogy based on marshalling resources, accessing information, swapping details of data and assessments; in short, of doing more quickly, reliably and interactively what teachers have always done. And because there is no attempt to raise the vision of teachers beyond doing with new technology what has been done with the old, there is no attempt to encourage teachers to think what might be done better. We read how ICT must be used to support the development of language and literacy or to support the development of numeracy. We even read that ICT must support pupils' creative development through the use of computer programs which encourage them to explore and experiment with pattern, shape, pictures, sound and colour. But we read nothing of the need of the children of the twenty-first century to acquire new knowledge, solve new problems and employ creativity and critical thinking in the design of new approaches to existing problems or, indeed, to new ones.

THE TRANSFORMATION OF KNOWLEDGE

The ways in which ICT interfaces with the learner obeys certain rules and conventions and elicits from her specific responses. Accordingly, teachers and learners have to be aware of them (Moro, 1997, p. 69). In today's information-rich society, learners grow up in an environment which is semiotically diverse and complex and which requires of them new skills and broader forms of literacy than were required hitherto (Heppell, 1993, p. 233); an environment, it could be argued, in which access to information and its active cognitive processing rather than passive consumption are essential. The key point is that in mediating the flow of information to the learner, the information itself is transformed:

> The 'dialogue' between 'information author' and 'reader/viewer' has grammar, ground rules, aural and visual cues and clues which are used to signify meaning, to indicate generic structure, and to reference the information web.
>
> (Heppell, 1993, p. 234)

The design structure of information through hypermedia shows a trend towards plurality – the user is no longer required to take a prescribed route but can determine her own path. The design can differ significantly from traditional, sequential and linear taxonomies and can be made up of a convergence of textual, visual and audio components. Random access to information is a characteristic of content-rich hypermedia such as CD-ROM and the Internet.

Bernard Moro suggests that the emergence of 'zapping' is linked to the retreat of the sequential mode and describes this phenomenon as 'nothing short of a revolution affecting how the media are both designed and consumed' (Moro, 1997, p. 72). He describes zapping as 'multiple tapping from a variety of sources which the child handles in a synecdochical way, i.e. by constantly reconstructing the whole from fragmented glimpses, so that he (sic) is capable of reading several programs at the same time' (Moro, 1997, p. 72); this is considered to be akin to natural, random information gathering.

Moro suggests that the rapport between the learner and knowledge is in the process of being re-defined:

> admiration . . . for the erudite has become obsolete, what matters is that intellectual energy must be devoted to the real tasks at hand. What matters is no longer to massively store facts, but to sort them, integrate them and reveal their relationships. . . . Facts are now instantaneously accessible, they are no longer the first and foremost object of learning. Handling them is what matters.
>
> (Moro, 1997, p. 73)

'Critical media literacy' (Collins et al., 1997, p. 62) is becoming vital. Compared to books, with hypermedia 'it is almost as if authorship and ownership get lost' (Collins et al., 1997, p. 64). Consequently there is the danger that hypermedia 'will present itself as the "truth" rather than the truth according to a certain author or authors' (ibid.). This is coupled with the arguably high face validity of computers, particularly with (male) teenage learners.

The proliferation of information which ICT makes possible renders the notion of the teacher as the source of all knowledge untenable and potentially undermines the authority of the teacher. Similarly, the representation of knowledge and simulation of reality through hypermedia is problematic, despite the apparently greater authenticity in portraying 'reality' afforded by the 'multimodality'[12] of text, images and sound. Technology increasingly determines what knowledge is acquired and how it is processed; there is a danger of the medium determining the message. (Collins *et al.*, 1997, pp. 84–5)

> Just as the supermarket chains shape the commodities we buy and the way we eat, will the spread of multimedia determine the knowledge which is presented to us and the way in which we 'consume' it?
>
> (Collins *et al.*, 1997, p. 85)

The same possibilities and pitfalls abound in the sciences. We can now manipulate geometrical figures in ways which were unthinkable to Euclid; we can solve a substantial proportion of school mathematical problems by pushing buttons on hand-held devices; we can manipulate physical systems on screens, and explore relationships which were previously only accessible via mathematical equations. Yet simply to do these things – and they are an infinitely more inviting prospect than downloading schemes of work – is to miss the point. For each of these possibilities raises new problems, new forms of knowledge. Computer mathematics is not the same as pencil mathematics, the relationships between screen objects is not the same as the interaction between real objects. The relationship is close and complex: and we need to find ways to help teachers and students to problematize these relationships. They cannot be waved away by pretending these complexities do not exist, or by claiming the 'effects' of new technologies on learning as if what is to be learned remains the same.

Yet claims of this sort for ICT-based learning are wide-ranging. Wolff, for example, argues that ICT can help learners make the knowledge construction process transparent and raise consciousness as well as provide classificatory systems which simplify knowledge processing (Wolff, 1997, p. 20). ICT, it is claimed, can also allow for active participation and cognitive interaction of the learner in the learning process. Applications, such as modelling, simulation and emancipatory software with huge potential, for instance, for saving time, cutting out 'inauthentic labour' or exposing the learner to certain material and processes do now exist. Some writers, however, have pointed to the danger that these learning experiences may remain 'an inadequate substitute for the real thing' (Collins *et al.*, 1997, p. 124) – although we should be aware that our definition of 'the real thing' is itself subject to evolution in the light of presence of the new technologies.

Michael Bonnett rightly points out that the liberating potential, for instance, of the word processor (in helping the user organize and reorganize thoughts quickly, correct spelling and produce high quality products) and its facilitation of engagement with the meaning of information beyond the mechanics of writing does not, in itself, guarantee that the desired outcomes will actually occur. Furthermore, its liberating potential might lead to a pre-occupation with presentation at the cost of quality of content (Bonnett, 1997, p. 152). With regard to CD-ROMs, Bonnett (1997) makes the point that the random presentation of information makes it hard to assess what cognitive links learners have made or whether they suffered from information over-load:

> Volume of content does not equate with richness of experience. . . . One of the chief dangers of information overload is that it can, at one and the same time, inhibit authentic thinking and seduce us into believing that all we need to solve our problems is yet more information (*ibid.*, p. 155).

In the wake of the behaviourist drill and practice tradition characteristic of early educational computing currently instantiated in the weakly conceived Integrated Learning Systems (ILS), there is every danger of promoting, through the use of ICT, 'a passive mentality which seeks only the "right" answers, thus stifling children's motivation to seek out underlying reasons or to produce answers that are in any way divergent' (Bonnett, 1997, pp. 157–8). In part, ILS systems embody the failure to deliver what Artificial Intelligence (AI) has consistently promised. The latter has now retreated from the ambitious aim of Intelligent Tutoring Systems in education 'which aimed to model enough of the domain (*of knowledge*), the learner, and relevant pedagogy to be able to give detailed instruction, remediation, and explana-tion, perhaps eventually – although this aim was kept implicit – to rival a human tutor' (Cumming *et al.*, 1994, p. 109). Instead, a 'dual interaction view' appears to be gaining support. This can be described in terms of learner interaction at task and discussion level (Cumming *et al.*, 1994, p. 108). In this model, the computer is used to provide a context for meaningful learn-ing to take place; teachers in this model have a crucial role to play, for instance, in providing lead-in, interaction and exploitation tasks to render ICT-based stimulus material effective.

> Pupils should encounter computers as mediational resources incorporated within suitably rich settings of activity; that is, settings with authentic goals and pur-poses for those pupils, and settings that are explicitly integrated with other expe-riences of knowing and understanding as they get organized at other times.
> (Crook, 1994, p. 43)

Despite the sometimes negative images associated with educational comput-ing, (see, for example, Light, 1993, p. 41), one of the most fundamental impacts of the use of new technology in education is the potential it affords in providing a learning environment which is collaborative and communica-tive: the 'synchronous, located nature of the traditional classroom now has dimensions that extend to asynchronous and distributed' (Heppell, 1993, p. 234).

In other words, with e-mail and video conferencing, the need for teachers and learners to coincide in time and location recedes. Not only is this development conducive to the inclusion of learner groups which, up to now, have been excluded, it also affords the possibility of drawing increasingly on sources, including expert opinion, from outside the classroom and the school. It is this potential for joint project work which has caught the imagination of many teachers as it provides added value in terms of tangible learning objectives which tend to be perceived as relevant and real by learners.

Computer-mediated communication (CMC), as Bernadette Robinson rightly points out, requires users to adapt 'their social and linguistic behaviour to the medium in order to engage with other people' (Robinson, 1993, p. 125). This involves an awareness of differences in discourse patterns in CMC, such as a relatively informal colloquial style of written utterances akin to spoken language or multi-strand interchanges. Given the importance of language in the learning process across the curriculum, this potential has huge implications for the way we conceive teaching and learning.

Mark Peterson's summary of competing hypotheses of positive and negative 'effects' in Table 10.1 (Peterson, 1997, p. 35) gives a succinct overview of some of the challenges facing teachers exploring the application of CMC for classroom-based, formal teaching and learning purposes.[13]

Peterson's points clearly illustrate that the transformation of the learning process by new technologies comes at a cost. Whilst, for example, CMC makes educational project work amongst partners at a distance in place and time possible, unless these projects are planned and managed carefully, there is the danger of learning being 'dehumanized', learners becoming or remaining isolated, suffering from information overload or of them using inappropriate language ('flaming') because of the relative anonymity resulting from not knowing their interlocutors personally or from being 'in character' or 'in role'.

Viewed in this light, the impact of the introduction of ICT across the school curriculum will clearly affect not only the epistemologies of what is taught in schools and how but also the way in which learners construct personal meaning. This, however, is a lesson which is only slowly being learned. 'They won't have to change what they learn: You won't have to change what you teach' announces a recent advertisement for a particular brand of computer. The advert reassures: everything will stay the same, there is no need to engage critical faculties, only to 'deliver' and acquire sufficient 'skill'.

Yet the computer could – if we allow it – change everything. It could transform our classrooms, the kinds of things we teach and the things our students learn. And it could transform the teacher's role.

TRANSFORMING THE ROLE OF THE TEACHER

Managing ICT use in educational contexts requires decisions, such as choice between centralized delivery through networked computer rooms or

Table 10.1 Positive and negative effects of computer-mediated communication

	Positive	*Negative*
Asynchronous conferencing	• opportunity for reflection before responding • opportunnity to revise written work	• loss of impetus to reply • slowness in decision-making
Synchronous conferencing	• opportunity for more authentic dialogue • immediate response	• need for a skilled moderator to facilitate (control?) dialogue • technostress
Learner autonomy	• removal of time distance constraintss • promotion of interactive learning	• 'contextual deprivation' • reduced feedback
Anonymity	• increased written output • increased participation by minority groups • learners take control of their learning • 'empowerment' of learners • increased self-disclosure	• less reading • reinforcement of existing inequalities • information overload • lack of accountability • 'flaming'
Collaboration	• increased collaboration between learners and between teachers and learners • language skills enhaced through activity in the TL[14]	• 'aloneness factor' • greater regimentation of learning
Technical issues	• learners gain vital computer skills • new opportunities for inductive 'learning by doing'	• high costs of new technology, dangers of monitoring and control • 'dehumanization' of learning

Source: Peterson, M. (1997)

distributed approaches through stand-alone machines in classrooms (for a more detailed discussion of these issues as well as a framework for evaluating ICT applications see, for example, Pachler, 1999). But technical choices of this kind are relatively simple, compared to the organizational and classroom management questions posed for teachers, e.g. whether learners should work on the computer individually or in pairs/small groups. Work with new technologies invariably involves the delegation of responsibility to learners and successful learning outcomes will depend on learners' ability to work independently and autonomously from the teacher and, increasingly, to take control of the learning process themselves.

There is no evidence whatsoever to suggest that the introduction of technology will decrease the teacher's role, at least, not if any serious attempt is made to exploit technology. It is true that a typical use of an Integrated Learning System, for example, is one in which half of a class can be marginalized for all or part of a lesson while the teacher concentrates on those who are not tied to their computers by a set of headphones. But, in relation to uses of technology which genuinely exploit its potential, all research to date suggests that the teacher needs to spend a great deal of time monitoring, directing and assisting in the learning process. Whilst new technologies might diminish certain aspects of the teacher's role, such as the collation of material and information, her agenda will remain central to ensuring a well structured and sequenced learning process. Eunice Fisher sees this process as a shift of the locus of control and a movement towards less didactic and more open styles of teaching (Fisher, 1993, pp. 60 and 62).

It is difficult, in our view, to sustain the notion that the moderating force of teachers' professional judgement will no longer be required in an ICT–rich learning environment. In view of the randomness both of the information accessible through new technologies as well as the 'multi-stranded' nature of CMC, teachers will continue to play a key role in providing 'scaffolding', i.e. mediating support in the process of acquiring new skills, knowledge or understanding (Bruner, 1985, pp. 24–25). In fact, in order to maximize the effectiveness of the contribution of ICT to the learning process, teachers will need to develop higher order skills relating to, for instance, the selection and evaluation of appropriate resources:

> [the] very nature of multimedia, vast, non-linear and readable only through the computer screen, means that it is difficult to assess the scope and quality of a title or source without spending considerable time on it. There is no equivalent to picking up and flicking through a book which will give an experienced teacher a clear view of its coverage and relevance.
>
> (McFarlane, 1996, p. 4)

The teacher needs to ask herself in what way the respective technological aid will support learning objectives and what kind of teacher-pupil and pupil-pupil interaction is likely to take place. Invariably, ICT applications are designed with certain assumptions about the subject domain, the nature of the learning process, prevailing teaching methodologies and other relevant knowledge from adjoining fields and disciplines.

It is worth quoting from a report by the Committee of Advisors on Science and Technology (1997) Panel on Educational Technology to the US President on the use of technology to strengthen K-12 education in the United States:

> [the] panel believes that the principal focus of an education schools technology programme should be the ways in which elementary and secondary school teachers can use information technologies to facilitate thinking and learning by K-12 students.
>
> (President's Committee of Advisors on Science and Technology, 1997)

This statement is supported by asserting that the choice regarding technology is to determine whether American children are 'prepared to hold high wage, high skilled jobs that add significant value within the world market place, or are instead forced to compete with workers in developing countries . . . for the provision of commodity products and low value added services.' (Executive Summary, President's Committee of Advisors on Science and Technology, 1997). That choice confronts the British system as well and, it seems, at least as judged by recent government pronouncements, that the focus will be on basic numeracy, basic literacy and, now, basic skills in relation to ICT. Whether this is a deliberate policy, and one which runs counter to that of the United States, or whether it is simply a failure to understand just how technology might change the educational process is unclear.

In the US, the view is unequivocal: in the words of the Director of Learning Technologies at the Council of Chief State School Officers, 'The US work force does not need knowers, it needs learners' (Section: Potential Significance, President's Committee of Advisors on Science and Technology, 1997). If, on the other hand, policy commitments are aimed at the low wage basic skill end of the spectrum, it may indeed be that the huge potential of the technology can be channelled into drill and practice sessions focusing on the acquisition of isolated basic skills downloaded from the Internet. In that scenario it will be likely that pedagogy would become unproblematic, time (and money) would be saved, and teachers further de-skilled. But in any other scenario, and particularly those in which the technology is fully integrated into the learning process, the teacher's role will be altered fundamentally and there is no sense in which the teacher will be relegated to mere support of ICT-based learning. New skills will be needed to help children make the most of the information they have at their fingertips; new conceptual frameworks will be required to encourage children to make sense, for instance, of the mathematical and scientific visualizations that are now routinely accessible on computer screens; and new complexities of pedagogy involving, for example, collaborative learning with computers will have to be addressed (just how complex this question is, even in one learning domain such as mathematics, has been amply illustrated by Healy *et al.*, 1995).

CONCLUSION

In this chapter we have considered the potential impact of ICT on the teaching and learning processes. We have suggested that the potential of new technologies has considerable implications for our current notion of knowledge and the teaching and learning processes as well as for the relationships and roles of teachers and learners. Whilst we have tried to demonstrate what ICT use means for currently prevailing concepts of education and schooling, we have also called these concepts into question by stressing the importance of preparing the teachers of the twenty-first century adequately so as to be able to provide the relevant knowledge, skills and understanding requisite of the new conceptual frameworks made possible by new technologies.

> [Computers] are redefining what capabilities their tasks require, and in ways that cannot but feed back eventually into the school curriculum. These changes are not only in individual techniques and skills, but are also altering the whole balance in thought and action between the intuitive and the explicit, and between the rationally simplified and the qualitatively complex. These are changes that teachers not only should not, but in practice cannot, ignore.
>
> (Scrimshaw, 1997, p. 109)

The challenges of new technologies for education are manifold. It would be too much to expect that educationalists and policy makers should, in a mere two decades, have faced all the complexities, developed the software and solved the problems which confront us as users of ICT. But we can at least recognize this complexity, and identify the new things that we can do, alongside the old things we can now do in novel ways. Anything less will lead, at best, to a waste of time and money as well as being a diversion from important educational tasks. At worst, it would lead to the further de-skilling of the teaching profession, the dumbing down of school knowledge and a shameful failure to equip children for the challenge of the new century.

REFERENCES

Bonnett, M. (1997) Computers in the classroom: some values issues, in A. McFarlane (ed.) *Information Technology and Authentic Learning. Realising the Potential of Computers in the Primary Classroom*, London: Routledge.

Bruner, J. (1985) Vygotsky: a historical and conceptual perspective, in J. Wertsch (ed.) *Culture, Communication and Cognition: Vygotskyan Perspectives*, Cambridge: Cambridge University Press.

Collins, J., Hammond, M. and Wellington, J. (1997) *Teaching and Learning with Multimedia*, London: Routledge.

Crook, C. (1994) *Computers and the Collaborative Experience of Learning*, London: Routledge.

Cuban, L. (1986) *Teachers and Machines: The Classroom Use of Technology Since 1920*, New York: Teachers College Press.

Cumming, G., Susses, R. and Cropp, S. (1994) The teacher-learner-computer triangle in CALL frameworks for interaction and advice, *Computer Assisted Language Learning*, 7 (2): 107–23.

DfEE (1997) *Connecting the Learning Society*, National Grid for Learning, consultation paper, London.

DfEE (1998) Teaching: high status, high standards. Requirements for courses of Initial Teacher Training. Annex B: Initial Teacher Training National Curriculum for the use of Information and Communications Technology in subject teaching. Circular

4/98, pp. 17–31.

Fisher, E. (1993) The teacher's role, in P. Scrimshaw (ed.) *Language, Classrooms and Computers*, London: Routledge.

Goodman, S. (1996) Visual English, in S. Goodman and D. Graddol (eds.) *Redesigning English: New Texts, New Identities*, London: Routledge.

Healy, L., Hoyles, C. and Pozzi, S. (1995) Making sense of groups, computers and mathematics, *Cognition and Instruction*, 13 (4): 505–23.

Heppell, S. (1993) Teacher education, learning and the information generation: the progression and evolution of educational computing against a background of change, in *Journal of Information Technology for Teacher Education*, 2 (2): 229–37.

Kaput, J. (1994) Democratizing access to calculus: new routes using old roots, in A. Schoenfeld (ed.) *Mathematical Thinking and Problem Solving*, Hillsdale: Lawrence Erlbaum.

Laborde, C. and Laborde, J. M. (1995) What about a learning environment where Euclidean concepts are manipulated with a mouse?, in A. diSessa, C. Hoyles, R. Noss and L. D. Edwards, (eds.) *Computers for Exploratory Learning*, Berlin: Springer Verlag.

Light, P. (1993) Collaborative learning with computers, in P. Scrimshaw (ed.) *Language, Classrooms and Computers*, London: Routledge.

McFarlane, A. (1996) Blessings in disguise, *TES Computers Update*, June 28: 4

McKinsey & Company (1997) *The Future of Information Technology in UK Schools*, London.

Moro, B. (1997) A pedagogy of the hypermedia, in A.-K. Korsvold and B. Rüschoff (eds.) *New Technologies in Language Learning and Teaching*, Education Committee: Council for Cultural Co-operation. Strasbourg: Council of Europe Publishing.

Noss, R. (1992) The social shaping of computing in mathematics education, in D. Pimm, and E. Love (eds.) *The Teaching and Learning of School Mathematics*, London: Hodder and Stoughton.

Noss, R. (1997) *New Cultures, New Numeracies: Inaugural Lecture*, London: Institute of Education.

Pachler, N. (1999) Theories of learning and information and communications technology, in M. Leask and N. Pachler (eds.) *Learning to Teach Using ICT in the Secondary School*, London: Routledge.

Peterson, M. (1997) Language teaching and networking, *System*, 25 (1): 29–37.

President's Committee of Advisors on Science and Technology, Panel on Educational Technology (1997) *A report to the President on the use of technology to strengthen K-12 education in the United States.*

Pyke, N. (1998) Obsolete computers jeopardise IT reform, *TES*, January 23: 3.

Robinson, B. (1993) Communicating through computers in the classroom, in P. Scrimshaw (ed.) *Language, Classrooms and Computers*, London: Routledge.

Scrimshaw, P. (1997) Computers and the teacher's role, in B. Somekh and N. Davis (eds.) *Using Information Technology Effectively in Teaching and Learning. Studies in Pre-Service and In-Service Teacher Education*, London: Routledge.

Stevenson, D. (1997) *Information and Communications Technology in UK schools. An independent inquiry*, London.

Teacher Training Agency and the Funding Councils (1998) *Lottery Funded ICT*

Training Programme for Serving Teachers: Specification for the Approval of Training Providers, London.

Thornton, K. (1998) Laptops 'will cut teacher workload, *TES*, April 24: 10.

Williams, M. and Burden, R. (1997) *Psychology for Language Teachers. A Social Constructivist Approach*, Cambridge: Cambridge University Press.

Wolff, D. (1997) Computers as cognitive tools in the language classroom, in A.-K. Korsvold and B. Rüschoff (eds.) *New Technologies in Language Learning and Teaching*, Education Committee: Council for Cultural Co-operation. Strasbourg: Council of Europe Publishing.

Wilensky, U. (1997) What is normal anyway? Therapy for epistemological anxiety, *Educational Studies in Mathematics* 33 (2): 171–202.

NOTES

1. For a historical (and somewhat quaint) review of this recurring pattern, see Cuban (1986).

2. For a detailed discussion of the notion of learning as a collaborative activity, see e.g. Williams and Burden (1997) and the role of computers within it, see e.g. Crook (1994).

3. Although we have no intention of exploring it here, this ubiquitous (in the UK) acronym nicely encapsulates the idea of the technology as a 'thing', easily summed up and delivered. Reducing the complexities of the technology to three letters is convenient but dangerous. In this chapter, we will opt for convenience while pointing to the dangers

4. DfEE (1997) *Connecting the Learning Society*. National Grid for Learning. The Government's consultation paper. London: DfEE; DfEE (1997) *Preparing for the information age*. Synoptic report of the Education Department's Superhighways Initiative. London: DfEE; McKinsey & Company (1997) *The Future of Information Technology in UK Schools*. London: DfEE; Stevenson, D. (1997) *Information and Communications Technology in UK schools. An independent inquiry*. London: DfEE.

5. Now the British Educational Communications and Technology Agency (BECTA; URL: http://www.becta.org.uk/)

6. URL: http://www.open.gov.uk/dfee/circular/0498.htm

7. URL: http://www.ngfl.gov.uk/

8. *Lottery Funded ICT Training Programme for Serving Teachers: Specification for the Approval of Training Providers*, Teacher Training Agency and the Funding Councils (1998).

9. Some indication of just how restrictive this is can be found at http://www.standards.dfee.gov.uk/literacy/theresourcearea.

10. See Noss (1997) for a discussion of the idea of numeracy and a critique of restrictive definitions of the term.

11. In case we are misunderstood: a facility with number is essential for any mathematical or scientific learning. Our point is simply that there is little evidence that the computer is especially useful in developing such facility, and even less that the technology is most usefully employed in this way.

12. For a detailed discussion of the notion of multimodality and the importance of visual literacy, see Goodman (1996).

13. Peterson's summary also includes the rubric 'teacher/learner' roles which are omitted here as it is the focus of a later section of this chapter.
14. TL = target language; in modern foreign languages teaching and learning the term refers to the use of the foreign language as the medium for instruction of and interaction with learners.

11

The Common Strands of Pedagogy and Their Implications

Judith Ireson, Peter Mortimore and Susan Hallam

The chapters in this book present a rich diversity of approaches to pedagogy in different phases of education. In this final chapter we will draw together and comment on some of the themes running through the previous chapters. We will endeavour to answer the question 'What do we now know about effective pedagogy?'. We will also comment on what we still do not know about this important topic. We will draw on the arguments raised in the various chapters in order to explore whether the age or stage of the learner makes a difference to the pedagogy used. Finally, we will set out what we see as the major lessons and implications for pedagogy in the future.

Before addressing these questions, however, it may be helpful to comment on some of the economic and labour force trends which are affecting the context of learning currently. These are important because pedagogy cannot be considered in isolation. It has to be considered in relation to the aims of education. What should these be? Teaching people the basic skills of literacy and numeracy is crucially important but there are many additional cultural tools that they will need to master if they are to have productive and satisfying lives in the twenty-first century.

Four major developments have had an impact on the English education system and hence on its pedagogy. First, the world trade markets have become acutely competitive and are increasingly dominated by large and mobile multinational companies, able to relocate their business to areas with skilled but cheap labour. Second, higher education, once a small scale enterprise catering for about ten per cent of the age group, has expanded such that a third of all school leavers – and a significant number of older people – now expect to participate in it. Third, during the second half of the twentieth century there has been an explosion of knowledge. To take just two examples of radical scientific developments: the biomolecular and quantum revolutions have given mankind the ability to alter and synthesize new forms of life and, perhaps ultimately, to control matter; and the information and computing technologies providing instant access to information, are transforming much of our working and our social lives. Fourth, the emergence of international studies of educational performance have made governments acutely aware of comparisons of the outputs of different systems.

The impact of these factors on pedagogy has been considered in Chapters 4, 5 and 7. The authors argue that changes in the world economy will place different demands on students in secondary, further and higher education. New demands will also be made on teachers in these sectors. The expansion of higher education requires that pedagogy meets the needs of a greater diversity of learners. Moreover, it is no longer sufficient for learners to demonstrate that they have acquired a specific knowledge base from courses. They now enter the workplace with the expectation that their learning will continue and the realization that they will need the skills constantly to adapt to changing patterns of work. These requirements for continued learning and adaptation call for specific personal qualities and attitudes. The authors who have focused on adolescent, adult and lifelong learning have stressed that individuals must be willing and able to continue learning and they must be willing and able to adapt to new demands and challenges.

WHAT DO WE KNOW ABOUT EFFECTIVE PEDAGOGY?

If we take as our yardstick the most general definition of pedagogy used in any of the chapters – 'Any conscious activity designed by one person to bring about learning in another' – we can address the question of effectiveness through the idea of fitness for purpose. By this we mean that teaching methods are aligned with the needs of the learner and with the desired learning outcomes. The evidence from the different chapters suggests that a particular pedagogy will be effective if it is:

• clear about its goals
• imbued with high expectations and capable of providing motivation
• technically competent and appropriate to its purpose
• theoretically sophisticated.

A pedagogy which has clear goals

A major problem at the heart of our consideration of pedagogy is that there has been little explicit discussion of goals within the education system. The question 'What are we teaching for?' is surprisingly seldom posed or answered. There was little discussion of general principles when the National Curriculum was being designed during the late 1980s. Instead, separate Subject Task Groups were given responsibility for drawing up a framework of attainment targets and these focused on the curriculum structure and assessment. There was little debate about the aims of education, which in the very broad terms of the Education Reform Act were 'to promote the spiritual, moral, cultural, mental and physical development of pupils' (DES,

1988). In time, each of the Task Groups concerned with the curriculum subjects formulated aims for their subject but, even taken together, these do not add up to a set of overarching national aims for education.

There has been a similar lack of clarity about the aims of pre-school education, where there is debate as to whether academic achievement or personal and social development should be the priority. Likewise in further, continuing and higher education, there is a tension between needs for personal development, the needs of industry and commerce and the requirements of academic work. In the absence of clear aims, the competitive climate that currently exists at national and international level has a powerful influence. An increasingly common pragmatic – but none the less limited – view is that the sole aim of teaching is to improve learners' performance in those national assessments and examinations whose results are in the public domain and are therefore open to scrutiny at home and abroad.

We would be among the first to support the view that a principal aim of teaching should be to enable as many people as possible to achieve as much as they can during their life time. For too long, in our judgement, young people from less advantaged backgrounds have underachieved (Mortimore and Whitty, 1997). To make closing the gap between the achievements of the advantaged and the disadvantaged a major aim of teaching will require a restructuring of our current educational system. In higher education, Government initiatives such as the establishment of the Open University, the turning of polytechnics into universities and many of the developments in further and higher education, including the proposed University of Industry, have began to move in this direction.

We also believe that our democratic political system requires an education in citizenship. The responsibilities of the individual in a democratic system are both personal and social. The personal aspects include taking responsibility for maintaining oneself and one's dependants and abiding by the laws of the land. The social aspects include paying one's taxes, contributing to the care of those unable to work and fulfilling one's electoral duties. In addition, good citizens need to develop critical and reflective awareness, to make informed choices and to take responsibility for their own decisions. This requires the systematic acquisition of knowledge, understanding, attitudes and competencies. Within the educational system, therefore, individuals need to learn to deal with choice within a carefully structured framework of progression.

It is well recognized that choice and self-determination can also exert powerful, positive influences on motivation. Despite this, much of our current school system offers little choice for pupils. Where, at fourteen, pupils have been offered a modular curriculum with guided choice, the adoption of such a system is reported to have improved pupil motivation (Ireson and McCallum, in press). Beyond the secondary school years, learner choice tends to increase, although training is often task or job specific. However, some companies have recognized the importance of personal motivation and have developed successful schemes in which training has been broadened to accommodate individual interests (Hougham *et al.*, 1991).

This brings us back to the question of the aims of education. Should education encourage individuals to pursue their own interests or should the needs of society take priority over individual wishes? Are the two, in fact, mutually exclusive? One starting point for discussion of the aims of education might be to ask parents, teachers and students what they think are the important goals of education. Surveys carried out in America (e.g. Goodlad, 1983) demonstrate that pupils, parents and teachers rated four general goals as important for schools. These were academic (including critical thinking as well as basic skills), vocational (relating to employment), social and civic (relating to preparation for entry into civic society) and personal (relating to the development of individual responsibility, self-confidence, creativity and thinking for oneself).

In a similar exercise undertaken in Britain, Raven (1994) found that pupils rated most highly personal qualities such as being confident, able to take the initiative in introducing changes, and being independent. They gave priority to qualities which were self-determined, self-motivated and forward-looking. They valued high grades, but mainly because these provided access to occupational opportunities and privilege, rather than because they valued the subject matter itself. Teachers' values were broadly similar to those of the pupils but were generally more prescriptive and rated the content of the curriculum more highly. Parents and pupils tended to value school mainly as a preparation for the world of work. Similarly, a high proportion of students in higher education see their education as a means of improving their employment prospects (*The Independent*, 10th December, 1998).

It is clear that careful thinking and informed debate are needed on the nature of the aims of education in all institutions committed to furthering learning. The debate will also necessarily involve a consideration of the values underlying the issue of inclusion (as discussed in Chapter 6). There are few occupations which require the simple, repetitive actions of industrial production lines. Increasingly, robots are performing these tasks. Most occupations require self-motivation, ability to take the initiative and to solve problems; many also require leadership and management skills.

As we have seen in Chapter 2, the Movimento da Escola Moderna (MEM) set out its goals for early childhood with great clarity. These goals included: an initiation into democratic life; the re-institution of values and social meanings; and the co-operative reconstruction of culture. Pupils, parents and staff could be in no doubts as to what MEM was trying to achieve. At the other extreme, the Connective Model of vocational education (cited in Chapter 8) sets out its goals as helping learners to experience different combinations of theoretical and practical learning and enabling them to relate their formal programmes of study to trends in labour and work organization. In other words, the students were being offered the opportunity to learn about business organization and provided with an opportunity to develop personal and social skills in this setting.

Evaluation of the effectiveness of pedagogy can only be made in relation to its aims. Establishing clear aims within each educational phase would enable the development of an appropriate pedagogy for each phase. Further, establishing clear overarching aims which provide a lifespan framework within which all formal teaching and learning could be understood would facilitate the development of a structured learning progression for each individual.

A pedagogy which is imbued with high expectations and capable of promoting motivation

A number of authors stressed the importance of high expectations in all forms of pedagogy. The problem is that high expectations cannot be assigned; they have to spring naturally from the belief and aspirations of the teacher and learner. They have to be genuine or they become counterproductive. We know from empirical research that expectations are passed between teacher and learner in subtle, often undetected, ways (Mortimore et al., 1988). As outlined in Chapter 4, underpinning teachers' attitudes to the capabilities of their students is their belief about intelligence. If teachers believe that intelligence is largely innate and unchangeable and if their students find learning difficult, they are unlikely to be able to adopt high expectations for their students. If, on the other hand, teachers believe that intelligence can be modified by experience, they will be more likely to pitch their expectations positively. This applies throughout all phases of education.

The emphasis on high expectations marks out the approach of the High/Scope Project (reported in Chapter 2). A strong Vygotskian influence takes a stage further the emphasis on continuous planning and review that is found in Reggio Emilia (one of the other programmes reviewed in Chapter 2) and provides a structured approach in all its routines. The same positive approach can be found in the work of Bruner (cited in Chapter 3), in many of the accounts of studies of school effectiveness (Mortimore, 1998) and in the references to mastery learning in Chapter 4. High expectations also play a part in work experience, in 'on the job' training and in participation in university courses.

Learners' orientations to learning

An important theme running through all the chapters of this book is the need to develop pedagogies that will encourage and support learners to take control of their own learning. With appropriate support, active control over learning fosters a mastery orientation towards achievement.

A mastery orientation to learning is linked with numerous beneficial motivational characteristics, including a preference for challenging work, high persistence in the face of difficulty and a focus on learning as a goal in itself (Ames and Ames, 1992; Dweck and Leggett, 1988; Nicholls, 1989). Learners with a mastery orientation are more likely to use effective learning strategies; to monitor their own learning, checking that they understand the meaning of their work, and to relate learning in formal education to their own experience (Meece, 1991; Rogers, 1990). The concept of a mastery orientation, which has largely been developed and applied in relation to school-age learners, resonates with the concept of deep learning, studied in student populations in secondary school (Selmes, 1987), further education (Strang, 1997) and higher education (Entwistle, 1992; Marton and Booth, 1997). The student who adopts a deep approach to learning makes the effort to understand and connect ideas. In contrast to the mastery orientation, a helpless or 'work-avoidant' orientation is linked with numerous negative motivational characteristics, including an avoidance of challenge, low persistence in the face of difficulties and the use of superficial learning strategies. This pattern is one that leads learners into a downward spiral of achievement.

A mastery or deep approach to learning, however, does not always work to the learner's advantage. In an education system which is governed by fixed syllabuses and courses of study, students who become too absorbed in a topic or piece of work may leave insufficient time to cover the syllabus. Generally, learners adapt to the learning situations in which they find themselves and maximize their potential for success. For instance, as outlined in Chapter 7, the evidence suggests that to cope with the demands of higher education, students tend to move from the adoption of a deep approach prior to starting their course towards a more surface approach as they proceed through it. Learners have to regulate their interest and organize their time so that they complete the work set and obtain the best grades they can. This may mean adopting a surface approach to satisfy course requirements.

Grades can be a powerful source of motivation and undoubtedly spur learners on to make greater effort, who otherwise might give up. They can also provide useful information about one's performance relative to others in a class or subject which may subsequently feed in to decisions about choice of courses and careers. However, too great an emphasis on grades can undermine learning – particularly if grades form a major part of judgements about self-worth (Covington, 1992) or where the emphasis is on rote learning for regurgitation in examinations at the expense of understanding.

Metacognition and self-regulation

A first step towards self-regulation is to become aware of one's own learning. This awareness can be developed from a very early age, as Siraj-Blatchford has pointed out in Chapter 2. Programmes such as the Reggio Emilia provide a means for children to reflect on their learning and to see their efforts and ideas validated and considered important by their teachers. In a similar vein, Pramling has demonstrated that children in the first years of school can start to take control over their learning if the meta-cognitive aspects of learning are introduced to them in appropriate ways (Pramling, 1996).

Gipps and MacGilchrist (Chapter 3) comment on the current focus in primary education on the academic content of the curriculum and call for an increased emphasis on meta-cognition. In other countries, particularly the United States, programs have been developed to increase children's use of learning strategies and their awareness of their learning. Examples include Informed Strategies for Learning (Paris et al., 1984), Reciprocal Teaching (Palinscar and Brown, 1989) and Cognitive Apprenticeship (Brown et al., 1989). Although these programmes differ from one another in their theoretical roots, they are all embedded within a curriculum area. They also include pedagogic elements to enhance teachers' and learners' awareness and understanding of the process of learning and, in particular, of the need for positive expectations.

The evidence from secondary and higher education shows mixed effects of programmes designed to promote meta-cognitive skills. While some have been successful (Biggs, 1987; Weinstein et al., 1988) others have not (Howe, 1991). This is in part because learners tend not to transfer their knowledge of strategies between learning situations. The degree of success of meta-cognitive programmes, therefore, depends crucially on the extent to which they are embedded within the curriculum and the current learning environment. Where they are not integrated, they can increase the adoption of a surface approach to learning. Learning about learning cannot be successful if it is taught as an 'add on'. It must be integrated with the knowledge which is being acquired.

Learners' and teachers' beliefs in their ability to succeed

In academic situations, beliefs about their ability to succeed influence both students' and teachers' motivation and coping. For students, their perceived self-efficacy means their belief in their ability to regulate their own learning and to master different academic subjects. For teachers, it means their belief in their personal efficacy to motivate and promote their students' learning. Bandura argues that, in the current information age with the rapidly accelerating growth of knowledge, a major goal of education should be to equip young people with the intellectual tools, efficacy beliefs and intrinsic interests they need in order to educate themselves throughout their lifetime (Bandura, 1995).

Teachers' beliefs in their own personal efficacy also influence their classroom practice. Those who have a high sense of efficacy tend to support the development of students' intrinsic motivation and academic self-determination. They also have a positive impact on student attainment (Tschannen-Moran et al., 1998; Ashton and Webb, 1986). In addition, teachers' belief in their own efficacy offers them some protection from stressful experiences in schools. Those who have a strong sense of self-efficacy are more likely to deal with academic problems by directing their efforts at resolving the problems, whereas those who have a weak sense of efficacy are more likely to attempt to avoid the problems. A teacher's sense of efficacy is built up primarily through experience of successfully motivating and promoting students' learning. A student's sense of efficacy is built up primarily through experiences of successful self-regulation and learning. For this to occur, teaching must be appropriately matched to enable the student to experience reasonable challenge. While success in the early stages of learning is important – failure creates expectations of failure which may be difficult to dispel – setting very easy work which may guarantee success may also lead to boredom and therefore is not a long term solution.

For those who experience failure during their education, the emotional responses to learning linger on and may have to be confronted in later life. Common emotions are a lack of confidence in the ability to learn, anxiety or a general lack of efficacy, which may inhibit the learner from engaging in formal learning. In schools, pupils disengage in a variety of ways, such as playing truant or daydreaming; beyond school, adults simply avoid further formal learning. As Hodgson and Kambouri point out in Chapter 9, the lecturer's awareness of adults' previous learning experience is an important factor in their work, since adults frequently carry with them a sense of failure from their school days. The situation is similar in further education where part of the educator's work is to help motivate those who have become disaffected from learning (Young and Lucas, Chapter 5). Those who leave school with few or no qualifications are less likely to participate in continuing education than their better qualified peers. In England and Wales, it is estimated that only about half the adult population has engaged in any kind of education or training since leaving school. Those who do participate tend to be young, male, mobile and from higher socio-economic groups (McGivney, 1993).

A pedagogy which is technically competent and appropriate for its purpose

Teaching is a complex task. A number of the chapters in this book have attempted to identify the assorted components that contribute to its totality. Even though it is possible to list the characteristics of an effective teacher, the anecdotal evidence of newspaper columns such as 'My best teacher' (in the *Times Educational Supplement*) illustrates just how often it is the unusual or the quirky approaches which feature in people's recollections. Nevertheless, the preparation of teaching programmes, presentation of ideas and information, setting of suitable assignments and provision of appropriate feedback all require a high level of technical competence.

Fitness for purpose

Earlier in this chapter, we introduced the notion of 'fitness for purpose'. The term implies an alignment between the needs of the learner, the desired learning outcomes and the tasks and activities designed by the teacher to achieve those outcomes. It includes assessment appropriate for particular forms of learning. There are two aspects of alignment that we would like to highlight. The first is the alignment of the learning activity with the learner's capabilities. By this we mean that a reasonable match is achieved between the learner's current understanding and skill and the new learning presented. Within special education, as Corbett and Norwich argue in Chapter 6, considerable effort has been invested in the development of techniques of task and needs analysis to enable teachers more accurately to target their teaching to meet learners' needs. Behavioural analytic models exemplify this approach, with detailed analyses of the needs of the individual learner in relation to particular goals and objectives. Optimal teaching methods are then developed in order to help achieve those objectives.

These ideas have been adopted in recent years in relation to target setting for schools and in the National Literacy Strategy. Although behavioural methods may not be appropriate for all kinds of learning and learners, there can be value in the approach. Similar methods are used to teach complex workplace activities such as team working.

Formative assessment, combined with tutoring programmes, can also help establish learners' needs but, to be effective, it must be rigorous and theoretically well grounded (Young and Lucas, Chapter 5). Corbett and Norwich (Chapter 6) usefully point to the distinction between three types of educational needs: those that are common to all; those that are specific or distinct; and those that are individual. All learners will have some individual needs which would require a specific adaptation of any general pedagogical approach in order to achieve a perfect alignment of learning tasks with their capabilities.

In addition to their role in establishing learners' needs, techniques of formative assessment provide a very powerful means of providing support for learning. Used well, this type of assessment can help students to develop the capacity to undertake assessment of their own learning. Assessment techniques, such as profiling, also encourage older students to set up their own action plans, assess their own work, discuss curriculum goals and review progress with their teachers. Black and Wiliam (1998), in a comprehensive review, demonstrate that formative assessment can raise attainment to a remarkable level. It can also have powerful effects on student motivation and learning (Broadfoot, 1996). However, its importance is not universally recognized: for instance, the majority of lecturers in higher education tend to view the role of assessment as summative rather than formative and do not appreciate how much assessment can help students to learn (Ramsden, 1992).

Aligning teaching methods and learning outcomes

The second form of alignment we wish to consider is between teaching methods, tasks and learning outcomes. Certain teaching methods appear to be better suited to achieve particular learning outcomes. Methods that emphasize efficient one way communication, such as lectures and class presentations, may assist students in obtaining and understanding information – the lower order objectives of teaching according to Bloom's taxonomy, although the evidence from higher education (Chapter 7) suggests that this may not always be the case. Methods which utilize communication between learners, or that involve discussion between teacher and students, tend to be more useful in helping students to achieve the higher order objectives of analysis, synthesis and evaluation.

There is also evidence that teachers' task assignment tends to emphasize quantity rather than quality and concentrates on the lower, rather than the higher, forms of learning (Kerry, 1984; Stodolsky, 1988). This appears to be true across all phases of education. On the one hand, the preponderance of knowledge acquisition and comprehension is not surprising, given that a major role of formal education is to impart new information and skills. On the other hand, the challenge facing education as a whole (see Chapters 4 and 7) is to develop a pedagogy which will equip students to deal with the uncertainty and unpredictability inherent in the world today.

In similar vein, Noss and Pachler (Chapter 10) argue that access to the information available through new technology renders untenable the role of the teacher as the source of all knowledge. Other skills, such as organizing and making sense of large amounts of information, need to be given a higher priority. If we are to take up these challenges then teaching methods will need to be aligned to achieve more complex learning outcomes.

Challenge and interest in learning

Fitness for purpose also involves the teacher in presenting sufficient challenge for the learner. If the task merely repeats what is already known, the learner will find it boring yet if it presents too much that is unfamiliar, the learner will be overwhelmed. Finding the optimal level of challenge for the learner is a key pedagogical skill in all phases of education, although to date it has been given most attention in school level education. It is important to distinguish here between the types of learning defined by curriculum analysts and the level of challenge for an individual learner. From the students' perspective, the acquisition and comprehension of knowledge can present considerable challenges, even though such tasks may not be considered by educators to be the most challenging types of learning.

Whereas challenge and interest fuel learning, boredom detracts from it. Students in post-compulsory education have choices and can opt out or drop out of courses they find uninteresting or ill-suited to their needs. Pupils in schools, however, do not have this freedom. In a recent survey, more than half of Year 9 pupils said they were bored in some lessons (see Chapter 4). Lessons in secondary schools may be uninteresting because of the curriculum content, the teacher's approach or because pupils simply do not engage with the topic (Mortimore, 1998). But cognitive challenge, relevance, variety of activities including well designed discussions and thought-provoking activities can make even the most difficult subjects interesting.

A pedagogy which is theoretically sophisticated

If there are to be radical changes in pedagogy to equip young people for the future, then teachers and lecturers must have an understanding of learning processes and the factors which affect them (see Chapter 4). They must also be learners too, a point made in several chapters of this book. For example, if teachers are to enable learners to develop a better awareness of their own learning, they too will need to develop awareness of their own learning, along with pedagogic strategies to encourage it. As Siraj-Blatchford reported (in Chapter 2) children who attended pre-school centres where staff had a dynamic understanding of children's learning and a positive view of their own influence on their pupils made better progress in literacy and numeracy. But teachers and lecturers also need a positive environment in which to learn – one which is rich in knowledge and supportive (see Chapters 3 and 7).

Teachers and lecturers as learners

Developing pedagogies to assist students in developing skills for the twenty-first century, for instance, dealing with large amounts of information or using advanced technological tools, involves experimentation and provides some risk for both teachers and learners. Both parties have to leave the security of their structured lesson or lecture. Teachers may be asked to demonstrate their own processes of problem solving, including all the uncertainties and false starts involved in, for example, creative writing or solving mathematical problems. Learners may be asked to reveal and discuss their methods for essay writing, solving problems or writing a composition. They may be afraid of looking foolish if they fail or if their strategy is judged unfavourably. The creation of a safe, accepting, and non-judgmental environment is essential for this type of learning.

Connecting theory and practice

The theoretical basis of new pedagogic initiatives needs to be established, researched and debated if teachers are take on the role of the architects rather than the bricklayers of learning. Theory is an important element in any formal learning. It serves to order thinking and to provide explanations. Yet, in recent times, there has been an enforced separation between theoretical and practical knowledge and a public belittling of theory within education.

The establishment of a General Teaching Council and the newly formed Institute of Learning and Teaching may lead to a recognition of the need for all kinds of teachers to ground their teaching skills in theories of learning. It remains to be seen whether the theoretical knowledge underpinning pedagogy and the research evidence for particular teaching approaches are given sufficient priority in courses for teachers and lecturers. Teachers and lecturers in all phases of education require an understanding of the principles on which teaching is based, in addition to practical skills, if they are to be able to use their knowledge flexibly and intelligently. In the past, as Young and Lucas argue in Chapter 5, teaching methods based on reflection have underplayed the importance of a theoretical knowledge base. It is important that the new National Literacy Strategy does not fall into the same trap.

Connecting learning in different contexts

A number of authors in this book have stressed how academic learning is enhanced when it is perceived as relating to real life. However, learners sometimes experience difficulties in making the connections between formal learning and real life contexts. Formal learning situations generate expectations and understandings of acceptable ways of doing things which govern learners' approaches to the tasks that they may be faced with. For example, students use different strategies to solve the same problems in different lessons in school (Saljo and Wyndham, 1993) and adults use different strategies for arithmetical calculation depending on whether they are in informal or formal settings (Lave and Wenger, 1991). Griffiths and Guile (Chapter 8) point to activity theory, as developed by Engstrom and others, as a fruitful avenue for the development of pedagogies linking school and work contexts. Promoting ways in which learning can be generalized to other contexts is a problem that has long taxed educators. It continues to do so.

Currently, in England, there is a tendency to see learning in rather polarized terms, linked to different ideas about human potential and to different views of epistemology. In crude terms, on one side are those who consider learning to be mainly a process of acquiring knowledge. On the other are those who see learning as the development of understanding and of conceptual change. The former tend to view extrinsic motivation as the fuel for learning whilst the latter see curiosity and the desire for competence as primary sources of motivation. In reality, both are required for the development of expertise in any field (Glaser, 1984). Ways of thinking are, to a great extent, embedded within knowledge structures. While an individual may acquire a range of strategies for problem solving, learning, or achieving understanding these cannot be transferred successfully to other domains unless the individual possesses the relevant knowledge base. An expert problem solver in one field, e.g. psychology, will not be an expert problem solver in nuclear physics without developing an extensive knowledge base in nuclear physics. Many educationalists intuitively have recognized this and try to find a balance between these two extreme positions. Similarly, learners are motivated by a variety of factors, including the promise of rewards, fascination with a subject, the desire to please a 'significant other' or, for some, the desire to get ahead of peers. Different motivators come into play in different situations for different individuals and it seems to us that pedagogy needs to be sufficiently flexible to accommodate this variety.

WHAT DO WE STILL NOT KNOW ABOUT PEDAGOGY?

Despite the surveys undertaken by some of the authors of this book, there remain a number of key pedagogical issues about which we know very little. The following five examples illustrate the point.

- *Whether it is equally beneficial to teach those who find learning easy with those who find it difficult*
  This argument lies at the heart of controversies about inclusion, selection, streaming and setting. The evidence for and against integration or segregation of different sorts of learners is often contradictory. At present, segregation of learners increases through the primary and secondary phases of education. In the post-compulsory phases, selection segregates learners but learners, themselves, also select courses and exercise some control over their learning. As with so many policy issues, the question cannot be considered without taking account of the aims of education. What does society wish to achieve through its system of education? With a clear set of aims established, educators and those involved in research may then address how they might best be achieved. Controversy arises where discussions about educational and institutional structures are undertaken without relation to the purposes for which they are intended. For instance, evidence from accumulated research on streaming has indicated that it tends to increase the gap in achievement between those in the bottom and top sets and has a detrimental effect on the self-esteem of those in the lower sets. If society requires a small proportion of well educated individuals and a greater mass of unskilled labour then it may be the best way of achieving this end. If, on the other hand, a society is required where everyone has high levels of skill then it is unlikely that streaming will be the appropriate means to attain this aim.

- *How much the adoption of particular assessment techniques influences the pedagogy chosen by teachers and the strategies adopted by learners*
  In 1979, Elton and Laurillard argued persuasively on the basis of their research that assessment is the driving force in determining teaching and learning strategies. The American literature similarly asserts that 'teaching to test' and 'learning for test' are common reactions to formal assessment.

Where test data are taken as a measure of teachers' accountability, the more 'high stakes' the process becomes and the more likely it is that a 'backwash' effect will be discerned (Biggs and Moore, 1993). If learning is driven by assessment then to achieve the desired learning outcomes requires that the assessment procedures reflect precisely the aims of the pedagogy. In the UK, national testing throughout the school years is still in its infancy and opportunities to target it specifically on higher order attainments are often defeated by the need to produce reliable – and hence defensible – measures. This also influences students' behaviour. Not surprisingly, some adopt strategies solely to get through tests and examinations regardless of whether such strategies involve any real changes in understanding.

- *How much the features of a disadvantaged life (poorer housing, health care, diet and emotional stress caused by relative poverty) impact on the pedagogy of schools and colleges*
  There is mounting evidence that, in a competitive education system, socio-economic disadvantage has a negative impact on the learning of pupils. However, as Mortimore and Whitty (1997) point out, data do not yet exist which could document the amount of improvement that particularly effective schools are able to endow on disadvantaged pupils. Whether learners who experience material or economic disadvantage would benefit from a different – perhaps more structured – pedagogy is yet to be researched. Entry to higher education is also influenced by social class with the lower classes being under-represented. In further and higher education, increasingly students are taking paid employment to support themselves, particularly where financial help is not available from their families. Where long hours are worked this can have detrimental effects on studying (Hodgson and Spours, 1998). Economic disadvantage has effects which continue beyond the school years. The question for society is whether educational aims should encompass the promotion of equity of opportunity and if so how this aim might be achieved.

- *How much ICT should change traditional approaches to pedagogy*
  ICT offers an opportunity to transform the pedagogy traditionally adopted in formal learning situations, as Noss and Pachler argue in Chapter 10. In higher education, the Teaching and Learning Technology Programme has generated a number of multi-media and interactive packages and simulations designed to extend the quality of teaching. There are interactive educational programmes available for schools and for individual learners to use on PCs at home. Many relate to the National Curriculum, Key Stage tests or national examinations at 16 or 18. Schools are also making increasing use of the Internet and available software in a range of subject domains. Despite the increased availability of ICT, the question remains as to the extent to which ICT can and should replace more traditional forms of teaching. Is a scenario likely in the foreseeable future where most learning takes place individually through interactive learning packages and

institutions of learning as we know them, for instance, schools, colleges, universities disappear?

- *Whether it is equally beneficial to both parties to teach girls and boys together and if so in what phases of education*
Although this has not been raised directly in most of the chapters in the book, there are advocates of the idea that it is best to educate girls and boys separately in secondary schools. Because girls develop physically, emotionally and intellectually at a different pace to boys, arguments are made that progress for both would be better if their education was undertaken separately. The evidence to support these arguments is inconclusive at the moment and there are many possible confounding factors. There is also the question of why segregation should be in adolescence and not in other phases of education. Are there particular concerns about the education of adolescents that are distinct from learners of other ages? A fruitful approach might be to consider the common and distinct needs of boys and girls and how these might be met within a broadly co-educational environment. In addition, the personal and social development needs of young people must be considered alongside their academic attainment.

DOES THE AGE OR STAGE OF THE LEARNER MAKE A DIFFERENCE?

Teachers of different aged learners are often seen as very different. The stereotype personified in Joyce Grenfell's early childhood teacher is very different to that of David Lodge's university 'History Man'. Such teachers work in contrasting institutions, exist in different cultures and hold very different images of their status. Yet they share many of same aims and adopt similar pedagogical techniques. Both are trying to promote learning. Both are seeking to elicit motivation. Both have access to specialized knowledge. Both use feedback to guide and develop the learner's own skills.

As we have seen throughout this book, there are probably more similarities than differences between children's and adults' learning. The basic mechanisms by which we learn do not change over our lifetime although they may become less efficient in old age. This is compensated for by greater knowledge and expertise. The main differences are that children know less than adults and are less self conscious as learners. Adult learners have become expert in many everyday activities which they can perform effortlessly and without conscious thought. They have more knowledge of particular topics and much more general knowledge. Also, they may have gained more control over themselves and their emotions, although this is not always the case.

All learners, however, whether children or adults, appear to benefit from a sense of control over their learning and the chance to understand and to apply their knowledge. They also benefit from challenge and an ethos in which learning is valued. In the current education system in England there is little continuity in pedagogy from one phase of education to the next and little opportunity for learners to achieve continuity and progression in their control and self-regulation of learning.

At present, young people in primary and secondary schools have very little control over their own learning. Ironically, the secondary phase is probably the most restrictive of all, at a time when young people are striving to become independent and look forward to the time when they will support themselves. Yet they are seldom permitted to take any control or responsibility for their own learning, although in higher education this is an accepted and essential responsibility. An important aim for education in the future might be the establishment of a planned and progressive increase in the learner's responsibility in relation to their own learning as they progress through each phase of education.

THE LESSONS AND IMPLICATIONS FOR THE FUTURE

Patterns of employment in this country have changed dramatically during the past fifty years. We have moved from an industrial to a service-based economy. Fewer factories employ unskilled manual labour. Employment is less secure, with more part-time and temporary work and a concomitant requirement for flexibility and resourcefulness. This applies across all occupations, from the least to the most skilled. The shift to a service-based economy places different types of demands on those who perform less skilled work. Social and inter-personal skills are in greater demand. Team working and flexible, transferable skills are required in many occupations. Given these changes, we should now consider if it is possible to identify forms of pedagogy that will best equip our young people for the future.

One way of tackling this task is to consider the characteristics that will be required of young people in the future and then to establish overarching aims for the entire education system which will cumulatively enable them to develop the necessary skills and knowledge. We do not claim to have a ready list of such characteristics (indeed we would contend there is a need for them to be debated in the country as a whole) but there are probably several that most people would agree are essential. These would include a good general education, including literacy and numeracy, and a knowledge of science, humanities and the arts. Young people also need to have a range of learning and self-regulatory strategies and the confidence to use them effectively. To these we would also add creativity, flexibility and the ability to obtain and evaluate knowledge in new topics and subjects. These characteristics require skills in locating, interpreting and evaluating information from a range of sources, including the electronic media. Faced with an enormous variety of possible occupations and careers, people also need to acquire self-knowledge, so that they can find a niche where they will be satisfied and competent. Perhaps we should encourage personal development and 'spend less time ranking children and more time helping them to identify their natural competencies and gifts and cultivate those' as Gardner recently suggested (Gardner, 1996).

One of Vygotsky's ideas, subsequently developed by Wertsch (1985), was that cultures assist development by enabling members of society to appropriate and use a range of tools. For Vygotsky, tools were both physical objects (such as hammers) and conceptual systems or ways of thinking. Could this be extended to include pedagogic tools? Marton and Booth (1997) have argued that one of the most important ways in which we, as humans, differ from other animals is in how we explicitly and deliberately teach our children and each other. Alongside this is our ability to learn deliberately and to take conscious control of our own learning. Our knowledge and thinking about the complex and challenging process of teaching may provide us with powerful cultural tools to enhance learning in the next generations. These tools may be the key to our culture's survival.

So how can we respond to the Vygotskian idea of cultural tools, place them within a pedagogical framework, and make generalizations from the debates which have emerged from this book?

Six key ideas stand out:

1. *The term pedagogy is seldom clearly defined*
   Pedagogy has been seen by many within and outside the teaching profession as a somewhat vague concept. Even amongst continental educationalists – where the term is much more commonly used – it is seldom clearly defined and, as a result, is used fairly generally. Yet it could offer those involved with teaching a useful conceptual framework with which to examine their own professional practice and those outside of this group a way to understand the often complex approaches that are needed. Further, the time for a consideration of pedagogy is ripe. The technological revolution currently underway on the one hand demands and yet also offers an opportunity for a reappraisal and evaluation of current pedagogical practice with a view to examining its appropriateness for the needs of the future – with or without assistance from information and communications technology.

2. *There is no pedagogical panacea*
   Different learners at different ages and stages require different methods of teaching in order to achieve optimum learning of different kinds. There is no simple recipe for effective teaching in any phase of education. Teachers need to develop a full repertoire of skills and techniques designed to achieve different types of learning outcome. This process takes time and involves training, practice and reflection. It is ongoing throughout the careers of teachers whichever phase of education they work in and is optimized where teachers are in a supportive environment and can adopt a mastery approach to their own learning. Allowance needs to be made for this in the demands made on teachers' working lives.

3. *Teachers are important*

Whatever the age or stage of learners, it is clear that teachers are crucially important. They need to devote themselves to the needs of their students but must be aware they cannot do the learning for them. As so many of the authors have stressed, teaching is a highly sophisticated activity in which thousands of judgements are made in course of a single day. Teachers – in their attempts to promote learning – have to provide information, challenge their learners to find information themselves, assess understanding, measure skills and provide formative feedback. Most of all, they have to inspire in their learners the desire to learn and reinforce their self-confidence. They will achieve this more readily if they have high self-esteem themselves and are regarded as members of a respected profession rather than one that faces constant criticism.

4. *Context matters*

The arenas for learning, whether kindergarten, schoolroom, lecture hall, workplace or other 'life' setting, bring with them sets of expectations about learning and behaviour. Transferability of learning from one setting to another does not happen automatically. Learners have to develop the skills of boundary crossing. Such skills are enormously important to the ability to succeed in modern life. But for some young learners, feelings of powerlessness and of being a captive audience can get in the way and can inhibit learning.

For teachers, this often means that issues of power and control become mixed up with pedagogical concerns. Control can become the first priority, learning the second. Pedagogy may be selected to facilitate control and not necessarily be the best teaching strategy for the desired learning outcome. If pupils have to be wooed to learn – and punished if they refuse to conform to the norms of the school – what hope is there of enlisting them as active learners at school or in their future lives? And what hope is there of them benefiting from the natural learning that appears to occur in other aspects of life? Commentators sometimes juxtapose the ease of 'real life' learning with the difficulties of school learning. But this misses the point that for young pupils, it is *school* rather than the worlds of pop music, premier league football or super models that is the 'real world'. These other worlds may exist but for most pupils will be unattainable. Yet young people seem to learn about these worlds very easily. Is this because the concepts are relatively simple or because motivation is so strong? The evidence would suggest the latter (Morris *et al.*, 1985). The compliance expected of school pupils (for very good institutional reasons) can act as a barrier to effective learning. This, as we have seen, is very different to the position of the adult learner who has much greater personal power and is generally in a learning environment because they wish to be there. The increasing trend for work place learning may mean, however, that some adults lose the voluntarism that has been an important part of the adult learning tradition.

5. *There are some general pedagogic principles*

Some pedagogical principles for teachers can be formulated, though only at a very general level. From the literature searches undertaken by various authors it appears to be beneficial if teachers:

– are clear about their aims and share them with learners
– plan, organize and manage their teaching effectively
– try to formulate the highest expectations about the potential capabilities of learners and their level of progress
– endeavour to provide positive formative feedback to all their students
– recognize the distinctiveness of individual learners within a general context of inclusivity
– provide learning tasks which will challenge and interest and which are aligned to appropriate assessment procedures
– seek to relate academic learning to other forms of learning and promote 'boundary crossing' skills
– make explicit the rules and, at times, the hidden conventions of all learning institutions so that all learners become aware of ways in which they will be judged
– include an understanding of metacognition in their objectives so that all learners can benefit from this knowledge and – as they advance through their learning careers - take increasing responsibility for their own learning
– motivate and enthuse learners.

6. *Teachers are learners too*

Finally, as so many of the authors have argued, it is important that the teacher remains a learner. Not only is our knowledge about the world growing at an increasingly rapid pace, but our knowledge of how learning takes place is also developing. It is imperative that teachers – with their many skills and experiences – continue to increase their own capabilities. Governments cannot do this for teachers – no matter how much they may want to do so. The teaching profession, itself, must set about becoming a learning profession. In England, the creation of a General Teaching Council and the Institute for Learning and Teaching in Higher Education will provide opportunities for this to take place.

To conclude, a wide-ranging debate is needed which focuses on the aims of education as well as pedagogy. This debate should take a broad view of learning through the lifespan, to develop a coherent framework for the lifelong development of learning skills. At present, the changes experienced by learners, as they move from one institution or setting to another, are governed to a large extent by the structures and forms of the institutions, rather than by a coherent strand of development in learning. The debate about aims that we propose should seek the views of all those who have a stake in education, including learners of all ages and stages as well as employers and –

through the government – the wider society. But it must be led by teachers so that the profession will own the debate and will thus be most likely to take the conclusions into its own practice.

REFERENCES

Ames, C. and Ames, A. (1992) Classrooms: goals, structures and student motivation, *Journal of Educational Psychology*, 84(3): 261–271.

Ashton, P. T. and Webb, R. B. (1986) *Making a Difference: Teachers' Sense of Efficacy and Student Achievement*, New York: Longman.

Bandura, A. (1995) Exercise of personal and collective self-efficacy, in A. Bandura (ed.) *Self-Efficacy in Changing Societies*, Cambridge: Cambridge University Press.

Biggs, J. B. (1987) *Student Approaches to Learning and Studying*, Hawthorn, Victoria: Australian Council for Educational Research.

Biggs, J. B. and Moore, P. J. (1993) *The Process of Learning*, New York: Prentice Hall.

Black, P. and Wiliam, D. (1998) Assessment and classroom learning, *Assessment in Education*, 5(1): 7–73.

Broadfoot, P. (1996) Educational assessment: the myth of measurement, in P. Woods (ed.) *Contemporary Issues in Teaching and Learning*, London: Routledge.

Brown, J. S., Collins, A. and Duguid, P. (1989) Situated cognition and the culture of learning, *Educational Researcher*, 18(1): 32–42.

Covington, M. (1992) *Making the Grade: A Self-Worth Perspective on Motivation and School Achievement*, New York: Cambridge University Press.

Department of Education and Science (1988) *The Education Reform Act*, London: HMSO.

Dweck, C. S. and Leggett, E. L. (1988) Self-theories and goals: A social-cognitive approach to motivation and personality, *Psychological Review*, 95(2): 256–273.

Elton, L. R. and Laurillard, D. (1979) Trends in research on student learning, *Studies in Higher Education*, 4: 87–102.

Entwistle, N. (1992) *The Impact of Teaching on Learning Outcomes in Higher Education: A Literature Review*, Sheffield: CVCP.

Gardner, M. (1996) *New York Times Educational Supplement*, Nov. 3.

Glaser, R. (1984) Education and thinking: the role of knowledge, *American Psychologist*, 3: 93–104.

Goodlad, J. (1983) *A Place Called School*, New York: McGraw Hill.

Hodgson, A. and Spours, K. (1998) Pushed too far, *Times Educational Supplement*, December 11.

Hougham, J., Thomas, J. and Sisson, K. (1991) Ford's EDAP scheme: a round table discussion, *Human Resource Management Journal*, 1(3): 77–91.

Howe, M. (1991) Learning to learn: A fine idea but does it work?, *Education Section Review of the British Psychological Society*, 15(2): 43–57.

Ireson, J. and MacCallum, B. (in press) *Innovative Grouping Practices in Secondary Schools*, A Report for the Department of Education and Employment.

Kerry, T. (1984) Analysing the cognitive demand made by classroom tasks in mixed ability classes, in E. Wragg (ed.) *Classroom Teaching Skills*, London: Croom Helm.

Lave, J. and Wenger, E. (1991) *Situated Cognition: Legitimate Peripheral Participation*, Cambridge: Cambridge University Press.

Marton, F. and Booth, S. (1997) *Learning and Awareness*, Mahwah, NJ: Lawrence Erlbaum.

McGiveney, V. (1993) Participation and non-participation: a review of the literature, in R. Edwards, S. Sieminski and D. Zeldin (eds.), *Adult Learners, Education and Training*, Milton Keynes: Open University Press.

Meece, J. (1991) The classroom context and students' motivational goals, in M. Maehr and P. Pintrich (eds.) *Advances in Motivation and Achievement*, Vol. 7, Greenwich, Conn.: JAI Press.

Morris, P. E., Tweedy, M. and Gruneberg, M. M. (1985) Interest, knowledge and the memorising of soccer scores, *British Journal of Psychology*, 76: 415–425.

• Mortimore, P. (1998) *The Road to Improvement: Reflections on School Effectiveness*, Lisse: Swets & Zeitlinger.

Mortimore, P., Sammons, P., Stoll, L., Lewis, D. and Ecob, R. (1988) *School Matters*, Wells: Open Books (reprinted 1995, London: Paul Chapman).

Mortimore, P. and Whitty, J. (1997) *Can School Improvement Overcome the Effects of Disadvantage?* London: Institute of Education.

Nicholls, J. G. (1989) *The Competitive Ethos and Democratic Education*, Cambridge, MA: Harvard University Press.

Palinscar, A. M. and Brown, A. M. (1989) Classroom dialogues to promote self-regulated comprehension, in J. S. Brophy (ed.) *Advances in Research on Teaching*, Vol. 1, London: JAI Press.

Paris, S. G., Cross, D. R. and Lipson, M. Y. (1984) Informed strategies for learning: a program to improve children's reading awareness and comprehension, *Journal of Educational Psychology*, 76: 1239–1252.

Pramling, I. (1996) Understanding and empowering the child as a learner, in D. Olson and N. Torrance (eds.) *The Handbook of Education and Human Development*, Oxford: Blackwell.

Ramsden, P. (1992) *Learning to Teach in Higher Education*, London: Routledge.

Raven, J. (1994) *Managing Education for Effective Schooling: The Most Important Problem is to Come to Terms with Values*, Oxford: Oxford Psychologists Press.

Rogers, C. R. (1990) Motivation in the primary years, in C. Rogers and P. Kutnick (eds.) *The Social Psychology of the Primary School*, London: Routledge.

Saljo, R. and Wyndham, J. (1993) Solving problems in the formal setting: an empirical study of the school as a context for thought, in S. Chaiklin and J. Lave (eds.) *Understanding Practice*, Cambridge: Cambridge University Press.

Selmes, I. P. (1987) *Improving Study Skills*, London: Hodder and Stoughton.

Stodolsky, S. S. (1988) *The Subject Matters: Classroom Activity in Math and Social Studies*, Chicago: University of Chicago Press.

Strang, A. (1997) Motivation for effective independent learning, *Education Section Review of the British Psychological Society*, 21(2): 26–35.

Tschannen-Moran, M., Hoy, A. W. and Hoy, W. K. (1998) Teacher efficacy: its meaning and measure, *Review of Educational Research*, 68(2): 202–248.

Vygotsky, L. S. (1978) *Mind in Society*, Cambridge: Cambridge University Press.

Weinstein, C. S., Goetz, E. T. and Alexander, P. A. (eds.) (1988) *Learning and Study Strategies: Issues in Assessment, Instruction and Evaluation*, New York: Academic Press.

Wertsch, J. V. (1985) *Vygotsky and the Social Formation of Mind*, Cambridge: Cambridge University Press.

Index